SALT in Your SOCK

HOME REMEDIES

SALT in Your SOCK

AND OTHER TRIED-AND-TRUE

HOME REMEDIES

A PEDIATRICIAN SELECTS PARENTS' FAVORITE TREATMENTS FOR MORE THAN 90 CHILDHOOD AILMENTS

LILLIAN M. BEARD, M.D.,

with Linda Lee Small

THREE RIVERS PRESS • NEW YORK

This book is not intended to replace information, guidance, or the care provided by your child's physician. The mention, reference, or listing of any (medicinal) family recipe, home remedy, or therapy is not an endorsement, recommendation for use, or acceptance as beneficial by the authors, publisher, or any organizations in which the authors hold membership.

Published by Three Rivers Press, New York, New York.
Member of the Crown Publishing Group, a division of Random House, Inc.
www.randomhouse.com

Printed in the United States of America

DESIGN BY BARBARA STURMAN

Library of Congress Cataloging-in-Publication Data
Beard, Lillian M.
Salt in your sock and other tried-and-true home remedies : a pediatrician selects parents' favorite treatments for more than 90 childhood ailments / Lillian M. Beard, with Linda Lee Small.—1st ed.
1. Pediatrics—Popular works. 2. Children—Diseases—Popular works. 3. Medicine, Popular. 4. Traditional medicine—Popular works.
[DNLM: 1. Medicine, Traditional—Child—United States—Popular Works. 2. Home Nursing—Child—United States—Popular Works. WB 50 AA1 B368s 2003] I. Small, Linda Lee. II. Title.
RJ61 .B2985 2003
618.92—dc21 2002008346

ISBN 0-8129-3312-5

10 9 8 7 6 5 4 3 2 1

First Edition

To my sister,

Yvonne René McLean Moore

(1952–2001)

ACKNOWLEDGMENTS

FIRST AND FOREMOST, my sincere thank you to the countless patient families, colleagues, relatives, friends, and strangers who willingly shared recollections of their families' treasured recipes for healing. Without their generous contributions of aromatic concoctions—sometimes mystical, but always mixed with love—this book would not have been possible.

Of special note: Agnes Birnbaum and Bleecker Street Associates, thank you for seeing the big picture, embracing this project, and for gently but persistently prodding me all the way to the finish line.

When my co-writer, Linda Lee Small, and I began our collaborative work, we had no idea of the many parallels in our lives. Through personal peaks and valleys, we could always count on each other's support and we stayed the course. Thank you, Linda, my friend.

Many thanks to my editors at Three Rivers Press, Betsy Rapoport and Stephanie Higgs; your sharp wit, patience, insight, and red pencils have been greatly appreciated.

My sincere appreciation to many professional contributors: Daniel Mowrey, Ph.D., advisor to Rodale Press and nationally renowned author, lecturer, and advisor on herbal medicine, for his extensive professional review of the manuscript. Thanks to health writer and editor Norine Dworkin, for her research and review of the manuscript, and to Sharon McDonnell, for her research.

Thank you Mindy Green of the Herb Research Foundation, and naturopathic physician colleagues Dr. Christopher Fabricus and Dr. Bobbi Lutack, for your willingness to respond to our numerous inquiries and for your kindness in sharing.

Yvonne V. Jones, Ph.D., anthropologist, University of Louisville, many thanks for your invaluable assistance in researching writings on many cross-cultural practices in the United States.

On a personal note: Doris, Arnetta, and Hunter, thanks for your continuing prayers, smiles, and hugs. Brian, thanks for your encouragement through the years. To E.H.F., R.D.H., A.G.D., E.W.P., J.V.S., I.C., and all my friends and family, thanks for your continuing understanding. Mother, thank you for your tough love; Mesha, for my heart; and Larry, for your unwavering love and support.

CONTENTS

An A~Z Guide to Home Remedies

SALT in Your SOCK

HOME REMEDIES

INTRODUCTION

MANY YEARS AGO, while I was advising a young mother on how to manage her baby's facial rash, I was surprised by a question from the baby's great-grandmother, who was in the exam room with us: "Ma'dear," as she was called, piped up: "When are you going to tell my granddaughter about the urine paste?" I did not have the slightest idea what she was talking about—and the idea of urine on a baby's face was definitely not appealing. But the older woman proceeded to educate me about her rural Alabama custom of using a baby's own urine to treat various rashes.

Later, when I heard tales of Hannibal's armies collecting and using their own urine to treat their war wounds, I began to make the medicinal connections to "Ma'dear's" advice. And then the pieces came together: While I was comparing labels of some widely advertised facial creams in a drugstore cosmetics section, I noticed that urea (a component of urine) was a major ingredient of many of the costliest ones. Great-Grandma had known just what she was recommending, even if she didn't know exactly why.

As a pediatrician, I am doubly blessed; I get to see not just my patient—the child—but also the child's family. One of the most fascinating and rewarding aspects of my practice is the opportunity to become a virtual member of my small charges' families, learning their traditions, sharing their joys, and participating in the family's growth and development. As I now care for my second generation—the children of my original children—I continue to be amazed by and learn from all "my" families.

Often as I examine patients and listen to their parents' descriptions of the child's illness, the families will usually share with me what they've tried at home. I've learned to ask for families' recipes for healing. I am convinced that most of these home remedies actually do something positive. Some represent ancient folk wisdom that science is only now beginning to test. Others allow the user to feel as though she is participating in restoring and protecting her child's health. Some of these home-based prescriptions represent such a deeply felt part of a family's cultural heritage that if I were to frown upon or challenge them, it would create a climate of doubt and mistrust. As I listen, I have learned to keep a straight face even when my initial reaction—as with first hearing about the use of the baby's urine—would be to say that the practice is gross or unsanitary.

I have found that some families, although politely accepting my scientific wisdom in the form of a prescription, will not follow my advice or even return for a follow-up visit if I don't incorporate their own beliefs. So if I am working with a Pakistani family, for example, along with giving traditional medical-school advice and reassurance for their baby's jaundice, which is not uncommon in newborns, I will let them know that I have heard that a little diluted beet juice (2–3 teaspoons mixed into 2 fluid ounces of water) just might help.

As the healing pendulum swings, we have traveled a long way from leeches to lasers—with much in between. There are many closely held family and home remedies introduced in past centuries and still practiced around the world. Although these may not have been taught in medical schools, they have been used successfully, managing to survive and thrive through the age-old folk traditions of oral and written history.

I have discovered that there is definitely a place for folk medicine or natural healing in my practice. However, I *always* caution the parents of my patients to use common sense and never rely solely on these remedies without checking with me first. Some of the "cures" are just helpful ways to make a child feel better until a doctor can treat the little patient; they should *never* be a substitute for your doctor's advice and care.

Salt in Your Sock evolved over many years as I listened to thousands of families as their pediatrician. I've also asked friends and professional colleagues from various medical and health disciplines to share their therapeutic treasures from their families' histories. Whenever I travel for business or on family vacations around the globe, I pick up "sure-fire" family remedies from the people I meet.

Through the years, as I listened and observed, I began to recognize some familiar themes. Many of the practices not only were cross-cultural and transcended time but also sparked my own recollections of some family remedies from my childhood. This book documents the remedies I've heard, reflected through the prism of my medical knowledge and experience. I sometimes like to think of these remedies as the equivalent of "Doctor, have you heard the one about . . . ?"

Although many of these practices seem to have *some* biological and physiological basis for effectiveness, others are just fascinating, such as drinking beet juice to help erase jaundice. (Although I'm still not sure about the restorative benefits of beet juice, I know that a couple of teaspoons will not be harmful.) Most have never been tested in a laboratory. But others, like the proverbial chicken soup for colds, have been proven to work. Grandma was right: There really *is* a penicillinlike substance in chicken broth.

I've listed the most common childhood ailments from A to Z, including the health concerns most parents ask me about. I didn't include some concerns, such as knock-knee, because I hadn't heard any "natural" remedies for them. I haven't included any of the formerly common childhood diseases such as mumps and measles, because vaccines have virtually wiped them out. Nor have I included folk remedies for any life-threatening or otherwise devastating diseases. As with a number of behavioral issues such as stress and depression, I strongly believe that these are best addressed by your doctor or other health professional.

Under each heading, you'll find a brief description of the ailment, the most common or conventional treatments, and then a "parents' report" of what works. Many of these remedies and practices have survived the test of time because so many parents have found that they offer some relief and comfort. For some, I can theorize a biological/physiological basis for their effectiveness. Others I've included even though I cannot offer any current recognized medical explanation for any results, but they can't hurt. And lastly, when appropriate, I issue a warning. I've mentioned some folk remedies that should *not* be followed, because they're dangerous.

Not surprisingly, you'll find a special emphasis on food and nutrition; even the father of medicine, Hippocrates, wrote extensively about the therapeutic use of diet. The "recipes" fall under a large umbrella of categories: nutrition, vitamin and herbal therapy, acupressure, gemstones, aromatherapy, and more. You'll also find some remedies that I frankly find baffling—putting raw potato slices on a belly to cure stomachache?—but they make me smile when I hear about them and seem to cause no harm. However, I recommend parents take these remedies with, well, a grain or two of salt!

HOW TO USE THIS BOOK

Salt in Your Sock is not intended to be a substitute for your physician's advice. _Always_ check with your physician before using any herbal or other family remedy. There is scientific documentation that some commonly used herbal medications may cause problems if combined with prescribed medicines. Recent medical literature also cautions that using herbal or other less traditional therapies can increase the risk for unexpected complications if surgery is performed. Many herbal remedies stay in the body's systems for weeks after use, or may interfere with heart rate, blood pressure, bleeding tendencies, or the effectiveness of anesthesia during a surgical procedure. So always ask your doctor before giving *any* supplement to your child.

The "New" Medicine Cabinet

If you want to stock your cabinet, I've listed the most frequently mentioned foods and herbs below. The much-quoted "Take two aspirins and call me in the morning" can be replaced with: "Peel some potatoes for a headache, cut up some onions for fever, and *then* call me in the morning." Every culture cooks up its own cures, often based on what's growing out in the fields. My version of a natural medicine cabinet is one filled with foods, teas, herbs, and, as you'll see, plenty of onions and garlic!

Stock Your Pantry

- ✦ Ginger—fresh or powdered
- ✦ Fruit juice—only naturally sweetened
- ✦ Garlic
- ✦ Onions
- ✦ White potatoes
- ✦ Oatmeal
- ✦ Olive oil
- ✦ Cayenne pepper
- ✦ Yogurt (with live cultures; look for *Lactobacillus acidophilus* and *Lactobacillus bifidus* on the label)
- ✦ Black tea bags (orange pekoe, Earl Grey)
- ✦ Horseradish/wasabi
- ✦ Baking soda
- ✦ Pineapple (fresh fruit or natural juice)
- ✦ Limes
- ✦ Vinegar
- ✦ Honey
- ✦ Parsley

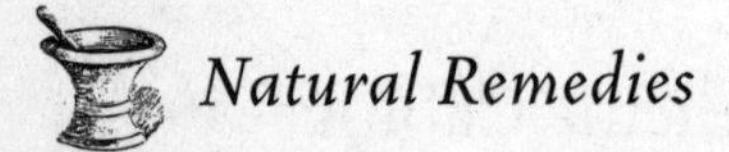

Natural Remedies

Herbs are nature's medicinals. From ancient times, there have always been herbalists who relied on the power of plants and their extracts. Following are the herbs and natural ingredients most frequently mentioned by parents.

- ✦ Activated charcoal—for food poisoning, gastrointestinal distress
- ✦ Aloe vera (gel or juice)—for minor burns, such as sunburn, cuts, scrapes
- ✦ Arnica ointment—for strains, sprains, and muscle aches
- ✦ Bentonite clay—for insect bites and stings

- ✦ Calendula cream—for cuts, scrapes, skin irritations, and bruises
- ✦ Chamomile (tea, tincture, and essential oil)—for stomachache, insomnia, and relaxation
- ✦ Clove (essential oil)—for teething and toothache
- ✦ Echinacea (tea, tincture)—for colds, flu, urinary tract and yeast infections, and acne
- ✦ Eucalyptus (essential oil)—for nasal congestion
- ✦ Eyebright (tea)—for eye infections
- ✦ Fennel (tea, seeds)—for gas and stomachache
- ✦ Goldenseal (tea, tincture)—for colds, flu, and gastrointestinal infections
- ✦ *Lactobacillus acidophilus* and *Lactobacillus bifidus*—for yeast infections and gastrointestinal distress
- ✦ Lavender (essential oil)—for cuts, scrapes, insect bites and stings, minor burns, insomnia, and relaxation
- ✦ Marshmallow (tea)—for sore throats and cough
- ✦ Peppermint (tea)—for stomachache, gas, and nausea
- ✦ Slippery elm (tea, lozenges)—for sore throats and cough
- ✦ Tea tree oil (essential oil)—for nail fungus, yeast infections, and acne

☛ WARNING: It's important to note that herbs can have side effects. As of now, the U.S. Food and Drug Administration does *not* regulate herbs. That means they are not held to the same standards set for foods, which require accurate labeling, or medicines, which must demonstrate their safety and effectiveness. Without regulation, they can easily be misused. Herb labels can proclaim a wide variety of results and cures without being substantiated. When an herb is good for an adult, it does *not* always mean it's safe for children, even when taken in smaller doses. Just because a product is described as "natural" does not make it synonymous with "healthy." Herbs need to be respected—they contain potent chemicals that function as medicines. When mixed with other substances, they can reduce or boost some drugs' efficacy. **Always check with your pediatrician first** before giving your child any herbal supplement. Look for herbs labeled "certified organic." This means that they are grown without pesticides, herbicides, or synthetic fertilizers. This makes the herbs safer for ingestion. Also check for standardized preparations—this means that every dose contains the correct (and same) amount of active, therapeutic ingredients. With nonstandardized preparations, even with measured amounts, it's just a "guesstimate" for getting too much or not enough of the herbal remedy. I recommend you avoid the bins of loose herbs found in many natural food stores, or preparations that do not list the specific amount of each ingredient.

Also keep in mind that many preparations that are safe for use on the body (say, in a poultice or inhaled during aromatherapy) are not safe for ingestion. *Most* essential oils, for example, can be harmful if swallowed.

Definition of Terms

Infusion

Infusion is just another word for tea. However, for therapeutic purposes, these teas need to be made stronger than the usual brew. Medicinal teas should steep for ten to twenty minutes to get the full effect of the herbs. These days most medicinal herbs come in ready-made tea bags that you can find in health food stores and supermarkets.

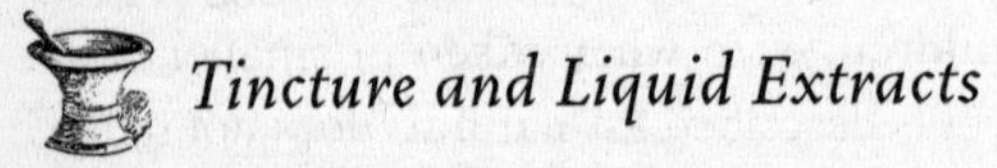

Tincture and Liquid Extracts

Tinctures and liquid extracts are more potent than teas, because they are more concentrated. Consequently, you need a smaller amount to get the job done, and they tend to work faster than teas. They can be stored for a longer time in your medicine chest. Even better, they're easily portable, so you can toss them into a diaper bag or travel medicine kit if you're going on the road. Tinctures are made either with alcohol or glycerin. You can make your own by putting fresh or dried herbs into a lightproof container with a tight-fitting lid. Aim for 2 ounces of dried herb or a handful of fresh herbs per pint (16 fluid ounces) of alcohol. Vodka works fine. Fill the container with the herb and the vodka. Allow the mixture to sit for a week or two, shaking it every once in a while and topping off the alcohol that may evaporate. After a week or so, strain out the plant material, then store the liquid in another dark, lightproof container, preferably one with a dropper. However, you'll find it much easier just to buy tinctures at the health food store. *Note:* If you want to avoid alcohol-based tinctures, you can make or purchase those with glycerin.

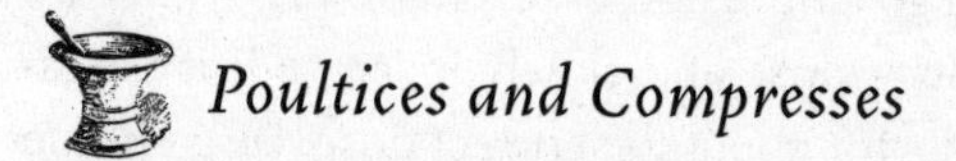

Poultices and Compresses

Poultices are very effective for cuts, scrapes, and other skin irritations. You can use fresh or dried herbs to make a poultice. If you use dried herbs, moisten them a bit. Simply crumble or crush (bruise) the herbs a bit to release the active ingredients, then apply gently to the affected area and hold them in place with a bandage. A word of caution: Unless you are a knowledgeable botanist, *do not* pick plants from the wild to use on your child's skin. Many plants look alike, and you may choose the wrong one. Also, plants from the wild may be contaminated with pesticides, herbicides, fertilizers, or car exhaust fumes. It's safer to buy certified organic herbs, either from a health food store or through reputable herb suppliers.

If you don't want to prepare a poultice or you don't have the fresh or dried herbs on hand, compresses work just as well. Use them hot or cold. To make a compress, simply brew a medicinal tea or infusion or put a few dropperfuls of tincture into some water. Then soak a clean cloth in the liquid, wring it out, and apply it to the wound.

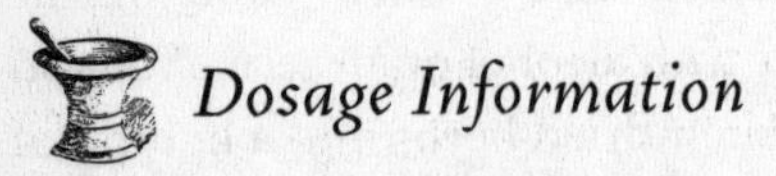

Dosage Information

Although herbal remedies also come in tablets and capsules, it's tough to gauge dosages because capsule size can vary from manufacturer to manufacturer. Teas tend to be gentler and less concentrated but easier to measure. Tinctures are more concentrated than teas and therefore more potent. That's mainly because they're alcohol-based, which speeds their delivery throughout the body. For this reason, a lesser amount is needed for effectiveness.

Herbal remedies are dosed according to age. However, size and weight are important considerations. If your child is small for her age, you should go a little lighter; even for larger kids, it's safer to start with a lower dose and slowly increase it if necessary. Check with your doctor about the correct dose. Discontinue any herbal remedy if the child has any reaction. Be on the lookout for changes such as skin rash, headache, diarrhea, stomachache, trouble breathing, or any other symptoms unrelated to the ailment being treated. Herbal remedies are generally safe when used correctly, but some children and adults may experience allergic reactions. If that happens, call your doctor, or proceed directly to the emergency room of the closest hospital if the attack seems serious.

Parents can report adverse reactions to herbal remedies by calling the Food and Drug Administration's Medwatch Hotline at 800-332-1088 or e-mailing www.fda.gov/medwatch.

The following are general doses based on age. Again, check with your doctor first to make sure they're appropriate for your child.

Birth to two years: Add 3 drops of herbal tincture or liquid extract to 2 ounces of water, infant formula, or breast milk. Or administer 2 to 3 teaspoons of herbal tea. Infants can take the remedy via bottle, eyedropper, or syringe. If nursing moms take the adult dose, a suitable dosage will probably pass to the baby in the breast milk; ask your doctor.

Two to six years: Add 6 to 10 drops of tincture or liquid extract to 2 ounces of water. Or administer 2 ounces (one quarter of a cup) of tea.

Six to twelve years: Take 10 to 20 drops of tincture or liquid extract, alone or in water or juice. Or administer 8 ounces (one cup) of tea.

Twelve years to adult: Take 20 to 40 drops of tincture or liquid extract, alone or in water or juice. Or administer 8 ounces (one cup) of tea.

Note: Herbal remedies can be bitter. Parents can make them taste better by mixing herbs with juice, water, or even some applesauce or hot cereal. Children over one year can have their herbs mixed with honey. **Never give honey to a child under the age of one, to avoid the risk of infant botulism.**

Pointers for Medical Urgencies

Sometimes, despite conventional medical treatment or the use of effective home remedies, a child will need urgent medical care. Keeping a cool head and planning ahead for emergencies will help you get your child the best care.

✦ Always keep your child's doctor's phone number taped to your telephone so that in a moment of excitement, the information is clearly visible and readily available.

✦ If your phone can store numbers for automatic dialing, program in your physician's telephone numbers, then tape a list of the speed-dial numbers on the phone so that all family members, baby-sitters, and caregivers can readily access a doctor if necessary.

✦ Know the location of the closest emergency facility (hospital) and the route to get there. Do they have a pediatric emergency team available?

✦ Tape the telephone number of the poison control center in your region onto your phone.

✦ The three-digit emergency medical rescue telephone code is often 911, but it may vary by region of the country; be certain that family members know the number for your area.

✦ If you have a cellular phone, program in these vital numbers (physician, poison control center, emergency medical rescue) for speedy access.

AN A~Z GUIDE TO

HOME REMEDIES

Acne

The Ailment

When most of us think of pimples, we associate them with the agonies of adolescence. The condition *is* most commonly experienced during the teenage and young adult years, when hormones fluctuate. But acne can occur at any stage of life, even in newborns.

Acne is a common skin disorder that is characterized by the development of pimples, whiteheads, and blackheads. Here's how it all works: Sebum, the waxy substance secreted from oil glands (sebaceous glands) within the skin's hair follicles, normally serves to lubricate the skin. However, if the channels from the glands to the skin's surface become clogged, pimples result. Closed pimples, where the intact skin stretches and has a whitish hue at its surface, are called *whiteheads.* When there is an exposed, darkened pinpoint opening on the pimple, it is known as a *blackhead*. If several channels beneath the skin are blocked, they may join together and form *cysts*. When many deeper lesions cluster together, hold bacteria, and become encapsulated, they form *abscesses*. These abscesses may be unsightly and uncomfortable, and they may result in scarring.

Acne most commonly occurs on the face, upper chest, and upper back and in the shoulder area.

Many factors, including stress, are involved in triggering the annoying breakouts, but primarily the increased levels of androgen hormones, present in both males and females, stimulate activity in the sebaceous glands. Sometimes touching or rubbing the skin or using certain medications can combine with the normal presence of bacteria on the skin's surface to set the stage for the development of acne. Although all of the causes are not known, eating chocolate or greasy foods or drinking soda does *not* cause acne.

There are measures that may help your child avoid acne and reduce the severity of an eruption if it occurs. The first step involves practicing careful skin hygiene.

- ✦ To minimize oiliness, the affected area should be gently washed twice daily with a mild, unscented soap, rinsed with plain water, and then patted (not rubbed) dry with a soft cloth.
- ✦ Keep the scalp and hair clean, and avoid styles that cause the hair to hang over or rest on the face.
- ✦ Avoid the use of oily creams and lotions, which may clog the channels and promote the formation of pimples.
- ✦ To prevent the spread of bacteria, more extensive eruptions, and lasting scars, teach your child to resist the temptation to squeeze or pick at the pimples.
- ✦ Encourage your child to consume a balanced diet with a wide variety of whole grains, vegetables, fruits, and lots of water.

☛ **WARNING:** There are degrees of severity of acne. If routine self-care does not improve the condition, or if the pimples become larger and more tender and change color, then your child may need medical attention. If lesions have progressed to the more serious cystic or abscess stage, he or she may need topical medication, antibiotics, or even a visit to a dermatologist for a minor surgical procedure or an injection of medication to speed resolution.

Conventional Treatment

- ✦ Many over-the-counter acne skin cleansers, acne lotions, and gels are found in the skin care section of your drugstore. However, cleansing with a mild unscented soap may work just as well.
- ✦ Prescription medications, including antibiotics, may be administered orally or applied topically and are quite effective when used as advised.
- ✦ Varieties of prescription-strength retinoic acid (Retin A) are remarkably effective in preventing new eruptions while hastening the drying and resolution of breakouts. But they are often too drying and irritating for some individuals to tolerate. (Many of the newer forms and preparations are milder.) There are over-the-counter creams, lotions, and gels that contain Retin A. However, read the labels carefully and exercise caution before applying to your child's skin. Avoid broken skin and areas around the eyes. Notify your doctor if tender spots or irritation occur.

☛ **WARNING:** None of these preparations should be used on an infant's skin. For infant acne, follow your pediatrician's instructions.

Parents' Report: What Works

Remember, although acne is not life-threatening, it can severely upset the life of your teen.

You may want to consider the advice of one grandmother in my practice who recommended "first urine." I have heard some teens mention this and pretend to gag, but a few swore it worked. According to the teens who have confided in me, you have to pee in a cup when you first wake up. Then dab a little of that "first urine" with a Q-tip and apply to your pimples. If you check the labels on some high-end skin creams, you may be surprised to discover that "urea" is listed as a major ingredient.

Most of the remedies that follow are based on working from the outside in—that is, they are applied to the skin. You might try these before calling the doctor or using expensive over-the-counter preparations.

✦ Try fluoride toothpaste. Just as the fluoride in toothpaste helps get rid of bacteria that cause tooth decay, fluoride can help battle the bacteria that encourage skin "decay." First, have your child wash her face with mild soap, rinse well, and pat dry. Then apply a dab of toothpaste on blossoming blemishes, allow to dry, and keep on overnight. Rinse gently in the morning.

✦ Here's a sweet solution: Have your child wash his face with granulated sugar and then rinse well. The sugar acts as an exfoliating agent and also has some disinfectant properties. It helps destroy bacteria and speeds heeling. After the sugar treatment, apply a warm oatmeal paste; allow it to dry, then rinse well with cold water.

✦ Use aloe vera juice or gel to counteract infection and to promote healing. Applying aloe vera juice morning and night for as long as necessary may help reduce acne scars and improve the skin's complexion and color. It is a drying agent, so if your child has dry skin, an aloe-based moisturizer may work as well. The pulp of the aloe vera plant is an excellent skin cleanser: Break off a portion of the plant leaf, cut it in half lengthwise, and rub the pulp directly onto the skin. If you see redness or the skin seems more irritated, discontinue use immediately.

✦ If your child has oily skin, use a cotton ball saturated with witch hazel, an astringent, and wipe gently over the entire face. This helps to dry and shrink pimples. Next, spread a thin coat of salicylic acid solution over face. (To make this solution, dissolve 4 adult aspirin in 2 tablespoons of water.) This regimen opens oil-clogged pores. It's not painful, although it does tingle, and the witch hazel has a clean, pleasant odor. Store extra solution in a labeled jar so you'll have some for future outbreaks. ☛ WARNING: Do *not* try this if there is any family history of aspirin sensitivity.

✦ Cleanse skin first, then apply either lemon juice or apple cider vinegar with a cotton ball. The acid in these common foods helps flush out the pores. You can also use apple cider vinegar to steam-clean the face. With your supervision, have your youngster lean toward a pot of water that has been brought to a boil, then cooled down a bit so that it is still steaming. Make sure her face is at least eight inches away from the water. Place a towel over her head to trap the steam for a few moments. Be sure her face feels comfortable. If it's too hot, pull away immediately. Remove the towel and apply the apple cider vinegar with a cotton ball to remove any dirt and oil buildup. Repeat, then dab more vinegar on the pores to close them.

✦ Liquefy a peeled cucumber in a blender and apply the resulting puree to the acne. Gently wash off with a soft cloth or with splashes of water. (You could also just slice some cucumber and place the disks on the affected skin areas for five to ten minutes each day.)

✦ Beat a few egg whites until stiff and allow the whites to sit out for several hours. Cleanse your child's skin thoroughly, then apply the egg whites with a cotton swab and let them remain on the child's skin for fifteen minutes before rinsing. The egg whites work as an astringent. ☛ WARNING: Do *not* use if your child has an egg allergy.

✦ Apply some cooled, cooked oatmeal (you can use unsweetened instant) to the entire face; allow it to remain on the skin for fifteen minutes, then wash it off. Oatmeal is an astringent and seems to draw oil and impurities out of the skin, helping to keep it clean and perhaps less prone to blemishes. You may need to use this remedy for a week or so before results are apparent.

✦ Boil buttermilk until it is thickened. Then add a tablespoon of honey to the cooled milk and apply the mixture to skin. Milk and honey is a soothing natural combination. It's okay to use this blend on children over the age of one.

The following remedies use herbs. ☛ WARNING: These suggestions are *not* for drinking, but are meant to be used as external skin washes.

✦ Bring 3 cups of water to a rolling boil, add 2 teaspoons of amaranth seeds, cover, and simmer for five minutes. Use the cooled tea as a face wash.

✦ To treat acne areas, obtain a basil-based oil from a health food store and apply as directed. Or make an infusion yourself by putting 2 to 4 teaspoons of dried basil leaves in 1 cup of boiling water. Steep for ten to twenty minutes, cool, and apply to the acne. This mixture has a pleasant aroma!

✦ Make a tea by boiling a handful of green beans in a quart of water for ten minutes, add 3 tablespoons of dried chamomile flowers to the tea, cover, and steep until cool. Strain and bottle. Use as a face wash three times daily.

✦ The herb burdock can be effective in treating acne because of its antibacterial properties. Make a tea by bringing 1 quart of water to a boil, then reduce to a simmer and add 4 teaspoons cut dried burdock root or a burdock tea bag; cover and allow to simmer for seven minutes, then remove from heat and let steep for two more hours. Use as a skin wash.

✦ Calendula, a natural antimicrobial and anti-inflammatory agent, is a gentle remedy for acne and other skin problems. Soak a clean towel in calendula tea and then apply as a warm compress. Washing with calendula-based soaps or applying calendula-based ointments may also help prevent and treat acne. Look for calendula preparations in the health food store.

✦ Tea tree oil, from the melaleuca tree of Australia, is another potent antimicrobial that's often used for treating acne. Tea tree oil is considered gentle enough to be used straight out of the bottle. Dab a little bit on pimples with a cotton swab. Since tea tree oil can also be drying, if skin becomes red, just dilute the oil in a little water. You can find washes, soaps, antiblemish sticks, and lotions made with tea tree oil in most natural food stores.

Allergies

The Ailment

An allergy is a lot more than just sniffling, sneezing, and wheezing. It's an abnormal reaction of the immune system to substances that generally cause no symptoms in most people. The role of the immune system is to recognize foreign, infectious, and other possibly harmful agents and to protect us from their effects. When the immune system becomes overly sensitive to foreign substances, mistaking harmless ones (such as house dust or pollen), or beneficial ones (such as dairy products), for dangerous ones, an allergic reaction results. Allergies tend to run in families and are found in about one in eight of us. And yes, natural redheads are more likely to be allergic.

There are several stages involved in allergies. The *sensitization* stage occurs when you are initially exposed to a substance (allergen). The *allergic* stage occurs when you are reintroduced to that allergen. During this stage, the body produces antibodies, which normally fight infectious organisms. But now those antibodies act as signals to certain blood cells and tissue cells to release chemicals (histamines) that cause a variety of familiar allergic symptoms, including runny nose, watery eyes, swelling, sneezing, wheezing, and itching.

The diagnostic labels for allergies depend on which body sites are affected and the system's reactions to the offending allergen. Most people who say they have allergies experience symptoms involving the *eyes and nose* (allergic rhinitis). Inhaled irritants such as pollen, dust, mold spores, and animal dander, to name just a few, can cause symptoms. Hay fever, the most common eye/nose allergic phenomenon, occurs seasonally when trees and grasses pollinate, triggering sneezing, nasal congestion, runny nose, itchy and tearing eyes, and an itchy sensation on the roof of the mouth and in the throat.

Pulmonary allergic reactions affect the major channels into the lungs (the bronchi) as well as the lungs themselves, causing breathing difficulties such as wheezing, coughing, shortness of breath, and chest tightness. Reactions to particular triggers such as tobacco smoke, dust, pollen, animal dander, cold, and exercise may also signal the presence of asthma, a chronic inflammatory disease of the breathing airways.

Intestinal allergic reactions are less common than those involving the eyes, nose, or lungs. Foods such as shellfish, berries, milk, wheat, eggs, and nuts, to name a few, may cause intestinal distress in some people. In highly sensitive individuals, an abnormal response to certain trigger foods may cause gas, cramping, nausea, vomiting, and diarrhea.

Skin reactions may be characterized by red bumps (fine or coarse), hives, itching, or painful rashes. These reactions follow direct contact with offending allergens such as poison ivy, certain chemicals, creams, gels, cosmetics, or metals, often topically but sometimes by internal absorption.

If you suspect your child has allergies, consult your physician or an allergist. You may be asked to keep a diary of your child's symptoms to try to detect which foods, substances, or situations trigger symptoms. When a food allergy is suspected, the doctor may suggest an exclusion diet to pinpoint the offending food. If your child's allergic symptoms become more intense, your doctor may arrange for a series of diagnostic allergy skin tests, followed by sequenced allergy shots (desensitization immunotherapy). Keep in mind, however, that the immune system matures with time, so it is possible for your child to naturally outgrow the tendency to react to some substances.

☛ **WARNING:** If you suspect your child has an allergy, do not devise your own diet for him or her. A restricted diet for children, without medical supervision, might leave them short of essential vitamins and minerals. And never attempt to devise your own allergy test. A mother in my practice who suspected her son had an allergy to pistachio nuts purposely fed him nuts and then waited for a reaction. Fortunately, he developed only a mild rash. But many allergy-prone children can have a very severe allergic reaction to nuts, particularly those in the peanut family. The result can be fatal.

If you have been advised that your youngster's allergies may be life-threatening, alert her school and other adults as necessary and make sure she wears a medical alert bracelet. Make sure your child's school has an emergency kit, including an Epi-pen to administer epinephrine, either in the principal's or nurse's office. Also have kits readily available in key places around your house and in your automobile. Your doctor can write a prescription for the Epi-pen. Make sure all responsible adults know how to use it, and teach your child to do so when she is old enough. Of course, the best treatment is avoidance of the allergen. This requires a lot of vigilance and education.

CONVENTIONAL TREATMENT

✦ There are many over-the-counter antiallergy medicines such as Benadryl that come in forms designed specifically for children and quickly get into the circulatory system. These medications are readily available for oral administration in liquid form for younger children or capsules for teens and adults. Some, designed to relieve the discomfort of the burning, itching, or stinging, are applied topically, in the form of gels, creams, or pastes, and act directly at the site of a rash eruption. (Examples are Rhuli gel, zinc oxide, calamine lotion, and hydrocortisone cream.)

✦ Prescription medications include more concentrated forms of hydrocortisone creams, injectable and oral corticosteroid preparations, antihistamines, nasal sprays, and inhalers.

✦ When prescribed after careful diagnostic testing, allergy desensitization serums have been proven effective.

✦ Cool water compresses on the itchy or swollen areas can make your child feel more comfortable during an allergic reaction.

Following are basic *housekeeping suggestions* to help reduce the possibilities of allergic reactions.

- ✦ Replace down and feather pillows with polyester or foam ones.
- ✦ Have your child wash his hands frequently, especially after handling pets.
- ✦ Wash bedding and linens in hot water weekly.
- ✦ Vacuum tufted mattresses and cover them with cotton blend mattress covers.
- ✦ Avoid upholstered furniture, which collects dust and mold spores.
- ✦ Use a dehumidifier with an air filter. (The optimum temperature is 70°F by day and 65°F at night.)

✦ Use air-conditioning at home and in the car to dry the air and reduce the formation of mold. Remember to wash or replace filters periodically.

Parents' Report: What Works

✦ Put one drop of peppermint oil on the base of your child's neck twice a day. I am not certain about the medicinal benefits for allergies, but your child should enjoy the soothing aroma.

✦ A father in my practice says he adds orange rinds to tea to relieve the stuffed nose his daughter gets with her allergies.

✦ In an effort to banish her daughter's allergies, one mother has turned to gems. Based on family custom, she believes that orange carnelian, a semiprecious stone, worn around the neck will shorten the length of an attack. But she tells me this *only* works with seasonal allergies involving the head and chest—those with sneezing and wheezing. According to her, the orange stone does nothing to help food allergies.

✦ One grandmother sternly lectured me, "You do know, of course, that bananas stop my grandchild's allergic reactions, don't you?" I had to admit that although I knew bananas provide potassium and other nutrients, I was not aware of their antiallergy benefits. Grandma was expecting me to give a stronger endorsement and was clearly not impressed. Later I asked a naturopathic physician about it. He said it's just an old wives' tale; bananas do *not* work to clear up allergies. In fact, they are actually contraindicated—bananas promote the production of a type of prostaglandin that's responsible for inflammation and smooth muscle contractions. This is *not* what you would want to experience during an allergy attack. Bananas are also a known trigger for migraine headaches in some children.

✦ One family recommended spreading sage on a piece of buttered whole grain bread. Although this recipe has the friendly aroma of Thanksgiving and stuffing, sage is a drying agent that could irritate the airway tissues during an allergy attack. Sorry, but I think this suggestion is a turkey!

Arthritis

THE AILMENT

Although this condition is not a common childhood malady, some youngsters do suffer with various forms of joint discomfort. Arthritis is a serious disorder and may lead to permanent joint deformities. There are many different types of arthritis, each involving some inflammation of one or more joints. It usually manifests as warmth, tenderness, stiffness, and sometimes swelling of the affected area.

The possible causes are not easily identified. Arthritis may be caused by trauma or by injury to a joint, or it can result from a viral, bacterial, or fungal infection settling in joints. An untreated strep throat, for example, can result in bacteria circulating via the bloodstream throughout the body, causing multisystem infection including joint inflammation.

Other causes may involve immunodeficiency disorders, diabetes, or allergic reactions. Sometimes joint discomfort becomes apparent after routine vaccinations. There are instances when the immune system malfunctions and produces antibodies that attack the body's own tissues. The result may be the joint discomfort and fever that characterize *juvenile rheumatoid arthritis,* one of the most common rheumatic diseases of children and a condition affecting children as young as age two.

☛ WARNING: Painful and swollen joints, limping, general aches and pains around the body, and fluctuating fevers are all signals to contact your doctor. Early treatment of arthritis can prevent long-term suffering.

Conventional Treatment

✦ Aspirin is generally considered a first-line therapy in children with arthritis today. (☛ **WARNING:** Children should *never* take aspirin without a physician's recommendation because of the risk of Reye's syndrome, a potentially fatal complication.) Other over-the-counter pain medications include those that contain acetaminophen and nonsteroidal anti-inflammatory preparations. Your doctor will recommend the pain reliever most appropriate for your child.

✦ Prescribed medications, including long-term oral antibiotics and occasionally intrajoint injections of corticosteroids, may be recommended for the progressive form of the disease.

✦ Physical therapy is often beneficial for many youngsters, as it allows them to participate in athletic activities and may prevent some of the possible long-term debilitating effects.

✦ Yoga is great for improving posture in a child with arthritis.

✦ Walking is great and swimming is an excellent activity to retain range of motion. Combine both by having your child exercise in a pool.

✦ Heat, by way of a warm bath, a hot shower, or a warm, moist towel applied directly to affected areas, can often relieve joint stiffness and discomfort.

Parents' Report: What Works

✦ Although arthritis may not be common, I have treated many children with joint discomfort. Often these children come in wearing a variety of copper ornaments, ranging from elaborate copper bangle bracelets to plain copper wire twisted around the wrists or ankles. Initially I questioned the rationale, but now I accept the jewelry. It is believed that copper absorbed through the skin provides temporary relief from arthritic pain. In general, rheumatologists haven't given copper jewelry an official seal of approval, although some give an approving nod to patients who have chosen these adornments.

✦ After years of translating aromatic offerings in the examining room, I can often anticipate the complaint of the child with just one whiff. Many grandparents, in particular, are fond of rubbing oil of wintergreen on a child with painful joints and then covering the joints with plastic. I remind them, however, that plastic bags should *never* be left in place on an unattended child because of the danger of suffocation.

✦ While my husband, Larry, and I were on a winter holiday in Mazatlan, Mexico, I fell under the spell of Francisco, a massage therapist. He swears his massage oil compound banishes arthritis pain. Although he would not reveal his exact recipe, he said he uses a handful of ground leaves of cat's claw, ruda, eucalyptus, cocao, sage, lavender, and arnica with 2 ounces of denatured alcohol, all added to 2 cups of sunflower oil and put into a quart jar. Most of these leaves can be purchased in health food stores. This mixture must sit for four to six months to mature for effectiveness. After straining it through cheesecloth, you can massage it into your child's aching muscles. Obviously, you have to plan ahead to use this remedy.

✦ This recipe was shared with me by a fellow pediatrician in Prague during an international symposium. Combine 2 teaspoons each of apple cider vinegar and honey in 8 ounces of water. Have your child drink this up to three times a day with meals. (Honey should *never* be given to children under the age of one because of the possible presence of spores that can cause infection.)

✦ For achy feet, microwave raw rice grains in a bowl for two minutes. Put this hot rice into a sock and knot the end. (The granules hold heat.) Make sure that the sock is not too hot. Place under the foot's arch and allow your child to roll this homemade bean bag back and forth. The soothing heat travels up the child's leg. I have tried this and it feels wonderful.

✦ A South Carolina native, Pearl, shared this family arthritis recipe with me as we chatted one afternoon in a hair salon. Soak a banana peel in rubbing alcohol for two to three days until the solution turns dark, then apply the resulting banana lotion to the painful areas. ☛ **WARNING:** Do *not* give this concoction to the child to eat or drink, as rubbing alcohol is poisonous.

✦ I have heard of families who feed their kids lots of salmon, tuna, and sardines in the belief that there is a substance in these particular fish that prevents the occurrence of arthritis.

Asthma

The Ailment

Asthma, the most common chronic disorder in children and adolescents, is an inflammatory disease involving the airways. The air passages from the windpipe to the tiny air sacs in the lungs become constricted, causing coughing, wheezing, shortness of breath, and chest tightness.

For reasons that are not entirely understood, the incidence and severity of asthma has been increasing in the United States. Asthma cannot be underestimated; untreated, it is a serious, life-threatening disease.

There are many factors associated with the extreme sensitivity of some children's air tubes in the lungs. A major risk factor is a family history of allergy and/or asthma. In kids with this greater sensitivity, irritants such as pollen, house dust, mites, animal fur, tobacco smoke, cold weather, viral infections, and emotional upsets can trigger an attack.

The irritants cause three major changes to occur within the lower respiratory system:

1. The tissues lining the inside of the bronchi (breathing tubes) swell, compromising the passageways' opening.
2. The muscles surrounding these tubes contract, making the passageways even narrower.

3. More than the usual amount of mucus is produced, plugging portions of the already narrowed openings, making it extremely difficult to get air through.

This all adds up to coughing, chest tightness, shortness of breath, and the characteristic wheezing sound as air is forced through narrowed, mucus-plugged airways.

Recurring episodes cause chronic inflammation of the bronchial structures. Multiple intermittent treatments help heal and repair the bronchioles, but at the same time they encourage thickening and other anatomic changes or "remodeling" of these structures. This repeated injury can be permanently damaging and lead to lifelong respiratory obstruction.

Contrary to popular belief, children do not truly outgrow asthma. The condition may become silent as their respiratory and immune systems mature. Also, as children grow up and learn to avoid certain environmental triggers they may have fewer episodes of breathing difficulties.

☛ WARNING: Asthma is *always* a medically urgent condition. All asthma sufferers require ongoing medical supervision. It is critical that your child take all prescribed medications as directed. Over-the-counter asthma relievers may actually cause a worsening of the condition and should not be used unless specifically advised by your physician. Severe breathing difficulties, chest pain, persistent wheezing, a darkening of the lips or gums, or any change in skin color signals danger and warrants immediate medical attention. All asthma sufferers may have recurring episodes. However, by following a physician's written treatment plan, asthma can be managed and controlled.

Conventional Treatment

✦ First, try to control factors that may contribute to the severity of your child's asthma. Where possible, minimize exposure to allergens and asthma triggers.

✦ As a part of controlling this disease, it is necessary to understand the importance of tools that measure breathing capability, such as the *peak flow meter.* Learn how and when to use it and check daily to see how well your child is breathing.

✦ Encourage your youngster to drink lots of fluids to help liquefy mucus.

✦ Reduce your child's consumption of foods that seem to increase mucus production. Milk is commonly thought to be a culprit in mucus production. Although there is little scientific support, many parents find reducing dairy products in the child's diet seems to help with their asthma. Check with your doctor.

✦ Increase the moisture in the environment. Use a humidifier to moisten the air. (Care must be taken to clean the humidifier frequently to eliminate mold and mildew, which can trigger an asthma episode.)

✦ Medications, some of which may be recommended for daily use, must be taken as prescribed for the most effective control of the disease. These may include oral anti-inflammatory tablets, medicines administered by a nebulizer (a machine that delivers medication in a vapor mist to the lower respiratory tract), inhaled medications for immediate and long-term relief, corticosteroid tablets, syrups, antibiotics for acute inflammation, and others as recommended and prescribed by your child's physician.

✦ Dietary therapies include reducing or eliminating common food allergens: milk, peanuts, synthetic food additives, saturated fats, refined foods, and sugar. Increased consumption of fish oils (omega-3 polyunsaturated fatty acids, found in coldwater fish such as salmon and mackerel) has been reported to lessen mild asthma symptoms. Other reported beneficial foods include vegetables, grains, onions, and garlic. Some health food advocates promote multivitamin therapy to enhance levels of vitamins B_6, B_{12}, and C, all of which are believed to benefit pulmonary function. I personally recommend that kids get their vitamins from a balanced diet rather than supplements. But I definitely endorse eliminating those foods from your child's diet that have been identified as probable allergens by your physician.

Parents' Report: What Works

If you talk with families living with asthma, they are likely to share all sorts of tales about what has worked, including some that are quite fanciful. One colleague, a pediatric allergist who has asthma, shared this story: When he was a child, his grandmother went into her backyard and hammered a nail into a tree. Family lore has it that when he grew to be the height of the nail, he outgrew his asthma. As he interprets this remedy, the idea is to hammer the nail *just* high enough to look forward to a positive outcome with growth, but not so high that the child feels doomed to suffer into adulthood. In the version he shared, the nail was "planted" at the adult height of the grandmother who drove in the nail.

I've heard one unusual remedy from several families with Latino backgrounds. I was told that if you have an asthmatic child in the family, you should get a Chihuahua dog. The belief is that asthma will transfer from the child into the dog. Does that mean that when the Chihuahua starts to wheeze, your child is cured? Playing amateur detective, I was able to find out that this custom is based on the folk culture of the Aztec Indians in Mexico, where Chihuahuas originated. The Aztecs believed that you could use a small animal to take on the breathing difficulties of a child. Unfortunately for the animal, once it was thought to have caught the asthma, it was then sacrificed.

The following remedies are *not* to be used *instead* of your physician's specific recommendations, but you may consider them a complementary addition to his or her advice.

✦ Offer tea. Theophylline, an ingredient in regular orange pekoe tea (not an herbal variety), is a known bronchodilator that helps widen blood vessels. Also, warm liquids are soothing and do not irritate the bronchial tubes. (Caffeine, found in small quantities in many teas, can also open the airways like an inhaler.)

✦ Mix together 2 ounces each of onion juice, carrot juice, and parsley juice. One mother of three asthma sufferers assures me that this blend, consumed twice daily, relaxes the bronchial muscles and prevents spasms. I must confess that I have never had the courage to sample this concoction, but I suspect the parsley helps to mute the taste of the onion. Actually, these ingredients might make a tasty soup base. (Another similar odorous mixture is raw red onion mixed with raw sugar—offer 1 teaspoonful every hour.) Onions help ease the constriction of the bronchial tubes.

✦ Green tea is believed to be an antioxidant and may be beneficial to those who suffer with asthma. You can buy green tea bags in most grocery stores.

☛ WARNING: Ma huang *(Ephedra sinica)* is a very potent cardiac stimulant and should *never* be used in children. I was dismayed to find that it is still popular enough that the warning needed to be repeated several times at a recent national pediatric asthma conference.

Note: Dosage information for any medicinal product is very important, particularly for children. (See the Introduction.) A naturopathic doctor may be better prepared to discuss the benefits and caveats of any herbal products. Remember, the use of herbal remedies is not currently regulated by the U.S. Food and Drug Administration, and has not been adequately studied in children. If you are considering using any herbs for your youngsters, it is *very* important to discuss your concerns and plans in advance with your child's doctor.

Athlete's Foot

THE AILMENT

Tinea pedis, more commonly known as althlete's foot, is a fungal infection of the epidermis, the outermost layer of skin. This fungus needs a warm, moist environment in which to thrive, such as that conveniently provided between the toes. It is characterized by annoying itching, scaling, and peeling between the toes and occasionally on the instep and soles of the feet. The fungus is contagious. It is generally acquired by walking barefoot in common areas where other infected feet have been, such as gym floors, communal showers, and pool areas. Preventive measures include good foot hygiene, primarily meticulous drying between the toes after bathing or soaking. Many parents find that hair dryers aimed at the feet can help dry those tootsies.

CONVENTIONAL TREATMENT

✦ There are many effective over-the-counter powders, solutions, and creams for the management and treatment of mild cases.

✦ Encourage your child to wear thongs in locker rooms and showers, and to change his shoes and socks regularly.

✦ Persistent peeling, cracking, and itching may lead to a more serious form of tinea that involves the darkening and deterioration of the toenails. This more involved stage warrants medical attention and prescribed medication.

Parents' Report: What Works

Most of the remedies that follow are based on eliminating the fungus that causes athlete's foot. Because the skin around the toes may be cracked and peeling, some of these preparations could sting a little.

✦ Clorox bleach mixed in water is a popular foot soak. Since bleach is not an antifungal, I'm not sure how it kills the tinea fungus that causes athlete's foot, but it does have disinfectant properties. Make a solution of 2 tablespoons of bleach added to 1 gallon of warm water and have your child soak his or her feet for ten to fifteen minutes twice a day. ☛ **WARNING:** Discard any unused solution and keep out of reach of children.

✦ A time-tested remedy is gentian violet, an antifungal tincture applied to the infected areas daily. It's generally available at your pharmacy over-the-counter. However, it is *really* purple and stains anything it comes in contact with; you must be careful not to get it on clothing or you may suddenly see everything through a purple haze!

✦ Another version of a soak is to crush 5 adult-strength aspirin and dissolve in 2 quarts of warm water in a soaking basin. The salicylic acid in aspirin has anti-inflammatory properties. (Do *not* use if there is a family history of aspirin sensitivity.) Remember: Soak, don't drink!

✦ Soak your child's feet in a mixture of half apple cider vinegar and half warm water for ten minutes daily or until symptoms disappear. This relieves itching and peeling. Also try rubbing the solution on the affected areas with cotton balls. An alternative is to add ½ cup of white vinegar to a gallon of water and soak your youngster's toes for fifteen minutes at least twice a day. Let his feet air-dry.

✦ Soak feet in a solution of 2 heaping tablespoons of baking soda in 2 quarts of warm water for thirty minutes daily. This changes the pH (acid/base balance) of the skin. Also sprinkle baking soda on the feet and in shoes and socks. This will absorb some of the perspiration and help neutralize the pH of the skin.

✦ Bring 4 cups of water to a boil, add 8–10 broken sticks of cinnamon, reduce heat to low, and simmer for five minutes. Remove and steep, covered, for forty-five minutes. Use as a foot bath. The heat and aroma are soothing.

✦ Rub a clove of raw garlic on the affected areas if your children don't mind the smell. You could also put some freshly crushed garlic on the sites, leave on for half an hour, and then wash it off with water. (You could even leave some garlic in place and cover with an old sock.) Do this once a day for a week, and the athlete's foot condition should be gone. If the garlic causes a burning sensation, remove it, wash with lukewarm water, and try again with diluted garlic juice. You can also dust with garlic powder or wash with garlic juice. Studies show garlic can kill the fungus that causes athlete's foot. Only consider these remedies when your child won't be in a crowd!

✦ Rub raw honey on the infected areas before bedtime, cover the feet with old socks, and leave on overnight. Honey is a good emollient that softens and soothes dry or cracked skin.

Back Pain

The Ailment

Back pain in children can be a diagnostic challenge, especially in the very young. Although it may require particular patience and skill, try to pinpoint the specific area of discomfort. Has your child had a recent fall, learned a new karate chop, tried a new sport, or performed any unusual movements? Ask your child: "Was the pain there when you went to bed last night? When you got out of bed this morning, did it hurt?"

Also observe:

- ✦ Has the pain interrupted or interfered with play activities?
- ✦ Does the pain move or radiate, and what action seems to offer relief?
- ✦ Does it occur when your child coughs or urinates?

Ask your youngster to demonstrate a few bends and reaches to determine if the discomfort is aggravated by any specific movement.

- ✦ Is the pain present or more intense at certain times of day or night?

- ✦ Have you noticed any asymmetry (crookedness) when looking at your child's back or walk?
- ✦ Does one shoulder appear higher than the other? Does your child carry a heavy book bag or purse on one shoulder?

Report all of these answers to your child's physician so that she will be in a better position to determine which diagnostic studies or referrals would be most appropriate. Sources of back pain may include pneumonia, appendicitis, kidney infections, ovarian cysts in girls, and, rarely, some childhood malignancies.

Note any increase in angle or any exaggeration of the normal plane of the back, such as occurs with the normal slight indentation (sway) of the lower back. When that sway is very pronounced, it's known as *lordosis.* If a curving of the backbone to either the right or left side is noted and appears as an S curve in any part of the back, it may be a condition known as *scoliosis*, which is commonly first detected in early adolescence.

Disc herniations, disc infections, and disc calcifications are very rare in children, but if they are diagnosed, they must be properly treated by an orthopedic surgeon, the medical specialist trained to deal with disorders of bones and their attachments to joints and muscles.

The most common causes of back pain in childhood are the sprains and strains associated with physical education in school, gymnastics, weight-lifting, dance, and other athletic activities. *Sprains* occur when a joint is pulled beyond its usual range of motion, sometimes tearing the ligament that holds the joint together. A *strain* is also called a pulled muscle and may occur when the muscle is overextended, sometimes tearing some of its fibers. Sprains are usually more painful than strains.

Congenital variations in back and spinal development, arthritis, trauma, or overuse injuries can also result in painful backs.

☛ WARNING: Any youngster who complains of persistent or prolonged back pain (for more than three consecutive days) or is awakened by the discomfort should have a full medical evaluation, which may include laboratory studies, X rays, bone scans, or other imaging studies.

Conventional Treatment

The obvious first step is to have your child limit activities that aggravate the painful area. If a strain or sprain is suspected, apply an ice pack to the painful area for three to five minutes. Remove for five minutes, then reapply, and repeat this process for the first several hours following an injury (some physicians recommend up to twenty-four hours). After this initial period, you can apply moist heat to that area and give your child an age- and weight-appropriate dose of acetaminophen or ibuprofen until your physician gives further advice. If your child's doctor suspects he or she has an arthritis condition, aspirin therapy may be one of the recommendations.

Parents' Report: What Works

If your doctor has ruled out a more serious condition, the following are some remedies for soothing children's aching backs.

✦ Many of the remedies families tell me rely on rubbing an oily substance onto a painful back. In some cases, it seems to be the penetrating odor that crowds out the "perception" of pain. Here's a southern recipe from the Reid family, which they shared with me after they relocated from North Carolina to the Washington, D.C., area. It's not for cooking ribs but for curing bad backs! Take ½ cup of fatback grease from a fatty strip of pork or beef and stir in ½ cup of turpentine from your local hardware store. Rub this mixture on the skin and massage into the muscles of the back. I have been told by more than one grandparent that motor oil can be used instead of fatback grease. However, turpentine and motor oil are toxic if consumed, so keep the remedies away from young kids, who have a greater tendency to put their fingers into their mouths.

✦ There are a variety of oils that many families have reported to be effective. They appear to stimulate dilation (widening) of the blood vessels when rubbed into the skin and increase circulation in that part of the body. The aromas themselves act as a distraction and perhaps as a counterirritant to the pain. Oil of wintergreen is very popular, but never use it with a heating pad or hot compress. The combination of the hot, tingling sensation created by the wintergreen oil coupled with the thermal effect of a heated pad or compress may cause irritation or even a first-degree burn at the site. ☛ WARNING: Keep this and all other aromatic oils out of reach of children. Swallowing any of these oils may be harmful.

✦ Some parents favor peppermint oil for back rubs. It tingles as it is applied and may stimulate the nerves. It has a comforting, cooling effect. ☛ WARNING: Do not use on child's face or nasal area or allow the child to swallow any of the oil. And don't use peppermint oil with any heat, as it may irritate or burn.

✦ A colleague who grew up in Greece recalls that his mother used cypress oil for many ailments. Cypress is known to strengthen blood capillary walls, improve circulation, and act as an anti-inflammatory. He suggests that it might be beneficial to massage 1 or 2 drops of cypress oil mixed into 1/4 cup of a carrier oil into a painful area.

✦ See **Arthritis** for more remedies.

Bad Breath (Halitosis)

The Ailment

Teens call it dragon breath. Whatever it's called, bad breath has many causes, ranging from poor oral hygiene to gastrointestinal disorders. The offensive rotten-egg odor comes from the hydrogen sulfide and other gases produced from a mixture emitted by the breakdown of food and bacterial compounds within the digestive system.

The breath of most infants generally has no odor, or it may be sweet with faint traces of the milk they ingested. Parents sometimes report unpleasant odors if the baby's tongue is heavily coated with milk.

As infants mature and their diets change to include a variety of solid foods, their burps begin to assume a more odoriferous character. Many parents are shocked when they discover that their cherubs also have "morning breath." This results from the child breathing, during sleep, with the mouth slightly open, causing dry mouth. A dry mouth allows odor-producing bacteria to flourish.

Look inside your child's mouth. Inspect the gums, tongue, soft palate, and inside of the cheeks for redness or any ulcers or sores. If possible, look beyond the back of the tongue to the large pinkish masses of tissue on either side at the very back of the mouth. These mounds are the tonsils. Are there white spots on these rounded masses? Are they a deep red color? If your child has teeth, do you wipe or brush them daily? Has your child had symptoms of a cold or upper-airway allergies, which might result in a stuffy nose or cough? Frequently, postnasal drainage from congested or infected sinuses causes unpleasant breath odors. Vomiting, diarrhea, or constipation can also contribute to mouth odor, as can inadequate liquid intake. If this is a persistent or frequently recurring problem, ask your pediatrician to investigate.

CONVENTIONAL TREATMENT

✦ Even if your baby hasn't yet sprouted teeth, proper mouth care is still important. Wrap a moist, clean washcloth or cotton handkerchief around your finger and wipe the inside of your baby's cheeks and tongue daily.

✦ As the primary teeth erupt, use a very small (less than pea-sized) amount of toothpaste on a soft baby toothbrush and gently brush the teeth. Don't let your child swallow the toothpaste. If possible, without causing choking, gently brush the baby's tongue daily. Remember, she can bite!

✦ Consider your youngster's diet. Is it well balanced, with vegetables and fruits? Is he drinking adequate liquids, including water? Check with your doctor to determine how much water your child needs based on age and weight.

✦ As you review the importance of good oral hygiene in your children, keep the steps simple and appropriate for their age and level of understanding. Most kids need their parents' reminders and follow-up on their teeth brushing, sometimes into their teen years. However, once they start brushing their own teeth, it is important to establish a morning and evening routine, and for them to learn to brush their tongue, followed by rinsing the mouth with lots of water.

✦ In my practice, I suggest regularly scheduled dental checks for all children before their molars erupt, generally between their first and second birthdays.

✦ There is debate over the wisdom of using mouthwashes in children as opposed to copious plain-water rinses. Many dentists feel that careful brushing, flossing, and water rinses are adequate. In fact, some feel that commercial mouthwashes—even those advertised with their flavorings as just for children—actually prepare the mouth for an overproduction of bacteria. Check with your pediatric dentist.

Parents' Report: What Works

✦ When sinuses become congested and inflamed, they can cause unpleasant breath. If you think your child has a sinus infection, first check with his pediatrician to determine if medication is warranted for the condition. However, for bad breath resulting from clogged sinuses, try this remedy using over-the-counter hydrogen peroxide (a 3 percent solution) directly from your medicine cabinet. Mix 2 ounces of hydrogen peroxide with 2 ounces of plain tap water. Use a nose dropper to put a few drops into each nostril. It may tingle a little as it foams and bubbles its way to the sinus areas. Repeat every eight hours. Don't let your child ingest any of the solution.

✦ Cloves are a powerful antiseptic. Make a tea by putting 3 whole cloves or 1/4 teaspoon of ground cloves in 2 cups of hot water and steep for twenty minutes, stirring occasionally. Pour through a fine strainer and use as a mouth swish.

✦ If your youngster is old enough to gargle, try mixing 4 drops of oil of cloves into 4 ounces of room-temperature water and allow him to gargle twice a day. The child should not drink the mixture, but it isn't harmful if a small amount is swallowed.

✦ Although chewing parsley and mint leaves has been one breath-freshening remedy used for thousands of years (and you may take delight in pointing out that the little pieces of parsley resemble little trees), most kids will not chew them. So put parsley or mint in a blender and mix with 1/2 cup of water and let it be a mouth swish solution. Parsley is especially good when garlic or onions are the source of the bad breath, as it is high in chlorophyll. Chewing a few parsley sprigs dipped in vinegar offers immediate, if only temporary, fresh mouth for adolescents who've just eaten a meal seasoned with garlic and onions. If the leaves are swallowed, they will be digested and continue to provide breath freshness. These plants also seem to reduce the production of intestinal gas by promoting better digestion.

✦ Tea tree oil contains antiseptic compounds that make it a powerful disinfectant. If it meets with your dentist's approval, try one of the toothpastes found in some health food establishments containing Melaleuca tea tree oil. Its strong aromatic flavor may combat unpleasant mouth odor.

Bed-wetting (Nocturnal Enuresis)

THE AILMENT

Once youngsters have become accustomed to responding to their toileting urges and can remain dry independently throughout the day, many parents expect them to awake in dry beds in the morning. However, most children master daytime bladder control before they can meet with consistent success during the nights. Still, some parents become unnecessarily anxious because of their youngsters' bed-wetting. The kidneys normally reduce their output of urine while we sleep. As the bladder becomes full, nerve sensor cells in its wall signal the brain, which transmits the urge to urinate. If, during sleep, the urge to urinate is either ignored or does not cause the child to awaken, and the bladder is unable to hold back the flow of urine, spontaneous bed-wetting results. There is no magic age when this mastery is spontaneously achieved. Many children remain dry through the night between three and four years of age. Girls generally achieve nighttime bladder mastery (for eight to ten hours of sleep) earlier than boys. Most youngsters outgrow bed-wetting by age six.

However, in some families it is not unusual for bed-wetting to persist into adolescence. Rarely a serious medical problem, enuresis (its medical name) is more of an annoyance for the youngster and his parents. If this is a problem in your household and you discreetly inquire among your relatives, you may discover a family pattern of bed-wetting. When I ask overwrought parents nonjudgmentally about their own recollections of night bladder control, I often hear that one or both of the parents was enuretic until late childhood or into early adolescence.

Once overnight bladder control has been successfully achieved for an extended period of time, a sudden recurrence of bed-wetting may signal other problems. I encourage parents to reflect carefully on recent life events. Is there a new baby, a new school, increased tension in the home, parental job anxiety, a recent death (family member or pet), or other family disruption? It is important to identify possible sources of stress and anxiety.

Determine if there is any association with increased fluid intake, an increase in the frequency of daytime voiding, or any discomfort with urination. Make a list of your observations and concerns and discuss them with your child's doctor. Your pediatrician may do a laboratory analysis of your child's urine to rule out infection, diabetes, or other disorders. It may be necessary to check for unusual anatomical variations or nerve impulse problems.

Conventional Treatment

✦ Attempt to restrict fluid intake in the evenings. As a first step, establish a time after which the child should not have anything more to drink, not even a bedtime glass of milk. For example, if bedtime is 8 P.M., no liquids should be consumed after 6:30 P.M. Also, take your child to the bathroom just before he gets into bed.

✦ Depending on the age of the youngster, a potty chair in his bedroom may help, so he won't have to travel any distance in a darkened home to get to the bathroom. If the potty chair idea isn't acceptable or doesn't work, I suggest the child be awakened, taken by the hand, and led to the bathroom about four hours *after* going to bed. This helps get rid of the beverages consumed with the evening meal. When counseling families, I always suggest that the last person up in the household be assigned that task.

✦ It's important that you not scold or punish your child for accidents, whatever his age. Shaming or making him feel guilty will only make matters worse and may shatter his self-confidence in other areas where he has achieved some success. Some children respond well to the wetting alarms available on the market, while others are terrified of them.

✦ Dress your child for sleep in a way that makes it easier to undress him if he does have an accident. Just put him in a T-shirt that can be pulled on and off. Some parents like to triple-sheet the bed; that is, they put a layer of plastic between two layers of sheet. If there is a wetting accident, you only replace the wet top layer.

✦ Many families have found that gradual bladder-stretching exercises are useful. To accomplish this, encourage the child during the daytime to overconsume liquids when you know you will be at home. With your assistance, encourage him to hold his urine for as long as reasonably possible. Over time, this bladder stretching should force his bladder capacity to increase, reducing the frequent full-bladder sensation during a sleep period of eight to twelve hours.

✦ After a careful assessment, your pediatrician may review the option of prescribed medications.

Parents' Report: What Works

✦ Use a chart or calendar system with smiley faces or stickers to mark dry nights. Have planned congratulatory rituals ready after you and your child have agreed upon reasonable periods of success.

✦ Corn silk tincture is a popular Chinese remedy that helps tone the muscles that help with bladder control. Herbalists often suggest mixing a few teaspoons with an equal amount of oats and St. John's wort and giving the resulting tincture to the child before bedtime. After a few nights of taking this combo, your child may wake up to a dry bed. The St. John's wort is believed to ease the anxiety associated with bed-wetting. Some pediatricians prescribe Tofranil, an antidepressant, for the same reason. Check with your doctor first.

✦ The Chinese also tout adding ginger and walnuts to your child's diet as a bed-wetting remedy. I'm not sure why, but ginger is tasty when made as a tea or even grated fresh into food, and walnuts are a great source of vitamin E as well as some healthy fats, so these foods probably can't hurt.

✦ A child psychologist recalls his Greek mother's remedy for preventing bed-wetting. She rubbed a few teaspoons of oil of cypress on his abdomen before bedtime, and he would awaken in the morning in a dry bed.

✦ Cinnamon is said to help prevent bed-wetting and promote sleep, so add a little to a cup of tea and allow the child to sip up to 2 or 3 tablespoons.

✦ Chamomile is another favorite with herbalists. One suggestion is to offer it as a tea. You can also put a few drops of chamomile essential oil into your child's bath or massage her lower back with a few drops mixed with some almond oil. Lavender essential oil has been recommended both in the bath and in a massage oil to combat bed-wetting. Remember, never let your child consume essential oils.

Birthmarks

The Ailment

A birthmark is not an ailment, but a skin discoloration caused by melanin, the pigment-producing cells, and very small blood vessels (capillaries) just beneath the skin. Birthmarks vary in size and shape. They may be flat or raised. Despite many folk tales, neither the size nor shape of a birthmark has any significance or any relation to a prebirth trauma or event. Some are obvious at birth, but many are not observed until after the first few weeks of life. Depending on their location and appearance, birthmarks are sometimes assigned various imaginative, though not accurate, names of identification.

✦ Stork bites: Red areas at the nape of the infant's neck are called stork bites because of the folk tale that the stork carries the newborn baby to her parents in its beak. The redness is actually a collection of small capillaries close to the surface of babies' thin skin. These reddened areas are called angel's kisses when seen on the eyelids or on the nose. They are harmless, and with time most disappear without treatment.

✦ Dark bluish areas on the shoulders, back, or buttocks of darker-skinned babies are frequently thought by parents to be bruises, but they are simply areas of melanin deposits. Sometimes referred to as Mongolian spots, these areas fade over time and frequently disappear entirely.

✦ A raised red area, sometimes irregularly shaped and perhaps resembling a strawberry, frequently enlarges before it gradually flattens and disappears. This strawberry patch is probably a hemangioma, a larger collection of blood vessels beneath the surface of the skin. Hemangiomas are generally painless and harmless. Most become flat and slowly fade after several years.

✦ A large flat red-purple area, which may appear on the face or any part of the body, is probably a port wine stain. A port wine stain on the face, although cosmetically upsetting, might be harmless or might be indicative of a more serious central nervous system disorder known as Sturge-Weber syndrome. If the doctor decides it's only a birthmark, expect it to spontaneously get lighter with time. However, it rarely fades completely.

Conventional Treatment

Most hemangiomas will shrink somewhat over time, but some may not fade quickly or completely enough for the family's satisfaction. After an evaluation and discussion with your pediatrician, a referral to a dermatologist may be necessary. Laser treatments are sometimes recommended to speed a resolution.

When present on the face or other exposed body areas, cosmetic camouflages are available to match the predominant complexion shade and serve as an effective concealer.

Parents' Report: What Works

✦ Castor oil massaged into the skin site is reported to erase birthmarks, but it may take months to see improvement.

✦ The juice from a lemon applied to any flat skin discoloration might help to lighten it.

✦ See **Blemishes** for other ways to bleach darkened spots on the skin.

Bites

Insect Bites

The Ailment

Insect bites occur most commonly during the spring and summer months. Though rarely dangerous, they are quite annoying and sometimes become the precursors of bacterial skin infections.

Bites from *mosquitoes* and *flies* usually cause a mild stinging sensation followed by a small raised eruption, which itches.

Flea bites result in raised areas that frequently occur in clusters, either in a line or in irregular patches on exposed skin surfaces closest to the source. Typical areas for flea bites are the feet on those who go barefoot or wear sandals and just above the sock line on shins and calves. Fleas live wherever family pets have been—on the carpet, in cracks in floors, sand on sofas and bedspreads.

Fire ants live in the southern regions of the country. They are found in pastures and meadows, and in lawns and park areas in cities and suburbs. Fire ants possess venom that causes immediate pain and swelling in the area of the bite. These bites also usually occur in clusters, especially on the legs and feet of barefoot children. If your child suffers extreme discomfort, unusual swelling, fever, nausea, or breathing difficulties after fire ant bites, call your doctor immediately.

Bees, wasps, and *yellow jackets* may cause stings that are immediately painful and quickly result in swelling and itching at the bite site. In some allergy-sensitive individuals, a severe reaction to bee and wasp stings may result in weakness, breathing difficulties, a sudden drop in blood pressure, collapse, shock, and in extreme cases death. If there is a family history of severe reactions to insect stings or bites, it is wise to have an emergency sting kit nearby. They are available, by prescription, from the pharmacy. I advise the parents in my practice to get three kits: one kit for the home, one to be kept in the family car, and one labeled with the child's name to be kept in the health office at the youngster's school. (See **Allergy** for more information.)

Tick bites usually result in painless small mounds. You may discover them, with the tick still in place, while bathing your child. If you live in an area where there have been reports of deer ticks or Lyme disease, do daily tick checks when your youngsters come in from play. Inspect the nape of the neck, the hairline, behind the ears, and all exposed body areas. If the tick is removed within twelve hours of attachment, there is less cause for alarm.

Conventional Treatment

✦ Wash the area with warm soapy water, then pat dry. Apply cool water compresses to reduce any swelling and to relieve the immediate itch associated with the bite. If itching is intense, apply an over-the-counter anti-itch preparation such as Aveeno anti-itch lotion or Caladryl lotion.

✦ Clip your youngster's nails as short as possible. If he is old enough to fan the itchy sites, encourage him to do so. This will reduce the likelihood of his scratching so much that he breaks the skin, resulting in a secondary skin infection.

✦ To reduce insect bites, avoid scented soaps, hairspray, and fragrant lotions. (Yes, "sweet" children do attract bugs.) When children will be outdoors for extended periods of time, avoid dressing them in brightly colored and flower prints; they attract insects. If your kids are going on a picnic or field trip, I suggest dressing them in long pants and lightweight long-sleeved shirts.

✦ DEET (diethyl toluamide) is a potent insect repellent that, if absorbed in great amounts through the skin, may cause serious toxicity. Although this chemical should *never* be sprayed directly onto your child's skin, if the child is over twelve months old, I usually suggest that parents lightly spray the youngster's outer clothing, including shoes, before sending them outdoors during high insect season. (Look for products specifically designed for children, which contain a lower percentage of DEET.) This will deter some mosquitoes, ticks, and fleas, but probably will not provide complete protection from the stings of bees and wasps. Over the course of many hours out-of-doors, periodic respraying is advised.

Parents' Report: What Works

Most of these remedies are designed to reduce the swelling and/or draw out the "sting." Some are so commonly used they may almost be considered conventional.

✦ Skin-So-Soft lotion, liberally applied on the skin, is the remedy most frequently mentioned by the parents in my practice. This Avon product now seems to be used more as an insect repellent than as the skin emollient for which it was designed. Avon smartly does not make any claims about its use as an insect repellant, but this belief has boosted product sales.

✦ Meat tenderizer mixed with a small amount of water to make a paste is one popular method for dealing with bites. Apply directly onto the itchy bite areas. Parents report that this paste minimizes the swelling and gives relief for the itching. Papain, an enzyme in the tenderizer, soothes and relieves the itching. Where feasible, remove any stinger present before applying meat tenderizer.

✦ Add 2–3 heaping tablespoons of baking soda into bathwater and then let the child soak. This reduces some of the swelling and relieves much of the itching, especially if there are multiple insect bites on the body.

✦ Aveeno oatmeal baths are very soothing to irritated skin.

✦ Jeff, a young tour guide my husband and I met in Bora Bora, shared his mother's family remedy after I got a lot of insect bites while on an excursion. He recommended lime or lemon juice squeezed directly onto the bite site. Unfortunately, when I did this, it stung! However, it did distract me enough from the itching that I stopped scratching.

✦ Ray Long, a Cherokee from the Mt. Ute Reservation in Pyramid Lake, California, told me that he applies the thin lining found inside an eggshell to the affected area and leaves it in place overnight.

✦ To avoid stings, Marie from Trinidad gave me her family's favorite homemade bug repellent. Mix equal amounts of pure coconut oil and rosemary; shake and apply to the body. It has a pleasant aroma but won't attract stinging insects.

✦ Wash the area and rub crushed aspirin on the site. Aspirin works as an anti-inflammatory. ☛ **WARNING:** Do *not* use if your child is aspirin-sensitive. Don't let children swallow aspirin because of the risk of Reye's syndrome, a potentially fatal complication.

✦ An acupuncturist, Sally, from Brooklyn, New York, shared a remedy that her mother learned while growing up in Austria: Crush several plantain weed leaves and apply directly to the sting site. It is believed that juice from the leaves draws out the stinger and venom. Plantain weed has pear-shaped leaves and grows prolifically in grassy places. Ask a botonist to confirm that you're using the right leaf. (Mullein leaves and yellow dock leaves also work well as poultices.)

Animal Bites

If your child has been bitten by an animal, the animal should be contained, if possible, until it can be evaluated for the presence of the rabies virus. If you can't identify or quarantine the animal, your youngster may have to undergo a series of rabies shots. Rabies is a life-threatening viral disease that can be prevented by inoculations during its incubation period. Any animal observed foaming at the mouth, behaving oddly, or walking or running strangely may have rabies. Many familiar animals in our environs, such as raccoons, skunks, squirrels, bats, dogs, and cats, may carry the rabies virus in their saliva.

Most bites from common animals (such as familiar dogs or cats) leave puncture marks but are generally harmless. If the bites are deep and involve tearing of tissue, the doctor should evaluate them immediately. If not properly addressed, these bites are likely to become infected and result in scarring. When possible, prevention is key. To reduce your children's risks for injury from animal bites, teach them never to pet or feed unfamiliar or stray animals. Do not allow them to disturb an animal, even the family pet, while it's eating. Children should never threaten, tease, pull the tail of, or corner any animal. Even if your child sees a cute dog on a leash, teach her to ask the dog's owner if it is okay to pet the dog. When you see stray animals in your neighborhood, notify the animal control authorities. Make sure you get your own pet its annual rabies vaccines.

CONVENTIONAL TREATMENT

Stop the bleeding from the bite by putting pressure on the area with a clean cloth. Flush the wound with lots of a warm soapy solution; rinse well, pat dry, apply a sterile bandage, then consult with your child's physician for next steps.

☛ WARNING: If redness, swelling, or tenderness lasts more than twenty-four hours, take your child to a doctor or the closest urgent care medical site for evaluation.

Human Bites

THE AILMENT

Human bites, most often inflicted by other children, are generally superficial puncture wounds. However, because of the many viral and bacterial organisms we harbor at any time in our saliva, deep human bites can be serious and sometimes require medical attention.

CONVENTIONAL TREATMENT

✦ Immediately wash the wound with soap and water, then rinse well under lots of cool running water to remove blood and saliva.

✦ Check your youngster's immunization records for the date of her last tetanus shot.

✦ Consult with your physician, describing the bite and your child's immunization status. Your youngster may need antibiotics to combat infection.

Snakebites

THE AILMENT

Each year more than forty thousand snakebites are reported in the United States. Most of these bites are from nonpoisonous snakes. If planning a camping trip or an outdoor adventure where you are likely to encounter snakes, check with the state or national park authorities to find out which types of snakes may be found in the region and what constitutes appropriate first-aid supplies for that area.

With your gear, be sure to pack a snakebite kit and a working cellular phone with an extra battery. Symptoms following a snakebite vary according to the type of snake.

Venom from rattlesnakes (found in every state except Alaska, Hawaii, and Maine), copperheads (found in eastern states), and cottonmouths or water moccasins (found primarily in the South) affects the cardiovascular system. Bites from coral snakes (found in the southeastern states) affect the central nervous system. You'll usually feel a sensation of stinging or burning pain at the bite site.

CONVENTIONAL TREATMENT

✦ If there is a snakebite, assume the possibility of venom injection. Look for immediate pain and swelling to occur. If possible, call for help and immediately transport the child to an emergency care facility. Until she can be moved, have your child lie still, avoiding movement, which can speed up the circulation and the spread of venom.

✦ If the bite is on an extremity, apply a firm tourniquet (but it should be loose enough to allow a finger to fit between it and the skin) *above* the site to slow the circulation of the venom from the bite. Immobilize the extremity.

✦ When possible, wash the site with warm, soapy water.

✦ If you have a snakebite kit, follow the instructions for using the vacuum suction device to extract the venom.

PARENTS' REPORT: WHAT WORKS

✦ Ray Long, a Cherokee living in California, offers a remedy that works only if you are in an area with cactus plants. If a member of your party suffers a snakebite, seek out a barrel cactus plant. Cut into the middle layer, which contains a milky sap that is said to immediately neutralize the venom injected by a snakebite. I know it's most unlikely that you'd stop to look for a barrel cactus when someone has suffered a snakebite, and I wholeheartedly endorse snakebite kits and medical assistance as your first line of treatment. But if you have no other resources, this is good to know.

✦ For rattlesnake bites: Wet the area, put salt on the wound, then wrap the site and immediately seek medical assistance.

✦ See **Stings** for more remedies.

Bleeding

THE AILMENT

Bleeding signifies the escape of blood from an injured vessel. The injury may be beneath the skin's surface, resulting in internal bleeding, which won't be immediately apparent. If you can see the bleeding, the outer layer of the skin's surface has ruptured.

At some point, every youngster will have accidents that result in skin breaks and bleeding. Depending upon the site and extent of the injury, bleeding may be negligible or quite profuse and prolonged. In general, the deeper the wound, the greater the blood loss, although some puncture wounds may not bleed too much. However, some superficial wounds, if located where there is a copious blood supply, such as the scalp, seem more extreme because they produce extensive bleeding.

Most minor bleeding injuries involve the tiny hairlike vessels known as capillaries that connect the arteries and veins and are present just under the surface of the skin. Bleeding from arteries is usually characterized by a bright red, pulsating flow. Veins are located a bit deeper and exude dark red blood when injured.

Many everyday injuries of childhood result in bleeding, including bumps, falls, cuts and scrapes, irritated or scratched insect bites, and tooth loss. Frequently when the air is warm and dry, the mucus membranes lining the nose become quite dry, and when they are rubbed or picked at, bleeding can result.

When the body's clotting factors are healthy, bleeding generally slows down and stops within a few minutes. Lowered levels or deficiencies of any of the blood clotting factors may result in a more prolonged bleeding time.

☛ **WARNING:** If bleeding or oozing persists for several hours or recurs after a day, notify your physician, who will evaulate the wound and order any necessary diagnostic studies to check blood clotting factors.

Conventional Treatment

✦ Cover the area with a clean cloth or tissues and apply pressure directly over the bleeding site. Hold for several minutes. Depending upon the location of the injury and the type of blood vessel (capillary, vein, or artery) involved, bleeding or oozing should cease after ten minutes of direct pressure. Once active bleeding has stopped, the site should be cleansed with cool running water, an antiseptic applied, and the area covered for protection. If you suspect your child may have severed an artery, call for emergency assistance immediately.

✦ The injured site should be kept clean and covered during the healing process. If there is redness, warmth, swelling, or extreme tenderness at the site days after the injury, it may be infected, so call your doctor for further advice.

PARENTS' REPORT: WHAT WORKS

✦ A physician's assistant explains that her Irish mother always put cobwebs right on the area that was bleeding. But that only works if you are an indifferent housekeeper and have the "supplies" handy! I've heard this remedy often, but I must admit that I worry about the dirt that clings to cobwebs.

✦ Here's a remedy from a travel writer: "I was once visiting a friend and my son's lip started bleeding and wouldn't stop. The friend tore off a piece of paper from a brown bag, wet it with my son's saliva, and put it on his lip. The bleeding stopped immediately." The explanation I gave is that fibrin, a tissue factor, helps blood coagulate. As paper is fibrous and a product of wood pulp, it perhaps has a fibrinlike quality. It could also be timing—her son's lip was ready to stop bleeding. And it could be the Band-Aid effect of anything applied to the site. Another variation I have heard is to cover the cut with brown paper that has been moistened with vinegar or lemon juice.

✦ A neighbor shares this memory: "My mother was told to put a wet tea bag on her bleeding gums, and it worked. After that she used a wet tea bag on my brother and me whenever we bled, and it always seemed to work." Just use a plain orange pekoe tea bag here.

✦ A number of people report using tobacco leaves for a variety of ailments, including to stop bleeding. Untreated ground tobacco works as a vasoconstrictor. If you live in Kentucky, Virginia, or the Carolinas and have access to tobacco leaves, you can consider it. ☛ WARNING: The leaves should only be applied by an adult. Tobacco leaves should *never* be left out where children can chew, swallow, or otherwise misue them.

✦ Here's a spicy recipe from a friend with roots in Louisiana: Sprinkle cayenne pepper directly on an external cut to stop bleeding. You can even completely pack the wound if you have enough pepper. Black pepper may be used instead if cayenne is not available. This remedy does not sting as you might imagine and is good in emergencies. Once the bleeding stops, rinse off the pepper and carefully clean out the wound site so an infection doesn't develop.

✦ Applying Saran Wrap to the skin for three to seven minutes will help clotting, and when it is removed, it won't take off the scab that's begun to form.

Blemishes

The Ailment

A red or deeply pigmented spot that scars in the aftermath of a break in the skin is a blemish. This generally transient stain results when one picks or scratches a lesion (bump) to the point of irritating the skin. If the irritation is superficial, only involving the outer (epidermal) layer of the skin, it is likely to fade with time. The greater the irritation (picking/probing), the greater the likelihood of a more extensive and longer-lasting injury. Then the resulting scars may need therapeutic intervention.

Conventional Treatment

With time and minimal effort, most blemishes heal and fade without residual damage. For the best results, keep affected areas as clean as possible. Discourage touching, scratching, or the removal of scabs. Over-the-counter first aid and antibacterial ointments reduce the bacteria and the itch factor at the site. Remember that a scab, though unsightly, is the body's self-made Band-Aid, which is meant to remain in place naturally until the healing beneath is complete and new skin forms.

Parents' Report: What Works

✦ Cocoa butter applied to the blemish daily is said to hasten the fading of these spots. Patience is required, but I know from personal experience that it works.

✦ Application of the juice of a fresh lemon to the healed but darkened area of skin has been reported to help bleach the darker spots and hasten their return to normal pigmentation. Lemon juice is aromatic and may leave a tingling sensation. The citric acid probably speeds the shedding of the outermost layer of skin and helps to lighten the scar.

✦ Elder flower, an herb, is another skin lightener. Try this combination recommended by the late natural beauty expert Dian Dincin Buchman: Mix equal parts of lemon juice with elder flower water, which is sold in stores that sell natural cosmetics. Dab onto the affected area.

✦ Strawberries are also said to have certain bleaching properties. You can try blending a few berries with a cup of lemon juice, then applying the mixture to your child's skin as a mask. Let it sit for fifteen minutes before washing it off. You can also mix lemon juice with the juice of a potato, parsley, and some rose hip powder, available in health food stores. All of these are high in vitamin C, which is also said to help repair skin. ☛ WARNING: If there are signs of skin irritation or itching, rinse off with cool water and do not reapply.

✦ Castor oil massaged into the skin usually feels good. I am not certain what causes the castor oil to reduce the scar, but I have been told that this works on birthmarks as well.

✦ See **Freckles** for more remedies.

Blisters

The Ailment

A blister is a collection of clear fluid in the outer layer of skin, which generally forms as a result of friction on the skin site or a burn from an extreme heat or cold source. This fluid serves as a protective cushion while a new layer of skin generates beneath the bubble. As the new skin forms, the blister surface dries; if it doesn't break, the fluid is gradually reabsorbed by the body. Eventually the outer surface of the blister sac peels away from the healed site, revealing newly formed skin. Usually blisters are not serious, but if they are punctured or squeezed, bacteria may be easily introduced and result in a serious skin infection.

Conventional Treatment

When the blister is located at a site likely to be bumped, rubbed, or reinjured, a clean protective shield or bandage should be applied. Otherwise keep the site clean and allow the stages of healing to occur. If the blister becomes filled with a milky fluid or if the skin surrounding the site becomes red, warm, or tender, it is time to consult your doctor, who may need to incise (open) and drain the site under sterile conditions or prescribe antibiotic therapy.

Parents' Report: What Works

✦ It's a good idea to keep an aloe plant or two handy. In addition to being an attractive, low-maintenance plant, aloe is a good first-aid supplement. Just snap off a leaf, cut lengthwise, and apply the sap. You can also use aloe vera gel, oil, cream, and lotions, which are available commercially.

✦ Many parents tell me they use zinc ointment twice daily on blisters for speedy healing.

✦ An Italian friend who seems to recommend garlic for just about every ailment rubs blisters with garlic oil.

✦ A few families have tried and recommend applying lavender oil. It's analgesic, anti-inflammatory, antibacterial, and soothing. But don't let your youngster consume any.

Boils

THE AILMENT

A boil starts with a small break in the skin (it may even arise from the base of a hair follicle). The skin break then allows for the entry of bacteria. As the broken skin attempts to heal and close above, bacteria and debris that enter are trapped and form a pus-filled sac below. This results in a red, tender, sometimes warm lump, which eventually comes to a head (points) and may spontaneously rupture and heal itself. As the body's defense mechanisms attempt to confine and contain the infection, surrounding tissues will "wall off" the site and form a distinct capsule, known as an *abscess*. The abscess contains the bacteria at a single site. Washing the hands after touching the affected area reduces the likelihood of new outbreaks on other areas.

CONVENTIONAL TREATMENT

✦ Warm water compresses ease the discomfort at the site, speed the rupture of the boil or abscess, and allow the healing process to take place.

✦ Consult your doctor if boils do not resolve. Antibiotics and surgical lancing may be required to drain the infected site and promote healing.

PARENTS' REPORT: WHAT WORKS

✦ Icthimol ointment is a tar-based compound that my mother applied to any boil-like eruptions when I was a youngster. I remember its pungent aroma and the messiness of this thick black paste. But I also recall its effectiveness. When the ointment was applied to the boil and covered with a bandage, within a short time the lesion came to a head, ruptured, and drained at the site. When I was growing up, we always had some in our medicine cabinet. Although it's not easily found, my local pharmacist recommended Boileze, an over-the-counter fish oil derivative that contains vitamins and coal tar. This product has that same memorable pungent aroma.

✦ Whisk raw egg whites, saturate a cotton ball, and dab onto the boil. Then cover with a Band-Aid. This is said to speed drying of the boil.

✦ A Native American friend offered me her family recipe for boils: Put slices of onion over the cut stem side of a thick tomato slice; place tomato slice with onion in place on the boil and cover with a bandage. This is said to speed drying of the boil.

✦ Annabel, my dentist's assistant from Kenya, has this suggestion: Use any powdered laundry detergent mixed with water to make a paste. Annabel called this paste Omo, and then applied it to the boil and left it in place until it drained and dried. Annabel also suggests mashing small green peas with a little water to make a paste, which can be applied and allowed to dry on the site.

✦ A nutritionist friend, Mimi, swears by this remedy: Open up a vitamin A capsule and apply the contents directly onto the boil.

✦ The heat of a hot compress can help draw out a boil. To make the compress even more effective, add some antibacterial herbs or essential oils. Try soaking a cloth in a tea made of goldenseal, ginger, and myrrh. If you can find usnea moss in your health food store, that antibacterial plant also makes a good compress that you can apply for ten to fifteen minutes three times a day until the boil heals. If you have some goldenseal tincture or even a goldenseal-echinacea combination formula, apply the liquid directly to the boil.

✦ Poultices are a little "gloppier" than compresses, but they are effective. Make a paste with powdered marshmallow root and slippery elm by mixing them with a bit of water. Spread over the boil; let it sit for twenty minutes, then wash off. You can also mix marshmallow root with plantain—another wound healer from way back—as well as with Oregon grape root, another plant with antibacterial properties. Apply to the skin for twenty to thirty minutes. You'd better have some activities to keep the child busy for this period of time! As always, make sure your child doesn't consume any of these mixtures.

Bronchitis

THE AILMENT

Bronchitis is an inflammation of the lining of the bronchi, the two large airways that lead into the lungs. Viral, bacterial, or allergic upper respiratory conditions (colds, sinus or postnasal drainage, sore throats) may irritate the tissues lining the airways, causing swelling. The swelling prevents the easy passage of air through the bronchi, causing breathing difficulties and coughing. The cough is usually deep, dry, and hacking—often occurring in cyclic spasms, sometimes resulting in vomiting. The continuing irritation of the vocal cords with this type of cough usually results in hoarseness or deepening of the voice. After several days, phlegm (mucus) may develop and the cough becomes productive (wet). Parents, in general, become very concerned when the phlegm is yellow or green. This is a sure sign of chronic irritation and inflammation, but not always the sign of a bacterial infection requiring antibiotics.

Prolonged fever, diminished appetite, rapid breathing, wheezing, and darkening of the tongue or the skin around the lips are urgent reasons to have your child medically evaluated.

Conventional Treatment

Try to make your child as comfortable as possible. To improve his breathing, elevate his head and chest for sleeping. If he is old enough for pillows (check with your pediatrician), try two under his head. If he is not likely to remain on his pillows while sleeping, put a couple of telephone books under the head of his mattress to achieve an approximately 45-degree angle. Increasing the humidity of the air with a cool-mist vaporizer or humidifier also helps. Even if his appetite is diminished, drinking more liquids will help to lower any fever and avoid dehydration.

Parents' Report: What Works

☛ WARNING: Some of the home remedies for bronchitis (many of which have been around for a long time) are dangerous and should never be used. Stay away from any remedy that involves flames. One method I've heard about from some Jewish grandmothers is called bonches and involves heating tiny glass bottles and placing them on the chest. Obviously there is a risk of burns. Don't ever use them on your kids.

Also, in other parts of the world, sedating narcotics and alcohol are often part of over-the-counter drugs. Belladonna, for example, is easily obtained in Italy and much of the rest of Europe, but it is available here only by prescription. These remedies are definitely *not* for children. A mother of three I met while traveling in Italy in the Tuscany region shared some of her family's medicinal recipes. One involved chamomile tea (fine) plus sage (also fine) and some belladonna (the no-no). A narcotic may stop the cough, but it also depresses the central nervous system, slowing many body systems, including breathing. Stay away from all narcotics and alcohol.

✦ Here's one remedy I do approve of: My friend's Hungarian grandmother's cure for all sorts of respiratory ailments was chamomile tea—not to drink, but to inhale. It's the steam that worked. "She would brew up a large pot of tea, make me lean over it, and then put a towel over my head to trap the vapors. Grandma would hug me at the same time to keep me still. It felt like I was there forever, but I always felt the hugging contributed to the cure." Make sure your child's face is a comfortable, safe distance from the steaming liquid.

✦ Many remedies involve mixing products and putting them on the child's chest. I've heard of everything from linseed poultice to lard. My mother frequently used old-fashioned mustard plasters. Here's her recipe: Mix one part dry mustard with four parts of flour. Add just enough water to make a paste. Put the mixture on a piece of cotton cloth or cheesecloth. Apply a layer of Vaseline over the chest and neck and around the nose for a protective coating. Then apply the cloth with the mustard-flour mixture to the chest and cover with a pillowcase. Tent a blanket very loosely over the child's head and chest; have her breathe in and out through her nose for twenty minutes while you supervise. Her mouth must be closed. She will perspire, but it breaks up congestion.

✦ Other remedies include all sorts of teas. The truth is that *any* hot liquid can help thin out secretions. When I traveled in Mexico, I was told to put bougainvillea into hot water to make a tea and then add lime and honey. (*Never* give honey to children under the age of one because of the risk of botulin spores.) Myrtle leaves, which contain myrtal, an antiseptic, are effective when brewed as tea. You can safely try a tea made with thyme, which is antimicrobial. The Chinese herb astragalus, an immune system booster, mixed with marshmallow root, an anti-inflammatory, is a combination tea that soothes the respiratory tract.

✦ Using essential oils, most of which have antibacterial properties, in a vaporizer can also help. Try lavender or chamomile. If your child is over six months, you can also use tea tree oil and eucalyptus. Remember not to let your child ingest any essential oils.

✦ Have your child consume foods rich in capsacin, such as hot peppers. This triggers the lungs to water, just as your eyes do. Hot mustard and curry also stimulate the same reflex actions as popular expectorants.

Bruises

The Ailment

A bruise is a discoloration (red, purple, blue, or green) of an area of skin occurring after a blow great enough to rupture small vessels beneath the surface of the skin. Bruises are common occurrences during childhood. They are usually harmless, but have your doctor investigate any recurring unexplained bruises; they may signal more serious conditions such as a low platelet count or a bleeding disorder.

Bruises may take up to two weeks to disappear. They go through a series of color changes (red, purple, blue, black, green, yellow) as they are resolving. The varying colors represent the breakdown of the blood pigments as they are reabsorbed by the body during healing. A lump may remain at the trauma site for an additional week or two.

Conventional Treatment

Apply cool water compresses and slight pressure to the site as soon as possible after a trauma. This step will help to lessen the bleeding under the skin and control the amount of swelling.

Parents' Report: What Works

Many of these remedies come right from your kitchen.

✦ Make a poultice of 2 teaspoons of dry mustard mixed with a little bentonite (a special kind of clay available in health food stores) and water and then apply to the bruise. It will draw the blood away from the bruise.

✦ Make a poultice of roasted onions mixed with a little water and apply to the bruise.

✦ Applying black pepper oil to the bruise helps draw blood away, but be especially sparing when you're applying it to children.

✦ Make a compress and soak it in vinegar to help the swelling. Avoid the child's eyes.

✦ Apply a tincture of witch hazel to relieve swelling and bruising.

✦ To alleviate dark, swollen bruises, apply any gel containing arnica every three hours. Arnica traditionally has been used for muscle aches, sprains, and bruises. Some people have a reaction to it, so if your child's skin becomes red, itchy, or inflamed, discontinue use. Do *not* take arnica internally.

✦ A writer acquaintance came up with this recipe from his Romanian uncle who was a farmer. In late spring, go out to the field and collect the yellow flower goldenrod. Put it in a jar with olive oil and let it sit all summer. This forms an ointment with a sweet aroma that can be used to heal bruises. The problem is, you *really* have to plan ahead. Also, many people have allergies to goldenrod. Obviously, if you're one of them, don't try this remedy.

Burns

The Ailment

A burn is damage to the layers of the skin or mucous membranes caused by exposure to heat, fire, hot liquids, steam, sun, hot metals, extreme cold, chemicals, or electricity. The severity of burns is determined by assessing the extent of damage and is defined by degrees.

✦ **First-degree burns** are considered superficial, causing minimal damage only to the outer layer, or epidermis, of the skin. There may be redness at the site, but without blister formation. Mild sunburn or brief skin contact with a hot liquid or object may result in a first-degree burn.

✦ **Second-degree burns** injure the epidermal and the underlayer (dermis) of skin. This level of greater damage is characterized by redness and blistering at the site of injury. Splatter from hot cooking oil, scalding from hot liquid, or severe sunburn are common causes.

✦ **Third-degree burns** are the most severe. They generally result from direct contact with flames or prolonged contact with a very hot object. This level of burn damages all layers of the skin and underlying tissues including superficial blood vessels and nerve endings. The third-degree burn area is insensitive to touch.

You cannot always judge the severity of a burn by the level of a child's discomfort; when the nerve endings have suffered damage, one's ability to sense pain is altered, so the worst burns may not hurt as much as less severe burns.

☛ WARNING: All burns, except the most superficial, must be considered potential sites for infection and scarring and should be treated appropriately. The steps you take immediately can make a big difference in how the burn heals. The first goal is to bring down the temperature of the skin.

Conventional Treatment

Immediate first-aid measures for first- and second-degree heat burns include:

✦ Cool the burned site with a cool compress, place it under cold running water for 2 minutes, or, if a larger area is involved, submerge it in a tub of cool water. Gently pat the area dry, then cover with a clean cloth or loose bandage.

- Elevate any affected limbs.
- If blisters form during the healing process, do not rupture them. Once blisters are opened, they become sites for possible infection.
- For mild discomfort, give acetaminophen or ibuprofen. If your child has severe or prolonged discomfort, consult your physician.
- Once healing begins and the new protective layer of skin has formed, use aloe or any skin-softening lotion.

Immediate first-aid measures for burns caused by acidic or alkaline chemicals are different from those administered for heat burns:

- Chemical burn areas should be gently flushed with cool running water for several minutes.
- Check the label on the chemical's container for specific instructions for the particular substance.
- After thorough flushing, cover with a clean cloth until you can get medical attention.

Immediate first-aid measures for third-degree burns include:

- Call for emergency medical transport to a hospital.
- Lightly place cool, wet compresses on burned areas.
- Cover the compresses with several thicknesses of clean cloth.
- Try to keep the burned individual as still as possible until help arrives.

Do not apply ice to any burned area; it may intensify the burn or provoke shock. If someone's hair or clothing is aflame, immediately have them drop and roll, and throw a heavy coat or blanket over the area to smother the flames.

Parents' Report: What Works

☛ **WARNING**: Because of the possibilities for severe infections, always check with your physician before trying any family recipes for burns. And do *not* put butter or any other grease on a burn—it will only increase the likelihood for infection.

✦ For burn scars, try shea butter. It has the consistency of cocoa butter—but it is *not* butter. It's from the seeds of the shea tree, native to West Africa. This is well known in Senegal as a remedy to fade the scars from a burn.

✦ For sunburn, have your child bathe in any regular tea, as recommended by a mother in Papeete, Tahiti. (Don't ask about the tea stains in the bathtub!)

✦ For sunburn, try an oatmeal soak. Fill the tub with cool water and add oatmeal bath soak.

✦ Apply milk. For a minor burn with unbroken skin not yet blistered, soak affected areas in whole milk for fifteen minutes. Then apply a cloth soaked in milk for ten minutes. Repeat every four hours. (You can also use cold, fresh dairy cream, if that's what is on hand.) ☛ **WARNING**: Do not use milk on an open wound. It may promote bacterial growth.

✦ Vermont Udder Balm or Bag Balm can be applied to the dry site while it's healing. It doesn't matter which state the udder balm comes from—it is exactly what it sounds like and is more readily available in farming communities.

✦ Try Preparation H—it contains a live yeast derivative that can speed healing. However, some forms also contain phenylephrine or phenylmercuric nitrate, which may not be suitable for some kids. Check with your pediatrician.

✦ Don't overlook aloe, a good burn remedy, especially for sunburn. You can also mix aloe with lavender oil, which is antibacterial, anti-inflammatory, and analgesic. (Modern aromatherapy was founded on the discovery of lavender as an excellent burn remedy. René-Maurice Gattefoss, the French chemist who developed modern aromatherapy, had just distilled some lavender oil in his lab when an explosion burned his hand. He plunged it into the nearest liquid, which happened to be the lavender oil. The story told is that by the time he got to the hospital, the burn was already starting to heal.) Parents can use lavender oil straight out of the bottle or they can make a compress with a few drops of lavender oil added to water. Don't let your child ingest any of the lavender oil.

✦ Calendula (also known as pot marigold) is another burn remedy; it has many components that help skin heal. Calendula ointments can be found in any natural health store.

✦ St. John's wort, the same plant that helps with mild depression, can also help with burns. Add 1–2 dropperfuls of tincture to a cup of cooled, boiled water and then soak a compress in the liquid and apply to the burn. Bandage the area.

✦ I have heard people recommend using beaten egg whites to soothe, but I have reservations about this cure. This could also introduce infection at the site.

Canker Sores (Apthous Ulcers)

THE AILMENT

Have you ever inadvertently nicked your gum while vigorously brushing your teeth? Can you recall the discomfort that followed for the next several days? Any mouth irritation can set the stage for a canker sore or mouth ulcer. It is a break in the lining of the mouth with some sensitive points that are intensely painful. These blisterlike lesions, with a grayish red rim, develop on the soft tissues inside the mouth and the gums. Most are viral in nature. Severe episodes of canker sores may be accompanied by fever, swollen lymph nodes, and fatigue. There may be more than one uncomfortable sore, which makes eating particularly difficult. Teething infants and toddlers often drool more than usual during an outbreak. Children often find it easier and more comforting to drink liquids rather than eat solid foods during painful periods. Don't panic; as long as your little ones are well hydrated, they should be fine. The acute painful phase usually lasts for just a few days.

Nutritional deficiencies, particularly shortages of iron, vitamin B_{12}, and folic acid, predispose some people to developing these ulcers. Potential triggers may be varied. Some teens are more prone to develop them when they are under stress, eating poorly, or have lowered resistance.

☛ WARNING: If frequently recurring or persistent, canker sores may signal a weakened immune system and should sound an alarm for further diagnostic evaluation. If they are more than an occasional annoyance to your child, it is important to seek medical attention.

CONVENTIONAL TREATMENT

Careful oral hygiene reduces the pool of likely suspects that could infect accidentally injured gums.

✦ Over-the-counter preparations such as Anbesol or Orajel contain small amounts of topical anesthetics; when swabbed onto painful areas, they offer temporary relief. Check with your pediatrician; some object to their use in very young patients.

✦ Mouthwashes with antiseptic and anesthetic components such as Chloraseptic or Listerine are soothing. However, many mouthwashes contain alcohol, so ask your pediatrician which one she recommends.

✦ Sometimes prescribed antiviral medications in the form of tablets or cream applied topically on the lesions can shorten the time for infection and discomfort.

✦ For youngsters over the age of twelve, a prescription dose of a "tetracycline swish" will speed the healing of the mouth sores. This is not recommended for children under the age of twelve because tetracycline causes discoloration of the secondary (permanent) teeth, which are still being formed.

✦ Sucking crushed ice chips also provides temporary pain relief by numbing the lesions.

PARENTS' REPORT: WHAT WORKS

Remedies reflect many different cultures because canker sores are common the world over. Frequently mentioned remedies include eating yogurt, breaking open a vitamin C capsule and squeezing it onto the sore (vitamin C has anti-inflammatory properties and may be antiviral as well), and placing a wedge of raw onion on the sore. One of my Italian-American families applies a dab of toothpaste with fluoride every few hours, which seems to hasten the clearing of an outbreak. If you don't like fluoride, you can have your child hold a zinc lozenge on the sore a few times a day.

My friend Joann relies on burdock root. She makes a tea or takes a capsule; both can be found in health food stores. To make the tea, bring 1 quart of water to a boil, reduce to simmer, add 4 teaspoons of burdock root, and allow to steep for two hours. She suggests up to 2 cups a day on an empty stomach. The tea, served over ice and with a straw, may be more appealing to your youngster.

The following remedies are mouthwashes thought to reduce the bacteria and speed healing of the lesions. Try several until you find the one that works for your child. Mouthwashes (swishes) are meant to be held in the child's mouth for a matter of seconds and then spat out.

✦ I've had many German families recommend sauerkraut juice as a mouth swish. It's probably the acid content that helps.

✦ For children over four years of age: Open 2 to 4 acidophilus capsules (these can be bought over-the-counter) and mix the contents with one cup of milk. Offer a few sips to your child a few times a day. (Read the label; make sure the capsules contain living organisms.) The milk is an activating culture medium for the "good" bacilli. This may reduce the pain and speed healing. Eating plain yogurt that contains live cultures will add friendly bacteria and also helps healing by competing with the bad bacteria.

✦ Antacid formulas, such as Mylanta and milk of magnesia, used as a mouth rinse, were reported to be effective by a taxi driver in Des Moines, Iowa, where I was attending a seminar. According to the driver, who originally hailed from Russia, antacids reduce the pain. However, I worry about youngsters accidentally swallowing too much antacid; check with your pediatrician before trying this one.

✦ Baking soda is another time-honored remedy. Mix 1 teaspoon with ½ cup of warm water and offer as a mouth swish several times a day, especially after meals and before bedtime. The pain should lessen within twenty-four hours, and usually the sore will heal within three days. *Note:* Baking soda contains a high level of sodium (salt). Your child should rinse his mouth out thoroughly after using to avoid sodium overload. Obviously, don't give this to a child who is more likely to swallow than spit.

✦ You can also mix baking soda with a small amount of water to make a paste and apply it with a Q-tip to the lesions. Use several times daily. It may sting a bit, but it works by reducing the amount of bacteria in the mouth. However, when used in this manner, it always gets swallowed and raises the body's salt load, so I prefer the baking soda mouth rinse.

✦ Hydrogen peroxide may also be used as an effective mouthwash. Mix 2 ounces of peroxide with 2 ounces of water. Have your child swish this solution in her mouth twice a day, then spit it out. Hydrogen peroxide should be used sparingly unless otherwise recommended by your dentist. Although it can kill bacteria, it may cause other dental problems. (Your child should not swallow this mixture, though if a small amount is swallowed, it won't harm her.)

✦ Fresh papaya fruit is good; if you live where there are fresh papaya leaves, allow your child to chew on them.

✦ I have "juicer" families in my practice—that is, they juice just about everything. This recipe comes from a family that lives by juicing: Take two fresh plums with pits removed, and put into a blender or food processor. Two tablespoons of the resulting plum juice can be uses as a mouth rinse for several minutes, several times a day. Even if your child swallows it, this juice is nutritious. For a very painful lesion, soak a cotton ball in plum juice and use it as a compress directly on the site for a few minutes. It's a reasonably tasty way to relieve discomfort.

✦ Salt water is another remedy. Mix 2 tablespoons of salt in 6 ounces of warm water and use as a mouth rinse three or four times a day. Salt draws fluid from the canker and helps it to heal. Make sure your child spits instead of swallows so he doesn't ingest too much sodium.

✦ Goldenseal is an anti-inflammatory agent. Make a mouth rinse of 1/4 teaspoon salt, 1/2 teaspoon goldenseal powder, and 1 cup of warm water. Have your child swish several times a day. Make sure your child spits the mixture out. You may also try a "pinch" of powdered goldenseal directly on the sore. ☛ WARNING: If used over an extended period (over four days), this mixture can cause digestive problems and other complications, so check with your doctor.

✦ Another herb, myrrh, speeds the healing of canker sores. To make a myrrh tea, combine 2 sprigs of coarsely chopped parsley, 3 whole cloves, 1 teaspoon of powdered myrrh, and 1/4 teaspoon powdered goldenseal in 2 cups of boiling water. Steep until cool, stirring occasionally. Strain and use as a mouthwash, not as a tea to drink. (This combination can also be used for bad breath and sore throats.) Here's another version: 1 teaspoon each of powdered myrrh, goldenseal, and cayenne pepper blended in 1 quart of water. If your child can stand the heat this mixture generates (it may burn a little), it is a good counterirritant to the canker sore discomfort. ☛ WARNING: As noted above, don't use goldenseal rinses for more than four days.

✦ A Native American family told me that they use sage tea as a mouthwash. Believed to be effective in healing canker lesions, sage has astringent and drying properties. If you can find sage tea bags, brew like regular tea. If using fresh sage leaves, pour boiling water over a handful and let sit for twenty minutes. You can also apply a pinch of powdered sage directly to the sore.

Some remedies are applied directly onto the sore.

✦ From the Caribbean comes the use of sorrel. In addition to its astringent and antiseptic properties, sorrel has long been used for various skin ailments. A mother's helper from Jamaica shared her recipe for clearing up canker sores: Take a fresh piece of this bitter herb (which smells like ginger) and place it on the sore until the herb becomes soggy. Reapply a few times a day. It should ease the pain quickly and speed healing.

✦ Place a moist regular orange pekoe tea bag on the canker. Press it onto the sore and hold it in place as long as your child can stand it. The tannic acid in the tea aids healing.

✦ You can also squeeze a few drops of vitamin E from a capsule directly onto the canker sore.

✦ Empty two capsules of myrrh powder onto a clean surface, moisten a cotton swab, dip it into the powder, and apply directly to the sore. Applying this powder to the area twice a day may clear up the sore in less than a week.

Chicken Pox

THE AILMENT

Chicken pox, a communicable infectious disease, was commonly experienced in the United States during childhood prior to the widespread use of the varicella vaccine. Usually a benign but bothersome disease that is itchy and highly contagious, the chicken pox virus can cause serious conditions such as pneumonia and encephalitis. This virus has an incubation period of seven to twenty-one days before the disease is apparent. That means if an unvaccinated individual is exposed to someone with the disease, that individual may exhibit full-blown chicken pox anytime during the seven to twenty-one days after the initial contact. The initial symptoms of fever and headache are quickly followed by crops of tiny, itchy blisters filled with milky fluid. The blisters traditionally occur first on the trunk before spreading. Chicken pox blisters can erupt anywhere on the body—in the mouth, in the ears, and on every extremity. After a period of time, the blisters dry and form scabs. Once there are no more blisters erupting and the existing ones have scabs, the disease is no longer contagious. The usual course is seven to ten days. If the lesions are scratched vigorously, shallow sores may form and there is the likelihood of long-lasting scars.

Conventional Treatment

Keep a child with chicken pox away from unvaccinated individuals. Administer an over-the-counter aspirin-free liquid (acetaminophen) by mouth to lower fever and to make the child more comfortable.

☛ WARNING: With chicken pox or any other viral illness, never give a child aspirin, which may cause Reye's syndrome, a potentially fatal complication.

Keep your child's fingernails cut as short as possible, to reduce the likelihood of scars from scratching. For extreme itchiness, over-the-counter antihistamines such as Benadryl for children, taken by mouth, can help, as might a topically applied anti-itch cream or lotion such as calamine. Your physician may suggest a prescription antiviral medication, which can shorten the course of the disease by one to two days.

PARENTS' REPORT: WHAT WORKS

In general, family remedies do not shorten the time the pox lesions last; they simply help relieve the symptoms.

✦ Drinking warm orange pekoe tea is thought to bring the pox lesions out—the more quickly they erupt, the more quickly they dry up.

✦ Break open a vitamin E capsule and put the liquid directly on pox lesions. The vitamin E, an antioxidant, can be absorbed through the skin and reportedly prevents thick scar formation.

✦ Jamie, from the Dominican Republic, dabbed milk of magnesia on her kids when they had chicken pox, and she confidently assures me that it worked.

There are several homemade bath enhancers:

✦ Baking soda baths relieve itching and dry the blisters. Try 1 cup in a warm bath. If you like, you can add 2 drops of lavender oil.

✦ Oatmeal baths are soothing and offer some relief from itching. If you have the time, you can even grind dry rolled oats into a fine powder in a blender. Add 1–2 cups into the child's lukewarm bathwater. Have your child get into the tub and soak for 15 minutes. Just be careful, oatmeal can make the tub slippery. Pat skin dry, but do not rinse off.

✦ Try this soothing anti-itch delight: Into a lukewarm bath, combine 2–3 drops of lavender oil, 2 fluid ounces of chamomile tea, or 2 teaspoons of dry or fresh chamomile leaves, and 8 ounces (1 cup) of calamine lotion.

Cold Sores

The Ailment

These tiny blisters are caused by a virus (herpes simplex) and tend to appear in or near the mouth, nose, or genital areas. The lesions are initially noted as tender, tingly, or itchy spots. Very quickly these tiny spots evolve into fluid-filled sores, which ooze and form crusts before they eventually fade. Cold sores are not life-threatening, but they are unsightly and may be uncomfortable. This virus, when in an active state, is easily transmitted between individuals. A pregnant woman with an active virus can transmit infection to her baby during a vaginal delivery. After the initial eruption, the herpes simplex virus can remain dormant in nerve endings for years, causing no problems. However, a fever, infection, fatigue, stress, overexposure to the sun, cold weather, or other factors may trigger the virus and the appearance of lesions.

To reduce the likelihood of viral contamination or a recurring eruption, use sunscreen with at least 15 SPF on your child's lips and other susceptible exposed areas. Advise youngsters not to share towels, toothbrushes, or utensils with others, especially someone who has cold sores. If your child has an episode, replace his toothbrush and remind every member of the household of the importance of frequent hand washing, especially after touching any affected areas.

Conventional Treatment

Medical research reports from the United Kingdom found that many people with cold sores had low levels of vitamin B_{12}. The addition of B_{12}, folic acid, and other B complex vitamins to the child's daily diet rapidly improved their eruptions. Check with your doctor for recommended dosages, based on your youngster's need and age.

General diet may be another culprit. Researchers have found that the balance of amino acids, specifically L-arginine and L-lysine, play an important part in controlling (not curing) cold sores. Arginine aids the growth and reproduction of the herpes virus, while lysine inhibits it. Foods with a high arginine content, such as chocolate, peanuts and other nuts, grains, peas, seeds, oatmeal, and whole-wheat products, should be greatly reduced in the diet of those who suffer with outbreaks of cold sores.

Cool compresses applied to the site may calm the burning or itching sensation. I also advise parents to use hydrogen peroxide to keep the area clean and to help dry the sores. If the lesions are very uncomfortable, I prescribe acyclovir, an antiviral ointment, which lessens the discomfort and shortens the duration of the infection.

Parents' Report: What Works

✦ Eating plain yogurt with live acidophilus cultures daily is reportedly a healthy preventative measure.

✦ One parent, a professional makeup artist, shared this trick of the trade with me: Dissolve a capsule of acidophilus in a small amount of milk. The milk is an activating culture medium for the bacilli. Apply this mixture to the lesions three to four times a day. This will soothe the tender areas and speeds healing. If you do this when your child first feels burning or itching at the usual site of the cold sore, this remedy may actually inhibit the formation of the lesion.

✦ When the tingling starts, and before the appearance of the cold sore, try dabbing the sap from the leaves of an aloe plant onto the affected areas.

✦ Some Native American groups use the herb chaparral as a remedy for colds, sores, and viruses. Chaparral has antioxidant properties, which makes it a healing agent. It should only be applied topically. Use the tincture form; soak a clean cloth in the liquid and apply it directly to the cold sores.

✦ Mix a pinch of ordinary cornstarch with a few drops of water to make a paste, then apply it to the lesions.

✦ Ask your pharmacist to mix up some spirits of camphor for you and then dab it on the affected areas with a clean cotton ball.

✦ Another suggestion to ease the pain is to temporarily numb the area. Hold an ice cube covered with a cloth in place directly on the sore for a few seconds periodically over the course of the day. This is especially good to do at the onset of a cold sore. Applying ice with great frequency, every ten minutes for an hour, *may* prevent the movement of the virus from the nerve to the skin.

✦ A topical application of the herb melissa (a member of the mint family) reportedly speeds healing of the sore, often within five days. According to Mindy Green at the Herb Research Foundation, it's the top herb for cold sores. It's antiviral, so it helps knock out the herpes virus that causes the sores. I know parents who give their kids some melissa tea to drink or make a compress with a clean cloth soaked in tincture (a more potent form) and apply it directly to the sore. Parents can also get an over-the-counter concentrated melissa salve (found in health food stores) and apply it directly to the cold sore.

✦ Try a tincture of myrrh to relieve the pain. I've heard anecdotal stories about its value, but I'm not sure how it works. I have been told it has some antiviral properties, and myrrh is a powerful immunostimulant that promotes growth of healthy skin.

✦ Steep an ordinary tea bag (preferably Earl Grey, as recommended by Mrs. Covington, an experienced grandmother of six who has tried several varieties) in boiling water for a few minutes; enjoy a cup of tea while allowing the tea bag to cool down, then apply the tea bag to the lesions. Within four or five days, most lesions crust over and disappear.

✦ Zinc has been reported to reduce the duration of cold sores. Zinc is available in a lozenge form. Have the child hold the moistened lozenge right on the cold sore two to three times a day. Applied topically, zinc speeds healing.

Colic

THE AILMENT

Colic is not a disease. It is a condition that causes healthy babies to have cyclical spells of uncontrollable crying. The crying often prompts a call to the doctor: "Help, my baby won't stop crying!" Once you have checked for the usual sources of distress, such as a wet diaper, injury, or hunger, there are some steps that can be taken to try to make your little one more comfortable.

These crying episodes usually occur with some predictability—at about the same time in the evening, and for a defined duration—and last for two to twelve weeks. Without warning, colic may spontaneously stop as mysteriously as it began. Although there is no pinpointable cause, many experts attribute the baby's irritability to abdominal discomfort, either from intestinal gas or from the air that is swallowed with crying. Regardless of the cause, the colicky baby is easily recognized by the sudden onset of his loud, intense, high-pitched, and prolonged crying. His body language also says colic; his legs are drawn to his abdomen, his face is red, his back arched, and his body tense. The fact that the baby seems inconsolable is frightening to parents.

☛ **WARNING:** High-pitched crying accompanied by fever, vomiting, diarrhea, skin rash, or difficulty breathing warrants an immediate call to your child's physician. The same holds true if the baby is inconsolable or unusually quiet after a fall or trauma.

CONVENTIONAL TREATMENT

Do not take your child's colic personally. This condition is not a reflection in any way of "bad" parenting or a "bad" baby. Wait it out while trying to make yourself and the baby as comfortable as possible. Understand that a "tincture of time" sometimes is the best prescription that can be offered for this common condition.

There are a variety of over-the-counter antigas medications designed for babies; most are safe and may be quite effective, but before using any of them it is always wise to check with your baby's doctor.

Parents' Report: What Works

Many of these tried-and-true remedies help, either to relieve the symptoms or to distract the baby.

✦ A pacifier meets sucking needs and may help calm an irritable baby. Don't use a plain bottle nipple. The pacifier should have a sealed back, because an open pacifier allows air to be swallowed, which causes the baby's digestive system to become filled with air and be even more uncomfortable.

✦ You can help relieve baby's gas or swallowed air with various burping techniques and changes of position. Try placing the baby over your shoulder or lying across your lap facedown while on her tummy. With either position, gently press her lower back as you rub it soothingly. Or try placing the baby on her back and gently rotating her legs in a bicycling motion.

✦ Wrap (swaddle) the baby firmly in a lightweight receiving blanket. Then some kind of rhythmic motion such as rocking back and forth, walking, or riding in a car can be the answer. You might also try an automatic swing.

✦ Have your baby lie on your chest to hear and feel your heartbeat, or carry her in a chest carrier or sling so she can enjoy both motion and closeness. Some parents report that the hum of their clothes dryer or vacuum cleaner quiets a fussy baby—and the bonus is that a little housework also gets done. Obviously, if you like this one, do not put the baby directly *on* the clothes dryer. She should be in your arms, in an infant carrier, or anchored securely in an infant seat (not on), only near the dryer.

✦ Gentle massaging of the abdomen while you sing or hum to her may distract her enough to relax her while she expels some trapped air.

✦ Place the baby on her tummy over a hot water bottle that has been wrapped in a towel or blanket to protect her skin from direct heat.

✦ A warm bath relaxes many babies. It relaxes adults as well. So take a bath with your baby. For safety, just make sure you have a waiting partner you can hand the baby to as you climb out of the tub.

✦ Many parents find that a 4-ounce bottle (½ cup) of very weak chamomile or peppermint tea cooled to room temperature does the trick. For very young babies, administer a few drops with a dropper or teaspoon.

✦ Add 1 teaspoon of fennel seeds to 1 cup of boiling water. Allow to simmer for ten minutes. Cool to room temperature and strain. Pour 1 teaspoonful of this tea into 2 ounces of water and give to the colicky infant. Fennel is aromatic and considered a *carminative;* that is, it causes gas to be expelled from the stomach and intestines, as do mint and chamomile. Fennel is particularly suitable for babies and younger children.

✦ Combine 1 drop eucalyptus oil, 1 drop lemon oil, 1 drop geranium oil, and 2 tablespoons almond oil. Rub onto the child's forehead. Perhaps the mellow aroma of this combination has a calming effect. ☛ WARNING: Do *not* give this to the child to take internally.

☛ WARNING: Gripe water (what an interesting name), used in British and Caribbean countries, frequently consists of a morphine derivative mixed with alcohol. Yes, it may calm your baby, but often at too great a cost, for it dangerously sedates her as well. The risk of the sedative effects outweighs any perceived benefits. I have seen gripe water on store shelves in London, and recently a Jamaican grandmother brought a bottle into the office, at my request, to allow me to review the ingredients. Do not give this to your child.

Common Cold

The Ailment

Colds are characterized by sneezing, sniffles, or nasal congestion; sore throat; coughing; a general lack of energy; and sometimes body aches and fever. The common cold may be caused by one of several hundred viruses. Viral particles can enter the body through our nasal passages—thousands of viral droplets are released into the air by sneezes and coughs, and we inhale that "loaded" air. Also our hands are major conveyers of viral diseases—with every touch, we pick up and transfer viral particles. Since most of us frequently bring our hands to our faces, there is a great likelihood of transmitting viral particles to our own nose or mouth. Hand washing is the number one preventive measure to avoid frequent upper respiratory infections. Teach your child to wash his hands properly.

Conventional Treatment

There is still no specific cure for the annoying common cold. Whether you try everything or nothing, it usually lasts seven to ten days. However, there are measures that can relieve some discomfort during this period. Your child may not feel like eating or drinking, but consuming lots of fluids is important to avoid dehydration and to lower fever, thereby increasing your child's comfort level. A nonaspirin liquid, such as acetaminophen or ibuprofen drops, effectively lowers fever and relieves much of the discomfort.

✦ There are many over-the-counter cold, cough, and congestion medications. You must carefully review the labels for specific claims and check with your physician with any questions. If your child exhibits one or two symptoms, it's better not to be tempted to use one of the combination preparations designed to treat every symptom under the sun.

✦ When upper-airway congestion makes eating and sleeping difficult, elevate the child's head and chest to at least a 45-degree angle. This can be done by putting pillows under the head of an older child, if your doctor approves. For infants and young children, try putting a few telephone books under the head section of the mattress.

✦ Increase the humidity in the child's immediate environment with a humidifier or a cool-mist vaporizer. This added moisture in the air will relieve some of the nasal stuffiness and soothe her scratchy throat.

✦ For stuffy noses, try normal saline (salt water) nasal solution; put a few drops into each nostril and use a nasal bulb syringe to clear an infant's nose. It's not hard to use a nasal bulb. After putting two or three drops of normal saline into each nostril, first hold and squeeze the bulb of the aspirator before putting its tip into one nostril, then release the bulb to allow negative pressure to suck out the secretions. Repeat this process with the other nostril. Babies don't like this, but it makes breathing less labored.

PARENTS' REPORT: WHAT WORKS

The common cold has obviously been around a long time. Over the years—make that centuries—different cultures have cooked up their own remedies. Many are based on drinking a warm, soothing liquid. I've heard of teas based on everything from ginger to onions. Choose a brew your child is likely to find tasty.

✦ Many parents still insist on giving cod liver oil to prevent colds. One version shared with me by a Native American family is cod liver oil (1 to 2 teaspoons daily) mixed in a cup of sassafras tea, which masks the unpleasant taste.

✦ From a Polish family comes this recipe: Mix 2 or 3 cloves of garlic with 2 tablespoons of honey and the juice of 1/2 lemon. Put into a covered glass container to sit for three days. Give 1 teaspoon for kids age two years and one tablespoon for kids five and up. (Under age two years, check with your pediatrician, but remember, **no honey for children under one,** because it may contain botulism spores.)

✦ Don't forget chicken soup! Your grandmother was right; there are healing ingredients in the broth. This hot, salty, delectable liquid makes you feel better and provides some nutrition.

✦ When I visited Israel, a few families told me that elderberry extract cuts the duration of a cold or flu by half. They told me to mix 1 tablespoon into 2 ounces of water. I have since found that there is very good research to back this claim.

✦ One of my colleagues, Ken, shares his grandmother's secret recipe for soothing colds: "My Greek grandmother would take three egg yolks and place them in a cup with a couple of tablespoons of sugar. She would whip it up for several minutes until it was creamy and changed color. It tasted great." ☛ WARNING: Today we are more aware of the risk of salmonella infection associated with ingesting raw eggs, so if you want to try this, use only pasteurized eggs.

✦ Usually kids with colds lose their appetites and do not want to eat. If your youngster will bite, many parents report that celery increases appetite, and it's a good way to "feed a cold."

✦ Boil some white and red onions to make a soup, then season with tamari or chicken broth.

Some remedies are designed to prevent the child from getting a cold.

✦ Ray Long, a Cherokee, reports that in his family it was believed that wearing garlic cloves in a pouch around the neck prevented colds or shortened the length of one. As he says of this practice: "I hated to go to school, because I stank." (Once you have a cold, garlic clears up a stuffy head.)

To relieve cold symptoms:

✦ In a large bowl add 1/4 cup salt to steaming water. Make a tent by covering the child's head and the bowl with a towel. Allow the child to inhale the vapors for at least two minutes with his head a comfortable distance from the steaming bowl. Repeat. The salt and steam thin secretions, relieving the stuffy nose.

✦ For a chest cold: Mix a few drops of turpentine or tea tree oil with coconut butter, then rub onto a warmed flannel cloth and apply to the chest. (You can warm the cloth in the dryer or for one minute in the microwave *before* adding the turpentine mixture.) ☛ WARNING: Do not leave the turpentine in an area where little fingers can undo the top and drink this aromatic but toxic liquid.

✦ There are many variations of the familiar hot toddy, but check each ingredient carefully: Most include lemon (for the vitamin C) and honey (as an expectorant and to soothe the irritated throat and to loosen the mucus), which are okay for children over one year of age (never give honey to children under age one because of the risk of botulin spores). But make sure they do *not* contain any whiskey or narcotics. (Some contain paregoric, a narcotic, which depresses the cough reflex and induces sleep.)

☛ WARNING: In other parts of the world, it is still common to give children alcohol and narcotic derivatives. Remedies that contain alcohol, paregoric, belladonna, or other known sedating substances, although commonly available over-the-counter in some other countries, cannot be safely recommended. With these substances mixed in home brews, the risks of oversedation and respiratory failure are far greater than any possible benefits. Please, never give your child any preparation with alcohol or narcotic derivatives unless prescribed by your doctor.

☛ WARNING: Echinacea, a popular herbal cold remedy, can trigger a rash, facial swelling, and diarrhea in a child allergic to ragweed. It is not advised for use in children under the age of three. (After that age most parents will know if their child is allergic.)

Constipation

The Ailment

Constipation describes the consistency of stools, not the regularity of bowel movements. It is the presence of hard, dry feces in the lower end of the large intestines, and is usually associated with discomfort when attempting to have a bowel movement.

Constipation rarely occurs in infants who are exclusively breast-fed. Contrary to some beliefs, constipation is not related to iron-fortified formula. In toddlers and older children, it is sometimes related to an excessive intake of milk and milk products. Less commonly, constipation may be a symptom of an underlying metabolic disorder, a nerve or muscle problem, or an anatomical structural defect.

Sometimes, as a result of overly aggressive toilet-training attempts, some children may begin a pattern of holding on to bowel movements, allowing large amounts of dry feces to fill the rectum (called *encopresis*). If this practice persists, fecal leakage may occur, resulting in brownish stains in underwear. Once this pattern develops, attempts to have bowel movements become more difficult and more painful. With this stage of constipation, rectal tears and fissures may appear, causing bleeding.

Call your doctor immediately if:

- ✦ Constipation is associated with severe abdominal pain or fever with or without vomiting.
- ✦ Constipation is associated with severe pain lasting more than two hours.
- ✦ Constipation is associated with blood mixed in or surrounding the stool.

Conventional Treatment

Keep in mind that when adults have bowel movements, we are usually sitting on the toilet, using our back, leg, and abdominal muscles. We have a firm surface, the floor beneath, to offer resistance when we push. When infants have bowel movements, they expend a lot of energy utilizing the same muscles, but more effort is required, as they are either lying on their backs, lying on their tummies, or reclining in an infant seat. They do not have the advantage of a firm surface against which they can push to assist in their efforts.

For infants under one year:

- ✦ If baby is grunting and straining with attempts to have a bowel movement, try putting his legs in a knee-to-chest position and rest the soles of his feet against your palms. This allows the infant to push more effectively, as if he were in a squatting position.
- ✦ Add 1 teaspoonful of Karo syrup to 4 ounces of water or formula. This may be effective in softening the stools, making them easier to pass.
- ✦ Once juices have been introduced into baby's diet, try prune juice diluted with equal parts of water (1 ounce prune juice mixed with 1 ounce water). It is also an effective stimulant.

For older children:

✦ Encourage your child to eat more vegetables, fruits, and whole grains, and to drink more water. Certain foods, such as raisins, prunes, and prune juice, have a natural laxative effect.

✦ If you have a child with chronic constipation, consider cutting back on milk, which tends to replace other solid foods. Add other fluids, especially water.

✦ Gentle massaging on the lower left part of the abdomen can help to stimulate some colon activity and facilitate colon emptying.

✦ Lubricate your rubber-gloved pinky fingertip or the tip of a rectal thermometer with petroleum jelly. Insert your finger or the thermometer gently into your child's rectum. This may stimulate a neuromuscular reflex (the anal sphincter reflex), allowing the feces in the rectum to be pushed out reflexively. If in attempting to do this you feel any resistance, *stop.* Do not risk injury to your child by attempting to push through any resistance. Beware that this same stimulation can have a reverse effect and cause the sphincter to get even tighter, not allowing any contents to be expelled. Follow this method with caution and only if approved by your child's doctor.

✦ Your child's physician may outline a treatment plan that includes the use of stool softeners, mild laxatives, or daily intake of mineral oil for a limited time to establish regular, easy, and painless bowel movements so that your child doesn't learn to fear the process and stops trying to hold on to his feces.

☛ WARNING: Enemas, laxatives, or rectal stimulation should be used only if recommended by your child's physician. These practices may be suggested on occasion for immediate action and relief but should not be administered frequently or on a routine basis.

PARENTS' REPORT: WHAT WORKS

✦ Castor oil, which comes from the castor bean, has historically been used as a body cleanser. This is a cross-cultural and very familiar family remedy for constipation that seems to have survived the test of time. And it is also the all-time favorite in terms of bad memories of childhood because of its thick, oily consistency. Castor oil does cause increased muscular activity of the large intestine, which in turn causes the lower colon to empty its contents more rapidly.

✦ Castoria, a by-product of the castor bean, is slightly milder than castor oil but causes the same stimulation, resulting in lower colon evacuation. With both, you need to be concerned about the loss of too much fluid, as hyperactive intestinal movements cause rapid emptying. Check with your doctor for recommended dosages.

✦ Joyce, an elementary-school teacher and friend who lives on the Eastern Shore of Maryland, shared her family recipe, which she insists always works: Mix 2 tablespoons of raw, not distilled, vinegar with 2 tablespoons of honey in a cup of hot tea. (Do not give honey to children less than one year of age. Honey can contain botulin spores, which can be toxic in infants' less mature digestive system.)

✦ Youngsters who find prune juice less than palate-pleasing may warm to a prune juice cocktail: 4 ounces of prune juice mixed with 2 ounces of lemon-lime soda or ginger ale and a few drops of lemon juice, served over ice with a straw. It's tasty, and because of the natural laxative effect of prune juice, you don't need to worry about laxative dependence.

✦ If your child is not fond of prunes, try a date cocktail. Soak six dates in a glass of hot water, allow to cool, and puree in a blender. Pour the nectar over ice and put in a straw, and your child will find this drink a treat.

✦ Finely chop parsley leaves and use liberally, either plain or mixed with foods.

✦ Apples contain pectin, which will add bulk to stools; the colon-cleansing action encourages bowel movements. Also apple cider, a fermented version of apple juice, has some of the same beneficial properties. Offer 2 teaspoons twice a day with a glass of water.

✦ Flaxseed oil is another traditional folk remedy. Try 1 to 2 tablespoons with lots of water *after* lunch or dinner. Or boil 2 cups of water and add 2 tablespoons of flaxseed; boil for fifteen minutes and then strain off the flaxseed and cool, leaving a jelly-like substance. Have your child try a cup of this *before* a meal, adding 1 teaspoon of apple cider vinegar. If problems continue, administer daily. Flaxseed is an excellent source of some of the essential fatty acids that our bodies need for proper bowel functioning.

✦ Take two small beets, scrub clean, slice, chop finely, and offer them to your child in the morning. If necessary, mix into a familiar food like applesauce. If lucky, a bowel movement should follow by the evening.

✦ The essential oils in carrots have an effect on the mucous membranes lining the stomach and digestive tract and help get the bowels functioning. Offer your youngster carrot juice several times daily.

✦ Garlic is effective for three reasons: It soothes, cleanses, and reduces inflammation. Because it is rich in potassium, it promotes the contraction of muscles, including those in the intestinal tract. Add diced garlic to foods or soups a few times a day. The entire family may benefit from all of the garlic's medicinal qualities if its aroma isn't a deterrent.

✦ Make a massage oil using black pepper, marjoram, and rosemary essential oils (1 drop of each added to ¼ cup of any carrier oil, such as sesame, olive, or jojoba) and massage into the abdominal area. Perhaps any therapeutic or medicinal effect is due to the hands-on stimulation of the abdominal area; this mixture's aroma and texture provide a pleasant vehicle.

✦ The parents of one of my patients were stationed with the military in Germany, and reported their baby-sitter's suggestion of a glass of warm sauerkraut juice. It seems to work well, although I don't know any kids who would tolerate the sour and salty taste!

✦ Sunflower seeds are a healthful snack. If your child is constipated, try a handful of raw, shelled, unsalted seeds. ☛ WARNING: Don't give seeds to young children; they could pose a choking hazard.

✦ I leave the strangest remedy for last. This comes from a colleague who is part of an informal group of women doctors. She suggests that you leave the water running in the bathroom sink while the child is on the toilet. She doesn't know how this works or why, but she insists it encourages a bowel movement. I had previously heard that running water in the sink encourages urination.

Cough

THE AILMENT

A cough is the reaction to an irritation in the throat or air passages. The body tries to expel a foreign substance from the trachea or lungs, mucus (phlegm) from the chest, secretions from the back of the nose that drain into the throat, or mucus from sinus congestion or the common cold that finds its way into the airway. A cough can also result from irritation of the air passages by smoke, dust, pollens, and other environmental triggers. If a cough is sparked by exercise or cold air or occurs when triggered by certain circumstances and progresses to wheezing, asthma may be the diagnosis.

☛ WARNING: If the cough is accompanied by rapid breathing, difficulty breathing, wheezing, fever, or dusky coloring around the mouth, lips, or fingernails, call your child's physician immediately.

Conventional Treatment

If your youngster can cough on demand and has a lot of phlegm, encourage him to "cough it up and out." If you can hear a rattling sound when your infant or toddler breathes, turn him onto his tummy on your lap and pat/tap him gently on the back to help him move or bring up the phlegm. At night, elevate his head and chest. For infants and toddlers, use a couple of telephone books to elevate the head of the mattress; for older children, try two pillows under the head if your doctor gives the okay. These measures will slow or stop most postnasal discharge into the throat. Encourage your child to drink lots of liquids. Add moisture to the air with a cool-mist vaporizer or humidifier to further soothe irritated respiratory passages and calm a cough.

Depending on the type of cough, your physician may recommend an expectorant to loosen the phlegm or a suppressant to soothe the throat, reduce irritation, and act on the "cough center" in the brain, quelling the cough reflex. Some compounds combine antihistamines (to dry nasal secretions), expectorant (to loosen phlegm in the chest), and a suppressant (to depress the cough reflex). If your pediatrician diagnoses an infection, your child may need an antibiotic.

Parents' Report: What Works

✦ Add 2 or 3 slices of bread to 1½ cups of milk and bring to a boil. Cool, then put this poultice *over* the child's throat.

✦ Slippery elm (despite its name) makes a tasty tea. You may be able to find some in lozenge form or in tea bags. Don't give lozenges to small children; they're a choking hazard.

✦ A mix of sage and thyme tea (made right from the spices in your kitchen spice rack) will also clear out mucus, according to Ms. Andrews, a great-great-grandmom.

✦ If you can find it, osha root is also said to be great for coughs. It helps to clear phlegm and works for dry cough. Children can drink it as tea or take it as a tincture.

✦ Mullein, slippery elm, and marshmallow are all demulcents, which means that they soothe irritated throats and respiratory tracts. They can be offered to children as a tea. Mullein, an expectorant, encourages coughing it up and out; marshmallow reduces inflammation.

✦ Lemon and honey in hot water has been offered for generations. Not only is the hot water soothing to the throat, but the heat makes it more difficult for germs to thrive. Also, the honey is anti-inflammatory. (Don't give honey to children under one year of age.)

✦ Rub a few drops of lavender oil diluted in a vegetable oil such as almond, olive, jojoba, or sesame on your child's chest. Other safe and effective essential oils for chest rubs include sage, rosemary, thyme, peppermint, and eucalyptus. (These last two are the same ingredients included in mentholated rubs and lozenges.)

A word about essential oils: All essential oils are said to be inherently antibacterial. Massaging them into the skin allows them to get into the body faster, perhaps because their molecules are small enough to penetrate the skin, allowing them to be absorbed into the system. Inhaling the vapors from these oils is also helpful. As they are inhaled and reach the throat and respiratory system, they may exterminate some germs in their path. You can also put these oils into a warm bath or even into a vaporizer in the child's room. Even dabbing a few drops on a hankie and tucking it into the child's bed or a few drops on the pillow will help the child breathe in the vapors.

Many families in my practice have shared with me their own recipes for homemade cough syrups. Most are based on similar ingredients. Here are just a few versions.

✦ For a dry cough, sweeten boiled potato peelings with honey. Give 1 teaspoon every four hours. This is not for children under one.

✦ Boil 1/2 cup cut-up onions in 2 cups of apple cider vinegar; add honey to taste. For children over the age of three, offer 1 teaspoon every hour. Never give honey to children under the age of one.

✦ Here's another onion recipe that comes from a career military family, the Pritchetts, who have lived around the globe for the last twelve years: Take one yellow onion and core the onion about halfway down. The hole should be about the size of a dime. Fill the hole with honey. After about one hour, brown syrup comes out. Offer 1 teaspoon of the syrup every three hours. This onion/honey combination offers the Pritchetts relief for their change-of-season coughs. (This is not for children under one year of age.)

✦ See **Bronchitis** and **Common Colds** for more remedies.

Croup

The Ailment

Croup is a respiratory infection, usually caused by one of the common cold viruses or one of the bacteria that cause ear infections or pneumonia. Either may cause inflammation of the larynx (voice box), the trachea (windpipe), or the bronchi or bronchioles (breathing tubes). It usually occurs in very young children (infancy through three years) because at this age their air passages are quite narrow and can become easily blocked by mucus. Croup is recognizable by the high-pitched wheezing sounds made when the child takes in air through swollen vocal cords and a narrowed windpipe. A characteristic dry, barking, or croaking cough usually follows.

Croup, which usually appears suddenly and in most instances at night, is a mild respiratory disease of childhood. However, croup can produce severe swelling and blocked airways and cause breathing to be extremely labored, with the chest caving in with each inhalation effort. When this occurs, croup quickly becomes a medical emergency.

☛ WARNING: If you look at the back of your child's tongue to inspect his throat and see a large round cherry-red mass of tissue, it may be an inflamed epiglottis. Epiglottitis is a life-threatening medical emergency.

Conventional Treatment

Elevate your child's head and chest when he is resting; this may make breathing less labored. This can be achieved by raising the head of the child's bed or mattress. In very young children, do not use pillows, but place two telephone books under the head section of the mattress. Also, keeping babies upright in their infant seats allows them to breathe with greater ease.

Humidify the room; breathing the moist air will ease coughing and wheezing. This can be done with a cool-mist or warm-mist vaporizer; both are effective. Today, many families have a humidifier attached to their home heating unit.

☛ WARNING: Consult your physician immediately if your child's breathing continues to be very labored and results in any duskiness around the child's mouth, if fever persists, or if you feel that your youngster is not taking in enough fluids. A brief hospital stay may be necessary to ensure that your child gets adequate oxygen into her circulatory system and receives intravenous fluids for hydration and antibiotics medications to speed her recovery.

Parents' Report: What Works

These are remedies to open stuffed nasal passages and help the child breathe a little easier.

✦ Fashion a *mist tent* by safely positioning your child with a large towel covering his head and a large container of hot water with 3 tablespoons of salt. Allow him to breathe in the steaming air. Of course, this must be done with caution; do not leave a young child unattended during the process because of the real dangers of accidental injuries from hot water.

✦ Run the hot water from the tap in the bathroom sink and shower; close the door and windows to trap the steam. Sit with your child in this steamy setting for twenty-to-thirty-minute periods throughout the acute course of coughing and difficult breathing. With your doctor's okay, give your child a mug of orange pekoe tea.

✦ The theophylline component in traditional teas has a bronchodilator effect (relaxing the muscles of the breathing tubes), making the bronchi and bronchioles wider, permitting more air to go through the airway with less effort. Theophylline is closely related to caffeine, which some parents may find objectionable.

✦ If it's a cool night, some parents find it effective to wrap the child up and take her outside. It's said the cool air helps reduce swelling and inflammation of the airways. On the other hand, I've been told that warm, wet air works too.

✦ For calming a child with croup, try chamomile, catnip, or peppermint tea.

✦ A mustard foot bath is also said to reduce croup. I'm not sure why, but it surely seems harmless, since it's topical. Just add 2 teaspoons of dry powdered mustard to a basin of warm water and allow the child to soak her feet for ten minutes or so.

✦ Since a major component of croup is the cough, many of the remedies listed under **Cough** work as well. You can use marshmallow, mullein, or osha root teas. Offer the all-time favorite, lemon juice and honey in hot water, for children over one year of age (no honey for children under this age).

Cuts

THE AILMENT

A cut is a break in the skin, and sometimes the underlying tissue, usually associated with bleeding. Appropriate treatment depends on many factors, including the length and depth of the cut.

CONVENTIONAL TREATMENT

Surface cuts are usually not serious. Clean with cold water and soap, pat dry with a clean cloth, apply a first-aid cream or an over-the-counter antibacterial cream or ointment (Neosporin, for example), pull together the edges of the skin, and cover with a bandage to prevent contamination and to allow healing to occur. Deeper cuts may require direct pressure over the wound to stop the bleeding before an assessment can be made about the extent of the injury and the need for stitches. If the wound is gaping or jagged, or if it continues to bleed after ten minutes of applying direct pressure over the site, a medical evaluation is necessary. The need for a tetanus booster depends upon the date of the last immunization, the extent of the injury, if there is dirt in the wound, and where on the body the injury occurred. Antibiotics and follow-up care may also be warranted.

☛ **WARNING:** If the wound is very bloody, proceed to an emergency department for evaluation. If too much blood is lost, lightheadedness, fainting, or shock can occur. If two to three days after the injury you notice red streaks, heat, swelling, or extreme tenderness over the injury site, see your doctor to determine if there is an infection and to tailor the treatment to the complications of the injury.

Parents' Report: What Works

✦ Our gracious tour guide in Tahiti advised this treatment for a cut: Take a young banana plant and cut the center of the stalk lengthwise. Put the clear juice (sap) directly on the wound. Or soak a broad leaf from the banana plant with the sap, wrap the wound with this leaf, and leave it on for three to four days. According to local beliefs, the sap stops the bleeding, is an anti-infective, and reduces discomfort.

✦ The antiseptic properties of cloves and clove oil have been known to relieve the pain of a cut. (See also **Toothache**.)

✦ When I was in Seattle, Washington, certainly a region that likes its apples, I was told by a chef that a mixture of apple juice and olive oil works well when applied to a cut. (Do *not* offer this as a drink.)

✦ If you have an aloe plant handy, snap off a leaf, cut lengthwise, and apply the sap directly to the wound.

✦ Sugar is a disinfectant. When I was visiting Whistler, British Columbia, a Canadian couple shared this use of sugar: For open wounds, sprinkle on granulated sugar to help kill the bacteria and speed healing. Smear a ring of petroleum jelly around the edges of the wound to hold the sugar in place, then put a little sugar directly on the wound. Cover with a bandage and change once or twice a day. Another sweet solution they suggested is to spread raw honey on the cut, but I don't recommend this for children under the age of one.

✦ Melaleuca (tea tree) oil is a potent antiseptic, which is why it's good for cuts and scrapes.

✦ A marathon runner from Barcelona, Spain, touted the healthful benefits of yogurt. His remedy: Apply plain yogurt, the kind with active cultures. These have the good bacteria that can help guard against infection from harmful ones. It also helps skin to heal.

✦ Vitamin E can help prevent scarring once a scab has formed. Break open a capsule and apply the oil directly to the scabbed-over area.

✦ Calendula helps the skin knit together, and it's antibacterial. Look for calendula ointment in health food stores.

✦ Echinacea alone or with goldenseal can disinfect cuts and promote healing. Just dab a bit of the tincture right on the cut. You can often find these herbs already mixed together in a combo form.

✦ This family pet remedy was shared by a friend who had me swear to keep her name a secret. She recounts: "Whenever my sister or I had a cut, my mom would have the family dog lick the wound. Once we were at a neighbor's house when I got a nick on my leg, and Mom had the neighbor's dog lick my wound." In human saliva, there is an enzyme, ptyalin, that aids in the digestions of carbohydrates and reportedly speeds the resolution of scratches. I wondered if there is such a substance in a dog's saliva, which could account for any healing effect; in a best-selling mystery novel I read, the heroine mentions that she has heard that there are healing properties in dog saliva! ☛ WARNING: This remedy doesn't meet the approval of a veterinary colleague, who tells me it's unsanitary. She reminded me that dogs eat everything and that their mouths host many more bacterial contaminants. So licking wounds may bring back memories for some, but it may add more than just a warm, wet, comforting feeling.

Dandruff

The Ailment

Scaling of the scalp can be caused by a wide variety of disorders, including atopic dermatitis, psoriasis, fungal diseases, and systemic diseases. However, most common dandruff is the result of normal exfoliation (shedding of skin cells) on the scalp. When the scalp is dry and sheds too often, white flakes may be visible in the hair or on the forehead and shoulders.

Diffuse scaling of the scalp may be seborrheic dermatitis. This is characterized by raised, scaly, greasy, grayish plaques seen on the scalp, perhaps the forehead, in the eyebrows and lashes, and behind the ears. When seen in infants, it is usually called cradle cap. If left untreated, the crust does not allow the scalp to "breathe" and may result in hair loss.

Conventional Treatment

Periodic and regular cleansing with a mild shampoo designed for dry scalp and careful rinsing of the scalp and hair with water may be the only measure necessary to remedy the condition. Antibacterial skin cleansers and shampoos containing salicylic acid should not be used by those with aspirin sensitivity. Coal tar or antifungal agents are quite effective for truly problem cases of persistent dandruff, but use them only with your doctor's approval.

PARENTS' REPORT: WHAT WORKS

✦ Apply the gel (sap) of aloe vera leaves into the scalp and leave on overnight. The next morning, wash scalp and hair with a mild shampoo and rinse thoroughly.

✦ Ms. Griffin, a day-care provider, suggests that apple cider vinegar will help restore the proper acid/alkaline balance of the scalp and kill bacteria that clog the pores that release oil. (The clogged pores result in scales and crusts.) With cotton balls, apply a mixture of apple cider vinegar diluted with an equal amount of water to the scalp and allow to dry. I have been told that lemon juice may also be used. It is the acid content that helps restore the chemical balance.

✦ An accountant friend's answer for dandruff is to add 1 cup of diced white beets to 2 cups of water. Then he covers the pot and boils the mixture until the water is almost gone. He strains the mixture and uses the remaining beet water residue to moisten his scalp.

✦ For mild cases of dandruff, one of my families uses the mouthwash Listerine on their kids' scalps because of its antiseptic properties. Do not use where skin is broken or it will be irritating.

There are many homemade variations of hot oil treatments:

✦ Combine 2 ounces of olive oil and 2 teaspoons ginger root and heat for 2 minutes. Apply the cooled-off mixture with cotton balls to the child's scalp before shampooing. If the dandruff is really bad, leave the mixture on for ten to fifteen minutes before shampooing.

✦ Massage warm rosemary oil or a mixture of olive oil and crushed rosemary leaves into the scalp and leave on for fifteen minutes; then use a mild shampoo to wash out the oil, and rinse well.

✦ Make another rinse by boiling 4 heaping teaspoons of dried thyme in 2 cups of water for ten minutes; strain and allow to cool. After shampooing and rinsing with clean water, massage this tea into your child's clean, damp hair. Do not rinse out. The oil from the thyme has antiseptic properties.

✦ Warmed coconut oil, applied in the same manner, also works.

Diaper Rash

THE AILMENT

Diaper rash is irritation of a baby's skin on the area of the body usually covered by the diaper. Many factors may contribute to the irritation of a baby's bottom. The bacteria present in the baby's stools and the ammonia compounds in the urine may be strong skin irritants. As contact with urine is extended, the skin initially becomes red and irritated, then raw. Also, if the baby is not dried well after bathing, especially in the upper thigh crease areas, dampness encourages skin breakdown and a red, raw rash may develop.

If there is extensive diaper rash, check your baby's mouth for white patchy spots on the inner cheeks or a coated tongue. If you see white patches, it indicates that monilia (candida), a yeast and the culprit causing thrush, is present and is probably the cause of the diaper rash. (See **Thrush**.)

Diaper rashes are also caused by some laundry detergents and fabric softeners used with cloth diapers. Allergic skin reactions may appear with some types of disposable diapers. The superabsorbent disposable diapers are great for absorption of urine. However, when they were first on the market, for some babies, these diapers' middle layer's special absorbent compounds were a major irritant to very sensitive skin. This problem has been resolved. Today, most babies' bottoms do very well with the superabsorbent disposable diapers.

CONVENTIONAL TREATMENT

Frequent diaper changes reduce the likelihood of diaper rash, so make sure to change soiled diapers as promptly as possible. Wash your baby's bottom with plain water and pat dry; whenever practical, allow him to remain diaperless for a while. Air-drying of a raw bottom is quite effective for healing. If you must cover the area, I recommend trying a cornstarch paste (mix 2 to 3 tablespoons of cornstarch with just enough water to make a paste, then apply liberally) to dry the rash. Once the rash subsides, coat the baby's bottom after each cleansing with a protective barrier such as petroleum jelly, A and D ointment, or zinc oxide. If the rash spreads and becomes more severe, consult with your physician, who may prescribe an antifungal or antibiotic cream to speed clearing.

PARENTS' REPORT: WHAT WORKS

Today there is a great variety of relatively inexpensive over-the-counter preparations. But here are some of the homemade remedies that my patient families have shared with me.

✦ A young Italian-American first-time mom, Donna, said her grandmother advised her to rub garlic oil on affected areas. But she admits her grandmother thinks garlic is good for just about anything that ails you!

✦ Over the years, many families have praised the curative properties of the sap from the aloe vera plant for a variety of skin ailments, including diaper rash. Just snap off a leaf, cut lengthwise, and apply the soothing sap.

✦ A grandmother and day-care provider says she always gives older infants 3 to 4 ounces of cranberry juice mixed with an equal amount of water over the course of the day. This seems to make sense; the juice drink probably alters the urine's pH (the acid/base balance), which may reduce irritation of the diaper area.

✦ This same day-care provider advises mothers of the children in her care to give cloth diapers a final rinse in a vinegar-and-water mixture after laundering them. This may work on a similar acid/base balancing principle.

✦ Apply a non-petroleum-based salve—ideally one with the herb comfrey or calendula as its main ingredient. Both herbs are well documented as skin healers and are safe for babies.

✦ Over the years, I have had a few mothers tell me that milk of magnesia also works to dry up diaper rash.

✦ If you are inclined to hang laundry on a line outdoors, dry cloth diapers in sunlight after washing. While you're out there, let your baby with diaper rash spend some time bottom up (naked) in the sunshine as well.

✦ One mother in my practice recommends using melaleuca (tea tree) oil for a variety of skin problems, including diaper rash. She is actually a sales rep for this product, but I have heard others tout its medicinal properties. She uses it for skin eruptions, abrasions, and irritations.

✦ Open a gelcap of vitamin E and rub the oil gently onto the raw diaper area. Vitamin C also promotes healing.

✦ A nanny from Georgia advised applying whole milk to the irritated areas with each diaper change. I wonder how this helps, since milk can encourage bacterial growth. So I give a thumbs-down to this one.

Diarrhea

THE AILMENT

Diarrhea is a condition characterized by the frequent passage of unformed, watery, sometimes explosive bowel movements. During this process, the digestive system is in a hyperactive state, and the intestinal contents (food and liquid residue) are rapidly expelled from the body while taking too much body water along with it.

Diarrhea is generally not considered a very serious condition for older children and adults. However, in infants and very young children, unchecked diarrhea can lead to great fluid losses, body mineral imbalances, and possibly dangerous dehydration.

Diarrhea, accompanied by vomiting and fever, may be a sign of infection. If loose and watery stools consistently follow your child's ingestion of certain foods, consult your doctor. This could be an indication of a malabsorption disorder, where specific body chemicals (enzymes) necessary for the digestion and absorption of particular food types may be deficient or absent.

Call your doctor immediately in any of the following situations:

- If stools remain unformed and watery for six hours or more in infants, twelve hours in young children, or twenty-four hours in older children and teens. Dehydration can be dangerous.
- If your youngster seems lethargic, if his lips and the inside of his mouth seem dry, if there are fewer or no tears when he cries, and if he is urinating less frequently. Again, the risk of dehydration exists.
- If your child's diarrhea is associated with fever, vomiting, or severe colicky pain lasting longer than you feel it should. There is the possibility of an intestinal obstruction.

✦ If diarrhea is bloody or mucus-filled. This may signal intestinal irritation and internal bleeding.

Conventional Treatment

Diarrhea is usually self-limiting. With a tincture of time, and allowing the gastrointestinal system to be inactive for a very short period, most symptoms begin to fade within one to two days of onset.

If your child is under one year: There are many opinions and approaches for the management of infant diarrhea. If you are breast-feeding exclusively, continue. If you are bottle-feeding, many experts now advise continuing formula. Others suggest that formula be discontinued temporarily and that you give an oral rehydration solution such as Pedialyte to replace the fluid and important minerals being lost in this process. Attempt to administer at least 3 fluid ounces of liquid per pound of child's body weight over a twenty-four-hour period. Your child's doctor will advise you which approach is best for your baby, and when and how to gradually reintroduce infant formula and other foods.

If your child is older: Alter the child's diet to allow the gastrointestinal system to become less active, work less, and to rest, while replacing fluid losses. A light BRAT diet may work: Bananas, Rice (boiled, with no added butter, milk, or other fat) or rice cereal, Apples (quartered or as applesauce or diluted apple juice), and dry Toast. Avoid high-fat and sugary foods during this period.

Don't give your child over-the-counter antidiarrheal agents unless advised by your child's physician. Antidiarrheals work by slowing intestinal muscle contractions and reducing the frequency of bowel movements. A safer choice is Kaopectate, which contains kaolin (a type of clay that attracts moisture and solidifies fecal matter) and pectin (a plant extract used to make substances jell). Sometimes this product does help to relieve symptoms. You can also try bismuth salts (Pepto-Bismol), which help to absorb the excess fluid in the large intestine. Most of the prescription preparations have antispasmodic properties as well, and some contain sedative substances or nerve impulse blockers, which slow the intestinal muscles' movements, thereby relieving the cramps that may accompany diarrhea.

Parents' Report: What Works

There seem to be as many remedies for diarrhea as there are families—each family has a recipe it swears by. Most are liquids, mixtures, or foods that bind and help solidify stools.

✦ Over the years I have heard dozens of apple remedies, many of which rely on apple cider vinegar. Gloria, a former neighbor, always touted the benefits of apple cider vinegar. She said to give children 2 teaspoons of apple cider vinegar in 4 ounces of water every two to three hours. This can be used for children as young as three years of age. The vinegar acts as a natural antiseptic and helps cleanse the intestines and entire digestive tract. Another variation is to grate an apple and let it stand at room temperature for several hours until well darkened. The apple contributes pectin (a water-soluble carbohydrate), which adds bulk to stools. The oxidized pectin may help stop the diarrhea. Offer children (and babies, with the doctor's okay) finely grated apples, followed by oatmeal porridge.

✦ Go bananas! Give some banana to your child a few times a day. It helps absorb the water in stool and replaces lost potassium.

✦ Another mother in my practice advises putting 1 teaspoon of allspice in a cheesecloth bag and allowing it to simmer in unsweetened blackberry juice for a few minutes. She gives her children 1 teaspoonful every four hours. Several tablespoons of fresh or frozen blackberries work well, too, as does blackberry juice. Just be aware that the mixture could stain fabric if spilled.

✦ Boil 1 cup of carrots, then puree. Give 1 teaspoon every fifteen minutes. The essential oils in the carrots have a salutary effect on mucous membranes in the stomach. Carrot soup is also believed to be helpful for children suffering with diarrhea caused by *E. coli* bacteria.

✦ It's long been accepted that activated charcoal stops diarrhea quickly by adsorbing toxins. It's widely available and is found in drugstores and health food stores. Parents should read labels for dosage instructions. For kids who don't swallow pills, the capsules can be broken open and mixed with a glass of water. But activated charcoal is not for everyday use, as it absorbs important vitamins and minerals as well. (*Note:* If you don't have activated charcoal, you can try burning a piece of white toast. Scrape the burned part into a cup of boiling water, cool, and offer it to your child.)

✦ Combine 2 tablespoons of cottage cheese and 2 tablespoons of sour cream and offer this mixture several times a day. Your child may find it more palatable put on a baked potato, saltine crackers, or toast.

✦ Make some potato soup from your favorite recipe and offer several cups during the day.

✦ Make a tea from the leaves of a pumpkin, hard squash, or gourd. (This seems especially appropriate if your child's upset stomach is due to overeating Halloween candy.) Boil 2 quarts of water, then snip several handfuls of leaves into the water, cover, and remove from the heat. Steep for thirty-five minutes. Offer ½ to 1 cup as a drink every couple of hours. (The only stumbling block is that to get pumpkin leaves, you have to go directly to a pumpkin patch!)

✦ If your child gets diarrhea as a side effect of oral antibiotics, encourage her to eat yogurt with live cultures.

✦ One of the nurses in the pediatric emergency department of a local hospital offered her recipe for a popular remedy: Boil a cup of rice in three cups of water for fifteen minutes, then pour off the water into a cup to cool. Administer several tablespoons of this rice water as frequently as possible.

✦ Children can be given mild teas. Black and green teas are rich sources of tannins, which have astringent qualities that help stop diarrhea. Peppermint, chamomile, sage, and tormentil teas can be used for stubborn cases.

✦ Try a tea made from caraway seeds. Put 1 teaspoon of seeds in a mug, pour boiling water over them, and let it steep for ten to fifteen minutes. Then strain the seeds out through cheesecloth or muslin. *Note:* To make your own version of a tea bag, use some snippets of cheesecloth or muslin and float the seeds in the boiled water in the homemade bag.

✦ Older babies with diarrhea can be offered ½ teaspoon of red raspberry leaf tea every four hours. Red raspberry leaf tea is routinely given to expectant moms in the second or third trimester because it is known to tone the uterus. Unless there is a family history of an allergy (and it's possible to be allergic to raspberries and not be allergic to red raspberry leaf tea), check with your doctor, but it's probably okay for older infants who have already been introduced to fruits.

✦ Meadowsweet is another popular herbal remedy. To make an infusion, use 1 or 2 teaspoons of the dried herb in 1 cup of boiling water and steep for ten minutes. If your youngster really likes it, you may offer up to 2 to 3 cups a day as needed. Meadowsweet is readily available in tea bags in health food stores. It's an analgesic herb, like white willow, which contains the same pain reliever as aspirin. ☛ **WARNING:** Don't give this if your child is aspirin-sensitive.

Earache

THE AILMENT

An earache is any type of ache or pain in the outer, middle, or inner ear. Earaches are fairly common in children under the age of seven.

Middle-ear infection (otitis media) is the most common cause of earache in young children. The familiar combination of fever, crying, and tugging at the ear is one of the most common reasons for calls to the pediatrician. In youngsters, the passageways that connect the middle ear to the back of the throat (eustachian tubes) are short and straight compared to the adult structures. This makes it easier for secretions from the back of the nose and throat infections to travel to the middle ear. Viral or bacterial secretions from runny noses or inflamed sinuses, colds, or other upper-respiratory infections may find their way from the back of the throat through the eustachian tube and get trapped in the area behind the eardrum (tympanic membrane).

Children left lying on their back with unfinished bottles are at greater risk for otitis media because these liquids are breeding grounds for bacteria, which can travel to the eustachian tube and cause a middle-ear infection. If ignored or left untreated, middle-ear infection can result in some hearing loss.

The increased middle-ear pressure resulting from trapped infected fluid can produce symptoms ranging from mild discomfort to excruciating pain. As the pressure in the middle ear increases, the eardrum may balloon outward, then spontaneously rupture, allowing fluid to escape into the ear canal. After such a rupture of the eardrum, most children begin to feel more comfortable. During an infection, because of increased middle-ear fluid and pressure, many children will experience minimal to moderate hearing loss. Hearing improves once the infection has cleared.

Middle-ear infections should be evaluated and treated by your child's doctor. Medical professionals disagree about whether each ear infection should be treated with antibiotics. Some studies have shown that ear infections generally clear up on their own with time. However, once I identify otitis media I usually treat it in the traditional way with antibiotics because of the small risk of progression of the infection, resulting in hearing loss. It is important to administer all prescribed medications through completion, as recommended by your doctor.

Other causes of earache include a foreign object in the ear, wax buildup, outer-ear infection (otitis externa; see **Swimmer's Ear**), teething, dental infections, an ear canal abscess, teeth grinding, jaw clenching, misalignment of the upper and lower jaws, and temporomandibular joint (TMJ) disorders.

Conventional Treatment

The first step is to determine the cause of the pain. Outer-ear infections usually involve a break in the skin of the ear. After careful cleansing of a visibly infected site, an antibacterial ointment and time will promote good healing. If you suspect a middle-ear infection, try to make your child as comfortable as possible. Acetaminophen will lower fever, and a warm pack to the ear offers some relief.

In my opinion, a middle-ear infection, where infected fluid gets trapped behind the eardrum, is best treated with prescribed antibiotics. Persistent, chronic, and recurring middle-ear infections that have not responded to antibiotic therapy may need to be resolved by the surgical insertion of ear tubes, allowing the middle-ear chamber to drain continuously. Since youngsters with ear tubes are at a higher risk for conductive hearing losses, hearing screens should be a part of their follow-up care.

Parents' Report: What Works

✦ A friend's grandmother from Italy treated all of her children and grandchildren who had an earache with her sure-fire remedy, which has worked for at least two generations in her family. Here's her recipe: Heat a cup of salt in a frying pan until all of the granules are hot. Pour the heated salt into a thick sock and knot the end. Test the warmth to make sure it's not hot enough to burn the skin, and hold the sock against the child's painful ear. I have recommended this to parents over the years, and many have reported that it works. My theory is that the heated salt retains the soothing warmth that eases the child's discomfort. Perhaps the salt also draws fluid from the painful ear. In doing so, it might decrease the middle-ear pressure, and if there was excess fluid behind the eardrum, the warm salt might help to create the climate for a spontaneous rupture of the membrane, which gives immediate relief. (Author Willa Cather mentions using "a bag of hot salt" for an earache in an early short story, "Old Mrs. Harris.")

✦ For a number of years, I had heard grandmothers and great-aunts of my little patients speak about the merits of sweet oil (oil of camphor). One day I finally got the lowdown from one kindly grandmother who brought her working daughter's toddler into the office. I had received a frantic late-night call from the mother, who described the classic otitis media symptoms and noted that her daughter was very lethargic. However, I wondered if I had misunderstood the mom as I watched this superenergetic child happily running around the office. When I wondered aloud how this child had made such a rapid recovery, the grandmother told me that after her daughter had called *her,* she'd immediately driven to their home and put warmed oil of camphor drops into her grandchild's ear. She warmed the oil by running hot tap water over the tiny bottle for a few minutes. Two drops of warm sweet oil are dropped into the painful ear every four to six hours for pain relief.

✦ Several parents have told me they take their hair dryer, turn it on the lowest heat setting, then hold it *at least* eighteen inches away and blow warm air over the ear for a few seconds. (This is best used with older children, who won't be so startled by the noise.) ☛ **WARNING:** Prolonged hot air forcibly blown into the ears may harm the skin and the delicate working parts of the inner ear.

✦ Mix vinegar and water in equal parts and put 4 drops into the painful ear with a dropper. Repeat every three to four hours until your doctor advises you on the next steps.

✦ Make garlic oil in advance if your child suffers from frequent earaches. (Garlic has anti-inflammatory properties.) Take ½ pound of peeled and crushed garlic cloves, put in a jar, and cover with olive oil. Cap the jar and shake a few times daily for several days. Strain this mixture through clean cotton. Label the jar FOR EARS and store in a cool place. Put 2 or 3 drops into the painful ear two or three times daily. Blot with cotton. Garlic oil is also available in health food stores. You can buy garlic oil and mullein oil, mix with olive oil in equal parts, then warm to room temperature. Put a few drops into the painful ear as needed.

Ear Wax

The Ailment

The buildup of ear wax (cerumen) is not a disorder, but a normal condition. This honey-colored, sticky substance is the ear's natural lubricant. It is produced by the glands in the skin lining the ear canal to protect inside the ears from dust, foreign objects, and infection. Some of us have an inherited tendency to be high wax producers. Our chewing motions usually move the wax along and out into the ear canal, where it can be accessible to a washcloth. On occasion, wax builds up, becomes dry and hard, and forms a plug that blocks the ear canal, causing some discomfort, ringing sounds, and possibly diminished hearing.

Conventional Treatment

✦ Wash the entire ear daily, including the inside of the ear opening. It is all right to push the tip of a wet washcloth into the small opening of the ear to remove some of the wax that does not move on its own, but don't push anything else inside the ear.

✦ For very heavy wax producers, put a couple of drops of hydrogen peroxide into each ear once or twice a week with a dropper. This causes the cerumen to liquefy, bubble, turn whitish, and drain out of the ear into the canal, where it dries and can be easily removed with a wet washcloth.

✦ If daily cleaning does not eliminate excess wax, or if there is a resistant wax plug, your child's doctor may have another recommendation, or she may remove as much as possible with an ear curette or with a suction device.

☛ **WARNING:** Do not poke around in your child's ear with a cotton swab, hairpin, or any other object. Remember that your child's ear canal is shorter and straighter than yours, and the risk of traumatic puncture of the eardrum is too great.

PARENTS' REPORT: WHAT WORKS

The remedy I hear most often involves olive oil and glycerin. Put a few drops of olive oil and glycerin into the child's ear to break up the wax, then flush it out with water using an ear syringe you can get in a drugstore.

Eczema

THE AILMENT

Eczema is a chronic, recurring allergic skin condition that produces a distinctive type of red, dry, scaly, itchy rash, especially in skin creases on the extremities—the folds of elbows and knees. It also occurs on the scalp, face, and neck, and occasionally on the chest and back. As with most allergic conditions, there is usually a family history of the ailment or sensitive skin.

Eczema rarely makes its first appearance before three to six months of age, sometimes revealing itself shortly after the introduction of solid foods into the baby's diet. The initial lesions may erupt as reddish areas on the face, which seem to itch because the babies typically maneuver their bodies into positions that allow them to rub the areas. This constant rubbing may produce raw, irritated spots, which may initially ooze and then form crusts. Constant rubbing or scratching causes breaks in the skin, allowing the entry of bacteria, which can cause infection. If this pattern of irritation is allowed to continue, these spots become visibly thickened, darkened areas of skin. To reduce the likelihood of eczema complications from scratching, try putting socks over your infant's hands during sleep. Also, keep your youngster's fingernails clipped as short as possible.

There are certain foods that may trigger eczema episodes, such as eggs, dairy, wheat, nuts, and seafood, although any food can be a specific irritant to an individual's immune system. Common skin irritants include animal fur or wool, nickel and other metals, detergents, and scented lotions and creams. Extremes in environmental temperature and emotional stress are also important factors in the eczema cycle.

Eczema itself is not dangerous, but it may signal the presence of associated systemic allergies, such as hay fever or asthma. People with eczema may be more susceptible to extreme reactions to certain medications or vaccines.

Conventional Treatment

✦ Always consult with your infant's physician for guidance on any formula or feeding changes. Follow your physician's advice on how to avoid all suspected triggers.

✦ Avoid using drying, scented, or deodorant soaps on your child's skin. Try gentle nonsoap cleansers such as Aveeno. Avoid harsh laundry detergents and, if possible, allow for an extra rinse cycle when washing clothes and bed linens.

✦ Apply unscented oil or lotion to your youngster's skin immediately following baths to help retain moisture. Moisturizing the skin while it's still wet reduces the irritation of towel-drying and allows some of the oil to be trapped in the skin, making it more supple and less dry.

✦ During cooler weather, when the indoor air may be warm and dry, reduce the frequency of complete baths to every two to three days; add unscented bath oil to lukewarm water. Keep your child clean with sponge baths in between.

✦ Your physician may suggest the use of an oral antihistamine such as Benadryl liquid or gelcaps to offer relief from the itching. She may also recommend hydrocortisone creams (over-the-counter or prescription strength) to reduce the inflammatory skin reactions and promote more rapid healing.

Parents' Report: What Works

✦ I recall hearing stories of parents' using coal tar, also referred to as black salve. It is still used in many soaps and skin preparations for skin conditions, including eczema and psoraisis. You can detect the odor in many over-the-counter preparations, such as Tegrin, which is used for itchy scalp.

✦ Evening primrose oil contains omega-6 essential fatty acids, which are quite soothing to the skin and relieve the symptoms of itching, flaking, and inflammation. Find a lotion that contains oil of evening primrose; don't let your child ingest any capsules.

✦ Some families use flaxseed, which is thought to contain healing oil. For children, I recommend that flaxseed oil only be applied to the skin. Flaxseed oil contains omega-3 essential fatty acids and has been used for arthritis and other conditions. Rub a little flaxseed oil directly on the skin. The oil needs to be refrigerated in a dark container, or it can spoil.

✦ If your doctor okays it, give your youngster a children's daily multivitamin with minerals, since many eczema sufferers are found to be deficient in zinc, calcium, and vitamin B_6.

✦ Parents can make a tea (*not* for sipping) with calendula, then soak a cloth in it and apply it as a compress. As noted before (see **Diaper Rash**), calendula is a good topical treatment for skin irritations.

✦ Try adding 1 cup of sea salt with a few drops of lavender oil to the tub; the combination is calming and healing. For children over the age of seven, it's all right to add a drop or two of bergamot oil.

✦ Mix a few drops each of lavender, geranium, and chamomile essential oils into rose hip oil, and then massage over the irritated area. Essential oils are *not* for youngsters.

✦ Put 5 tablespoons of oatmeal, which is healing to skin, into a muslin bag and let it float in the bathwater. This also works for poison ivy.

✦ Ken, a child psychologist, shared this story: "As a kid, I had eczema on my arms and feet. My Greek grandfather would take a glass of olive oil and place ground-up tobacco leaves in it from his pipe. This concoction would sit for days, and then he would spread it on my skin. It burned like hell and didn't help." So I strongly suggest you stay away from this one!

Fatigue

THE AILMENT

Fatigue is most easily defined as a lack of energy. It's not normal for kids to be fatigued, so a constant lack of energy should warrant a trip to the doctor. It may be an early symptom of something more serious, including depression, hypoglycemia, hyperthyroidism, anemia, or chronic fatigue syndrome.

Create a checklist to consider possible causes for fatigue:

✦ What other symptoms have you noticed—paleness, bruises, appetite or bowel pattern changes, irritability, shorter sleep periods?

✦ Are there any new complaints that seem to be lasting longer than you think they should—sore throat, headache, stomach pains, sneezing, runny nose, unusual thirst or hunger?

✦ Are there any new medications, pets, unusual school situations, or family disruptions? Could your child be using the complaint of tiredness as an escape route?

Investigating the cause of fatigue can be very challenging.

Conventional Treatment

Your pediatrician will need a complete history of the fatigue problem to do a comprehensive evaluation with laboratory analysis. If medications are involved, perhaps just a change in type and dose may do the trick.

For overall prevention, make sure your child eats a well-balanced diet that includes plenty of fruits, vegetables, and whole grains, and adds up to enough calories to meet the energy requirements for his growth and development. Often girls get tired because they are dieting. Ask your doctor about nutrient deficiencies—particularly the B vitamins and zinc. Kids who are tired may just be overscheduled, so cutting back on activities may help. So can simple steps such as making sure they go to bed at a reasonable hour to meet the demands of their full days.

Parents' Report: What Works

✦ Here's a recipe for a quick pick-me-up from Ms. McKenzie, an acquaintance of mine. Mix a handful of parsley and six carrots in the container of a blender or food processor and liquefy. Serve chilled or over ice. How this tastes may depend on the size of your hand.

✦ Ginseng is said to be helpful in any form, though some prefer the liquid extract. There are many types of ginseng, but I have a colleague who only recommends Siberian ginseng tincture. According to her, it has no side effects. She advises giving kids one measured dropper (1 cc) of this tincture by mouth twice a day, morning and afternoon, to stimulate the adrenal glands. She says you may have to do this for a few months until your child bounces back. Then gradually wean your child from the mixture.

☛ **WARNING:** You should discuss any remedies that reportedly alter or mimic adrenal gland actions with your child's physician *before* you administer them.

Fever

THE AILMENT

Fever is not a disease. It's a symptom—the body's defense mechanism for fighting infection. Fever is defined as an elevation of the body's temperature. Normal body temperature is somewhat variable. We customarily use 98.6°F (37°C) as the index for a normal core body temperature. However, I usually tell parents that any rectal measurement between 97.6°F (36.4°C) and 99.6°F (37.5°C) is within the acceptable range for normal depending upon the child's age and state of hydration. (The more dehydrated the child, the higher the temperature.) There will also be variations based on how and where you take your child's temperature. Your child has a fever if it is:

- Above 99.7°F or 37.6°C rectal or ear
- Above 100.4°F or 38.0°C oral
- Above 100.8°F or 38.2°C under the arm

The core body temperature changes with the time of day and the pace of activities. However, coupled with other symptoms, a fever is a signal of some adverse systemic change. The younger the child, the greater the concern about an elevated body temperature.

☛ **WARNING:** Any body temperature measure above 100°F (37.5°C) in an infant younger than two months old is a reason to call your pediatrician. If your child has an elevated body temperature and you see any rhythmic shaking or trembling, it may be a convulsion. Some infants and young children have such febrile convulsions during periods of high fever.

CONVENTIONAL TREATMENT

Consider the word CALM once you discover that your child has a fever.

✦ **C: Check** the body temperature with a reliable instrument, such as a standard oral or rectal thermometer, tympanic (ear) thermometer, or any of the digital ones. ☛ **WARNING:** Recent reports highlight the dangers of glass mercury thermometers.

✦ **A: Assess** for other symptoms (e.g., loss of appetite, irritability, change in activity).

✦ **L: Lower** the temperature to increase the child's comfort. Give your child sponge baths in room-temperature water (as water evaporates, it cools the body down). Today we advise against alcohol sponge baths, as the alcohol vapors can be an irritant when inhaled. Administer a nonaspirin remedy such as acetaminophen (Tylenol, Tempra) in liquid, tablets, or suppository form. Higher or resistant fevers respond very well to ibuprofen (Children's Motrin, Children's Advil, or the store brand) in dosages appropriate for your child's age. (Never give a child aspirin because of the risk of Reye's syndrome.) Offer liquids: It's important to keep your child hydrated.

✦ **M: Monitor** your child's behavior and temperature for changes, and report any concerns to your child's doctor. If the fever remains high and or prolonged, call your pediatrician, who may want to evaluate the child to look for the underlying cause.

If we consider a naturopathic view of illness, fever is not always seen as a cause for concern. Fever is a sign that the immune system is working and that the body is fighting back. So some naturopaths don't like to bring fevers down if they're below 100°F. In this view it's not how high the fever is, but how fast it rises that may necessitate a call or visit to the doctor.

Parents' Report: What Works

✦ One day, upon entering an exam room, I noticed the distinct aroma of something resembling a burger and fries wafting in the air. Despite our office signs requesting no eating in exam areas, I politely asked the mom if she had just eaten her lunch while waiting for her child to be seen. She replied, rather annoyed, that she was too upset over her child's fever to take the time to eat. As I proceeded to undress the child, I was astonished to discover half an onion on the sole of each foot, held in place with his socks. That explained the aroma of onions. The mother explained that the onions draw fever from the body: You put half a cut onion on the sole of each foot, leaving them in place until the onions turn brown, indicating that the fever has been reduced. Since then, I have heard similar onion-related tales and have pondered the medicinal properties of the popular vegetable. The onion is a member of the allium group of plants, as is garlic; we have long been aware of the healthful benefits of garlic on blood pressure and cholesterol levels. So sometimes in addition to recommending acetaminophen for fever, I will give a nod to an onion being thrown in—just for good measure!

✦ Vitamin C, one 250 mg tablet crushed and dissolved into 1½ cups of onion soup, is considered a healthy fever-breaker according to a chef who is a parent in my practice. The onion seems to help the vitamin C work more efficiently.

✦ A naturopathic colleague suggests treating the particular illness or infection that's causing the fever—not the fever itself. That means if it's an ear infection, you use ear drops; if it's flu, she advises giving Echinacea with vitamin C, a popular tincture found in health food stores. For adults or older children, follow the label's dosage instructions. For youngsters, check with the doctor for any special precautions. If your child has a history of pollen sensitivity or hay fever, don't offer echinacea, which may cause a reaction.

Flu (Influenza)

THE AILMENT

Influenza, more commonly referred to as flu, can be difficult to distinguish from the common cold. Both are caused by viruses, and both produce fever, chills, sore throat, congestion, cough, and sometimes vomiting, diarrhea, and fatigue. However, if it's the flu, these symptoms are more intense, last longer, and are often accompanied by higher and more prolonged fevers, extreme eye discomfort caused by light (photophobia), headache, and muscle and body aches. Both colds and flu may run a course of five to seven days before symptoms subside. One aftermath of flu may be a persistent cough, often lingering for weeks after other symptoms disappear.

Influenza is of greater concern for anyone who has asthma, cystic fibrosis, congenital heart disease, sickle cell anemia, diabetes, or any chronic disorder that can compromise the body's immune system. The very young and the elderly are the most vulnerable to any complications of flu, which include bronchitis, pneumonia, and infections.

Prevention, when possible, is key. Each year, the Centers for Disease Control and Prevention predict which viruses may cause the most people serious illness. Based on this yearly prediction, a new influenza vaccine is manufactured and readied for distribution and administration by early fall. Experts agree that high-risk populations should receive the vaccine, and children are a high-risk population. In 2002, The American Academy of Pediatrics recommended that children over six months receive the influenza vaccine. Discuss with your pediatrician whether or not your child is a candidate for this flu vaccination.

☛ **WARNING:** If you suspect your child has the flu, do *not* administer aspirin. Reye's syndrome, a serious disorder resulting in liver failure and sometimes death, is associated with viral illness and the taking of aspirin.

Conventional Treatment

✦ Encourage your child to wash her hands frequently to prevent the spread of infection to other family members.

✦ Give fluids and acetaminophen (not aspirin) to relieve elevated temperatures and body aches.

✦ Humidifiers may make breathing easier.

✦ Cough formulas may help quiet and lessen the frequency of annoying coughs. Fatigue and listlessness usually mean the child has no choice but to rest.

✦ There are antiviral medications available by prescription, which if taken promptly after influenza exposure may prevent the illness or lessen the severity and shorten the course of the infection.

Parents' Report: What Works

✦ Garlic and onion are mentioned frequently, both separately and together. Some of my families reach for garlic cloves and onions to add to their children's food at the first sniffle or cough.

✦ Echinacea with vitamin C, a tincture found in health food stores, may be helpful with flu. Dosing instructions are on the package. As stated before, if your child has allergies, avoid echinacea. Also, don't give this tincture to children under the age of three.

✦ Try the electrolyte solutions discussed under **Gastroenteritis:** Japanese miso soup, diluted Knudsen's Recharge, or rice water.

✦ Prepare a warm bath with 2 cups Epsom salts. Have your child soak in the bath for about five minutes. Because your child may be weak from illness, do not leave him unattended. Make the water just hot enough so that the child isn't uncomfortable.

✦ See **Common Cold, Cough, Fatigue,** and **Bronchitis** for suggestions for specific symptoms.

Foot Odor

THE AILMENT

Our feet have more than a quarter of a million active sweat glands. Moist feet, socks, and shoes are perfect vehicles for bacteria growth and the resulting unpleasant odors. For some, the tendency to perspire heavily through their feet tends to be an inherited family trait, and it does occur more commonly in males. For others, foot odor may be a by-product of poor hygiene or wearing dirty socks. If feet are not properly dried after bathing, the areas between the toes may become cracked, inflamed, infected, and eventually smell.

CONVENTIONAL TREATMENT

Remind affected family members to dry feet well after bathing, particularly between the toes. Also, children should get in the habit of changing their socks daily—100 percent cotton is preferred, because natural fibers are cooler for the feet and do not hold moisture as long as synthetic fibers. Allow shoes to air out in between wearings. Rubber-soled shoes retain moisture longer than leather-soled ones. Athletic shoes are the worst offenders and should be allowed to air out in an open area, untied, with the tongue out and without the socks left stuffed inside.

There are many over-the-counter foot powders. For some they are worth the cost, but any effective foot care program must begin with good hygiene.

PARENTS' REPORT: WHAT WORKS

✦ Try the family underarm antiperspirant spray. Just spray your child's washed and dried feet. It should keep feet reasonably dry for a period of time.

✦ Sprinkle baking soda into socks, and also into shoes after wearing. As we know from the good job an open box does in the refrigerator, baking soda is an effective "odor eater."

✦ Over the years I have suggested using cornstarch sprinkled lightly on clean dry feet prior to putting on socks, because cornstarch absorbs moisture. There will be small white clumps caused by the cornstarch that need to be wiped from the toes when the socks are removed.

✦ A mother of two active boys shared her family remedy for stinky feet. It is one her grandmother used when her dad and his brothers were growing up in Boston. Steep 10 tea bags in 1 quart of boiling water and allow to cool. Then soak both feet in the tea for twenty to thirty minutes several times a week. It worked for her family. It is thought the tannic acid in tea interacts with the protein in the outer layer of skin, temporarily blocking many of the feet's sweat pores. My concern is the potential staining of the feet by the tea. Perhaps for some the benefits of odorless feet are greater than the drawbacks of tea-stained feet.

✦ This comes from a friend with her own organic garden: Juice about two dozen radishes, add 1/4 teaspoon of glycerin, and put in a spray bottle. Spray feet a couple of times a day. Perhaps the smell of the radishes wipes out the foot odor!

✦ For older children, if they are taking a daily multivitamin, check the label for the mineral zinc. Zinc is said to help eliminate foot odor. ☛ **WARNING:** Don't give your child more than 15 milligrams of zinc daily for more than a week without medical supervision.

✦ Everyone seems to have a favorite vinegar soak recipe. Here's an easy one: Mix about a third of a cup of vinegar in a pan of warm water, then have your child soak his feet. Or mix 2 to 3 tablespoons of vinegar into 2 quarts of cool water for a cool dip.

✦ Soak feet in a pan of warm water that contains Epsom salts. The salts are drying and help to clean feet.

✦ Try grapefruit seed extract. You'll find this in the health food store. It's antifungal, antibacterial, and potent, but gentle. If you find liquid extract, apply it right to the feet. If you only find capsules, break open a few and mix into a basin of water and then use as a foot soak.

✦ Consider getting shoe inserts made with activated charcoal. These inserts can be found in your neighborhood drugstore. Trim them to fit your child's shoes. Activated charcoal is antibacterial.

✦ Here's another use for melaleuca (tea tree) oil, which can be found in health food stores. It's a strong antifungal and antibacterial agent, but it's gentle enough to apply right out of the bottle to feet. However, it can be drying, so if skin gets red, you can dilute it with water. Just put a few teaspoons into a pan of water and use as a foot soak. If your child won't use a foot bath, there are creams that have tea tree oil in them. Have the child massage the cream into his feet, then air-dry or put on socks and have him hop into bed. If the odor is coming from toenail fungus, use the oil straight out of the bottle around the nails. But if skin is cracked or raw, then use the cream, as the oil may be too harsh. You have to use the tea tree oil for at least a month after the fungus appears to have cleared to prevent recurrence.

Freckles

THE AILMENT

A freckle is a collection of brown pigmented spots on the skin due to an accumulation of melanin. It is not an ailment but a distinguishing characteristic. Freckles are common and run in some families. Those with reddish hair are more likely to have freckles. Although freckled kids are considered cute, a proliferation of those brown spots can be stimulated by overexposure to the damaging ultraviolet rays of the sun.

☛ WARNING: If a small brown or black spot appears on your child's face or body that differs slightly in appearance from the other freckles, it may be a mole. Most moles first appear in childhood and adolescence. A mole does not require any immediate action, but it should be watched carefully. Any change in a mole's size, shape, or color should prompt a visit to your physician or dermatologist for a more complete evaluation.

Conventional Treatment

Provide sun protection for your children regardless of family history of freckles. Always apply sunscreen of at least SPF 15 twenty minutes before your child goes outdoors. Further protect your children with brimmed lightweight hats, periodic reapplication of sunscreen, and sunglasses. When possible, avoid the peak sun hours between 10 A.M. and 2 P.M. Sand and the reflection from the water or snow make the sun's rays more intense.

Parents' Report: What Works

✦ To lighten freckles, try using the juice from fresh lemons—fruit acids have the same effect as many expensive cosmetic creams.

✦ I saw many freckled lasses during a visit to Schull, Ireland—and my friend Ava told me about a Gaelic remedy, which is to apply honeysuckle, which grows abundantly in the wild. Honeysuckle is a vine with yellow flowers. Pull off a handful of leaves and flowers and soak overnight in a cup of water. Splash on the resulting mixture.

✦ Mix 1 tablespoon of grated horseradish with 2 tablespoons of buttermilk. Let the mixture sit for a few hours and then apply. I haven't a clue about the rationale of this remedy, shared by Maxine, a pharmacy assistant, but if the aroma is not a deterrent and it does not cause the skin to itch or turn red, it can be tried for a few weeks.

Fussiness

THE AILMENT

Fussiness is less of an ailment and more of a state of being. Some ailments have fussiness as one of the symptoms. Fussiness may be a temporary state of minimal discomfort; it could be an infant's way of letting you know that she wants to be changed from her position, maybe from her crib to your arms. But it could signal the beginning of a serious malady. So it is important to regard fussiness in context. (Also, see the section on **Colic** to distinguish fussiness from colic.)

✦ If she is crying, is the cry at *her* usual pitch, or in this instance does the pitch of her cry alarm you?

✦ If you find that the baby is fussy, what does it take for you to calm her? Does she seem inconsolable, or if you hold her in your arms, does she wind down and become comfortable? Have you checked her diaper, her position, her body temperature, and whether she may be hungry? When was her last bowel movement and what was its character?

☛ WARNING: Extreme, inconsolable fussiness accompanied by any of the following warrants an immediate call to your baby's physician: fever, vomiting, diarrhea, skin rash, or difficulty breathing. Also call if you notice prolonged or unusual fussiness after a fall or trauma.

Conventional Treatment

If you are able to determine the cause of the fussiness, you can more easily fix it. Even if you can't determine the cause, if you have discovered what works to calm and settle your child, continue to do that when necessary. Just be sure to share your technique with your pediatrician so that she can okay it and pass it on as a possible answer for the next parent with a similar concern. If your pediatrician identifies an ailment and initiates treatment, be certain to complete the prescribed course as recommended to ensure a good resolution.

Parents' Report: What Works

Many of these suggestions are designed to get the baby's attention and calm her down.

✦ Many of the parents in my practice like the "football hold" to help reduce fussiness. Carefully hold the baby on her abdomen on your forearm with her head facing your elbow. Balance the baby with your hand on her bottom and gently rock back and forth. Of course, be careful not to "fumble."

✦ A pacifier often settles a fussy baby by meeting her need to suck. Make sure the pacifier has a sealed back, because an open pacifier allows air to be swallowed, which causes the baby's digestive system to become filled with air. Then you will have an uncomfortable baby, which defeats the purpose.

✦ If your baby is jittery, try swaddling him. Sometimes being wrapped up snugly encourages relaxation because it is like being back in the womb. Wrap the baby firmly in a lightweight receiving blanket.

✦ Massage is often very relaxing. Gently massage her while you sing or hum to distract her.

✦ A warm bath relaxes many babies; it has the same effect on parents. So take a bath with your baby on your tummy. For safety reasons, make sure you have an adult you can hand the baby to as you climb out of the tub.

✦ Many parents find that a few sips (up to ½ cup) of very weak chamomile or peppermint tea cooled to room temperature works quickly to calm a fussy baby.

✦ See **Colic** for other suggestions on how to distract a fussy baby.

Gas

The Ailment

Gas is a sign of intestinal activity and sometimes warns us of intestinal disorders. In general, gas is a normal by-product of life and is an expected by-product of ingesting food. Excess gas may be produced by certain types of foods—beans, foods in the cauliflower and broccoli family, bran and other foods with insoluble fiber, and carbonated beverages. In addition, some seasonings and spices ferment in the intestinal tract and produce flatulence.

Some babies are gulpers. They hungrily suck from their bottles, not getting the bottle's contents as quickly as they may like, producing lots of bubbles, and taking in air while swallowing the liquids. Also, when they have a cold, many infants and young children breathe only through the mouth and swallow a lot of air at the same time. This swallowed air gets into the esophagus and may produce more belching, or it progresses farther down the digestive tract and results in the air passing through the rectum. Also, gastroenteritis will cause some bloating and abdominal discomfort.

Gas can be expelled by burping or by being passed through the rectum. The force with which gas is expelled determines the noisiness of this activity.

Some ethnic groups, including many people of Native American, African, or Asian descent, develop lactose intolerance in late childhood, adolescence, or adulthood. Because of an insufficient amount of the lactase enzyme that is needed to digest dairy products, affected individuals experience abdominal discomfort and lots of gas when they consume these foods.

Conventional Treatment

Recognize that passing gas is normal. When the gas production seems excessive and causes discomfort, some manipulation of diet, manner and method of eating, or body position will usually bring relief.

✦ With infants, take time while breast- or bottle-feeding; look out for the gulpers, and burp at frequent intervals, perhaps every 2 ounces. Try not to upset the baby; some will cry when you interrupt the feeding. Excessive crying causes more air to be swallowed and uncomfortable ballooning within the digestive tract to produce still more gas.

✦ If your child's nasal passages are congested, ask your pediatrician for methods to open the airways so that less air will be swallowed by mouth while baby's trying to breathe and eat.

✦ Monitor your child's diet. If you note that his gassiness increases when he eats certain foods, eliminate or reduce those foods from your child's diet (or, if breast-feeding, from mother's diet). Also examine your child's eating patterns. Even older kids may eat too fast and then gulp excessive air, which can cause gas. Have your child slow down and see if that helps. As noted earlier, lactose intolerance results in gas. Food allergies too may cause gassiness. Ask your doctor about an elimination diet to figure out what foods may be triggering the gas, a good idea since food allergies can cause other problems as well.

✦ If your child has explosive vomiting and/or diarrhea, particularly if accompanied by fever, consult his doctor. This could be an infectious type of gastroenteritis. Sometimes a mild anti-gas therapeutic, such as over-the-counter Mylicon infant drops or, for older youngsters, an antacid such as Children's Mylanta, may be recommended. Look for over-the-counter remedies that contain simethicone. It basically breaks gas bubbles into tinier bubbles to help them pass.

✦ Easy remedies include placing a warm-water bottle on the child's abdomen to alleviate the discomfort. Also, it's amazing how just getting off the couch and moving around can help the body process gas more effectively.

PARENTS' REPORT: WHAT WORKS

✦ An herbalist friend who is well versed in India's ancient medicine, called Ayurveda, believes that fennel is the top gas reliever. (It may also help with colic.) To use fennel, make a tea by steeping about 1 teaspoon of seeds—right out of your spice rack—in 1 cup of boiling water. Let it sit for twenty minutes. Strain. Then offer 1 to 2 teaspoons a few times a day, if needed. You can also find fennel tea bags in health food stores. For older children, you can give 1 teaspoon of fennel seeds to chew on. ☛ WARNING: Don't give the seeds to babies, since they're a choking hazard. Nursing moms with colicky babies can drink fennel tea; the therapeutic elements pass through the breast milk.

✦ Another Ayurvedic remedy recommended by an herbalist is ginger. Since ginger is known to be good for nausea, it's not surprising that it's helpful for other digestive woes. You can prepare a ginger tea with tea bags, fresh sliced ginger, or grated gingerroot, or just mix a small amount of powdered ginger into hot water. Or mix 1 teaspoon of grated fresh ginger with 1 teaspoon of lime juice. While cooking, you can blend ginger into dishes that are likely to produce gas, such as beans.

✦ The herb peppermint, which kids can ingest either in tea form or by chewing the leaves, will relax the intestinal muscles, making it easier for gas to escape. Peppermint is considered a potent remedy for gas. You can steep fresh peppermint in boiling water or use peppermint tea bags. Give children one teaspoon of peppermint tea four to five times a day.

✦ Chamomile tea with catnip, fennel, and ginger added to make it more palatable often works well. If your baby has gas and is bottle-feeding, add just ½ teaspoon of the mixture to 8 ounces of her formula. If breast-feeding, the mother can drink some of the tea.

✦ Dill relaxes the digestive tract muscles and relieves gas. You can find dill tea bags or loose dill in a health food store. You can also steep fresh dill or the seeds in boiling water. (Strain out the seeds.) Offer ½ to 1 teaspoonful no more than twice a day.

✦ Carbonated water encourages belching, the passage of gas, which relieves the discomfort. However, for very young infants, I do not recommend more than one to two teaspoons of carbonated or sparkling mineral water.

✦ To help prevent gas when eating beans, soak dry beans and change the water several times over a twelve-hour period before cooking them. This may strip the beans of the long-chain sugar molecules that produce gas. Or you can give your child Beano, an over-the-counter remedy that contains plant enzymes that help the body digest the carbohydrates found in beans. A few drops on the first bite of food often does the trick.

✦ My friend Andy is into probiotics, the generic term for beneficial live bacteria supplements that can help repopulate the intestines to aid with general digestion. Look for *Lactobacillus acidophilus* and *Lactobacillus bifidus* supplements. Follow dosage instructions for children. Yogurt with live cultures (there is always a container or two in Andy's fridge) is another good source of probiotics. Even many lactose-intolerant children can eat some yogurt. Check with your pediatrician.

Gastroenteritis

The Ailment

Characterized by abdominal discomfort, loss of appetite, nausea, vomiting, fever, and sometimes diarrhea, gastroenteritis is an inflammatory reaction involving the stomach and intestines. The most common culprits are viruses, which can be transmitted with our hands. Frequent hand washing is easy and remains the best preventive practice in order to avoid and halt the spread of gastroenteritis.

Improperly handled, spoiled, or contaminated foods cause similar symptoms with more severe, sharp abdominal cramps, and may be identified as food poisoning. The most common bacteria implicated in food poisoning, staphylococci and salmonella, may cause explosive, watery stools within six and eighteen hours, respectively, of eating the tainted foods. More debilitating and possibly lethal for youngsters is *E. coli* bacteria from tainted, undercooked hamburgers. The onset and duration of symptoms, and the character of the bowel movements, may help to distinguish which type of contaminant is the likely offender. However, a stool specimen for laboratory analysis would be necessary to accurately diagnose the cause. Determining the severity of a bout of gastroenteritis can be a challenge.

☛ **WARNING:** Infants and young children are at higher risk for dehydration resulting from prolonged loss of body fluids during diarrhea and vomiting.

Conventional Treatment

There is some debate about the preferred treatment of gastroenteritis. Some child health professionals advocate not changing the child's diet through bouts of diarrhea or to return to the age-appropriate diet within a few hours once rehydration with an electrolyte solution is completed.

It is my practice to temporarily alter the child's diet. My goals are to prevent dehydration, allow the gastrointestinal system to rest, and yet abate hunger. I advise parents to stop milk and solid foods for twenty-four to forty-eight hours. I recommend electrolyte replacement fluids such as Pedialyte, which is available in several flavors and is easily administered by bottle or cup. Fruit-flavored Pedialyte liquids and ice pops offer balanced hydration and variety while quenching the thirst and pleasing the palate of the pickiest eaters.

A child needs approximately 3 ounces of replacement fluids for each pound of his body weight over the first twenty-four-hour period of gastroenteritis. Even beyond infancy, I still recommend holding off on milk and modifying the diet for twenty-four to forty-eight hours. In older children, it is easier to gauge their improvement by the return of their appetite. Certain foods and herbs, such as apples (the skin contains pectin) and peppermint, have a soothing and therapeutic effect on the digestive system.

Rice cereal mixed with water (or Pedialyte) or mashed bananas mixed with water (or Pedialyte) for a creamy consistency can be offered by spoon to a hungry infant whose routine diet has progressed to cereals and other solids. Older children can be offered chicken broth, plain boiled rice, or potatoes, boiled and mashed without butter, milk, or gravy. Also, flat (minus the fizz of carbonation) Coca-Cola or ginger ale, apple slices (with skin on), and bananas provide hydration and some electrolytes. If everything you offer is regurgitated, it may be too early for foods; if your youngster seems thirsty, it's a safer bet to offer ½ cup of crushed ice.

Occasionally medications in the form of liquids, tablets, or suppositories are prescribed for short-term use to slow intestinal activity and to resolve the problem.

☛ **WARNING:** Forceful or projectile vomiting during infancy warrants an immediate call to your baby's doctor. Prolonged or persistent vomiting at any age may be one signal that an intestinal blockage or some other medically urgent situation may be the problem.

Parents' Report: What Works

Dr. Bobbi Lutack, N.D., a naturopathic physician at the Evergreen Natural Healing Center in Washington State, shared these remedies.

✦ Echinacea/goldenseal combination formulas can be found in health food stores. Use the tincture because it's stronger than tea. The echinacea supports the immune system, and it's also antimicrobial. Goldenseal is considered the number one herb for intestinal bugs. (Another herbalist friend says it is the best remedy for Montezuma's revenge, and always packs some when traveling.) Remember, do not give echinacea to children who are allergic to ragweed or who are under the age of three.

✦ Encourage your child to drink fluids. Restoring the electrolytes is key. Offer miso soup, rice water, or a juice product called Knudsen's Recharge (found in health food stores) that's diluted with an equal amount of water.

✦ Ginger seems to be the herb of choice for nausea and vomiting. You can offer your child ginger tea or even ginger candy. If your child is old enough to swallow pills, you will find ginger capsules in health food stores.

✦ And remember that *Lactobacillus acidophilus* is the "good" bacteria that helps vanquish the bad bugs. Break open a capsule and mix with a little applesauce or in an electrolyte solution.

✦ See **Gas** for more remedies.

Hay Fever

The Ailment

Hay fever has nothing to do with hay or fever. It is the immune system's upper respiratory allergic response to irritating environmental substances such as pollen from trees, grasses, and flowers. Hay fever can occur any time during the year. In most regions with changes of seasons, pollen counts are highest during the spring and fall. Symptoms correlate with the pollen counts, exposure, and sensitivity to other identifiable allergens. The mucous membranes (lining) in the nose and sinuses swell, itch, and produce thin, clear secretions. Sneezing, sniffles, and difficulty breathing are the most common symptoms associated with the ailment. The eyes of susceptible individuals become red, itch, swell, and tear.

Substances other than pollens, such as dust and dust mites, mold, animal dander, fragrances, and other environmental irritants, can cause hay fever symptoms. When the symptoms are present all year and do not seem dependent on the presence of pollen alone, the condition is called *perennial allergic rhinitis.*

Although allergies tend to run in families, and the children of afflicted parents may eventually exhibit some aspects of the disorder, kids rarely get hay fever during the first three years of life.

Conventional Treatment

The best way to treat hay fever is to reduce exposure to the substances that trigger episodes. During periods of high pollen counts, close the windows in your home and in the car and use air-conditioning. Often on high pollen days (counts over 200), the hairs in our nose and on our head will trap pollen, causing sneezing, sniffling, and other symptoms to continue beyond bedtime as the pollen finds its way onto the bed pillows. To reduce the likelihood of nighttime symptoms, after you and your children come in from outdoors on high-pollen-count days, rinse faces with cool water and, with a wet washcloth, wipe through your youngster's hair. Avoid prolonged outdoor activities during the peak pollen hours of the day (between 5 A.M. and 10 A.M.).

Over-the-counter and prescribed allergy medications and nasal sprays may offer temporary relief. If symptoms significantly interfere with your child's ability to partake in his usual activities, ask your physician about an allergy referral for evaluation and possible desensitization shots.

I suggest plain cold-water compresses and salt water nasal washes for the pollen and dust that get trapped in the nostrils.

Parents' Report: What Works

✦ Several families in my practice have used fenugreek, an herbal decongestant. It can be offered either as a tea or swallowed as capsules. See the label for dosage instructions. It can sometimes cause gas or bloating.

✦ Here's another good reason to add yogurt to your child's diet. As a neighbor and I were lamenting about the pollen one spring, she said it rarely affected her kids because she gave them each a cup of yogurt twice daily to keep the proper flora in their digestive tracts. As yogurt populates the digestive tract with friendly bacteria, perhaps it makes the child less sensitive to environmental irritants.

✦ Cut up three carrots, cover with 1 quart water, and boil for twenty minutes. Encourage your child to drink this carrot broth. This might help a scratchy throat, and carrots are a good source of the potent antioxidants vitamin A and beta-carotene, which help the body fend off invaders.

✦ If you are into reflexology, like the Mason family from my practice, you could try this remedy: Gently massage the area near the instep on the bottom of the feet and the area at the base of the thumb near the heel of the hand. This is said to stimulate the adrenal glands. The big toe is another reflexology point for the head and sinus areas. You can stimulate your child's lungs by massaging the balls of the feet and the hand right at the base of the fingers. Do this regularly, not just when your child has hay fever. (If acupressure is more your style, then press in between the index finger and thumb and hold for one minute.)

✦ Many remedies for hay fever involve different essential oils. Put one drop of chamomile oil and one drop of lemon oil on a tissue and have the child inhale. If symptoms don't improve, add a few drops of peppermint, clove, rosemary, lavender, or geranium oil. Mix and match, but don't use more than five oils at a time—that can overstimulate the olfactory (sense of smell) nerves. Remember, don't let your child ingest essential oils.

✦ Make a steam inhalation by pouring boiling water into a bowl, then tenting a towel over the child's head. Supervise while your child puts his face a comfortable distance from the steam. The steam opens up nasal and bronchial passages. You can also put a few drops of chamomile or peppermint oil into the steaming water. You can do the same with a warm-steam vaporizer in a child's room.

✦ Garlic is an immune system booster; it's believed that after eating garlic, the body is better able to handle a hay fever assault. It can also help stop a runny nose. Older children may be willing to take over-the-counter garlic capsules. The Kyolic brand is deodorized, which some people tolerate better.

✦ Vitamin C is an antioxidant with natural antihistamine properties. If used as a supplement, one 250 or 500 mg tablet daily is sufficient. You can also put some vitamin C into a soothing bath for your youngster. (Just open 2 or 3 capsules and dissolve the contents into a warm bath or crush tablets into the water.) Also, look for ascorbic acid powder, which is powdered vitamin C, in your health food store. Drop about 3 tablespoons into the tub.

✦ Calcium and magnesium are said to soothe the nervous system, which goes into overdrive during a hay fever attack. Administer up to 250 mg of calcium and 125 mg of magnesium twice a day while symptoms persist; drop off to once a day for two months to make sure the symptoms are gone. Check with your doctor before administering any supplemental vitamins or minerals to your child.

✦ Omega-3 essential fatty acids added to your child's diet may help with hay fever. These good fats are believed to assist in counteracting the body's inflammatory responses, which occur during a hay fever attack. Omega-3s are found in flaxseed, either oil (1 or 2 tablespoons daily) or ground seeds; sprinkle over salads or put the ground seeds over cereal or smoothies. You'll find flaxseed in the health food store. (Flaxseed oil must be refrigerated.) Omega-3 supplements can be found in health food stores also. Follow dosage instructions on the package. Fish oil capsules are another good source. The capsules with a high concentration of EPA (eicosapentaenoic acid) are considered the most effective. Unfortunately, fish oil capsules do have a fishy aftertaste. As a way of reducing that unpleasant taste, look for ones with higher concentrations of EPA, at least 50 percent. Check with your doctor for the most appropriate dose.

✦ Stinging nettle is chock full of vitamin A and works as an anti-inflammatory. But don't pick from your neighbor's garden;

you can't be sure if they spray with insecticides. (Not to mention that you could be trespassing!) You can find stinging nettle in health food stores as teas, capsules, or tinctures. My British colleagues sometimes advise this to fend off hay fever attacks. However, Dian, a friend in Kent, England, said that she gives her three kids a daily dose of stinging nettle starting one month *before* hay fever season begins. All three have fewer attacks, only an occasional sneeze with sniffles. In some individuals, nettle may cause slight stomach upset. If this occurs, just stop offering it. (The amount depends on weight and age of child. See the dosage information on pages 10–11.)

✦ Echinacea/goldenseal, a powerful combination, is often administered two to three times a day for colds and allergies. It should not be used consecutively for more than seven days straight or it could lose its effectiveness. (See dosage information on pages 10–11.) ☛ **WARNING:** Echinacea can trigger a rash, facial swelling, and diarrhea in a child allergic to ragweed. It is not advised for use in children under the age of three.

✦ Astragalus is a Chinese herb believed to strengthen the immune system. You can find it in health food stores. A Chinese mother in my practice believes that astragalus is the key to her son's good health. She says that if you give it to your child daily for a month before hay fever season begins, symptoms are usually avoided. But don't give it if your child has a fever or infection. (See the dosage information on pages 10–11.)

✦ Another Chinese herbal remedy is minor bupleurum, said to work as an immune system booster. You can find it in Chinese herb stores. (And it's available through mail order or online.) Don't give it to your child if he has a fever or infection. (See the dosage information on pages 10–11.)

✦ My friend Joyce swears by eyebright, an herb that's great for eye disorders and for hay fever. She finds it especially effective for itchy, swollen eyes. She buys eyebright tea bags in her local health food store and uses the cooled tea as an eyewash. You can also use eyebright tincture: Put 5 to 10 drops into 1 cup of boiling water. When it's cooled, use it as an eyewash. I think this is fine for older kids (over age twelve) or adults, but ask your allergist about the use of eyebright—despite its name!—for younger kids.

✦ Saltwater flushing is universally believed to be therapeutic. In India's Ayurvedic tradition, a nose stuffy from hay fever can be unclogged by using a *neti,* which is simply salt water. Mix half a teaspoon of salt into 2 cups of water, tilt your child's head forward and to the side, and pour ½ of this solution into each nostril. Have your child spit out any water that runs down his throat. A drugstore nasal syringe makes this easier, and it takes some practice.

✦ Drinking freshly squeezed lemon juice in warm water with a little honey is said to head off an attack. It may work if you use locally harvested honey, which contains traces of pollen that may be pestering the child. Honey also contains a host of immune-stimulating components. Too, the lemon juice contains vitamin C. Or it could just be the placebo effect. In any case, it helps soothe the sore, scratchy throat you get with runny nose and other allergies. However, don't give this to any child under the age of one, because the honey may harbor botulin spores.

✦ Some Indian parents have told me that dabbing some clarified butter (ghee) inside your child's nostrils can also help. The butter may be soothing to a sore nose, but it also coats the interior and acts as a barrier so pollens can't directly aggravate nasal passages. Unfortunately, butter is likely to provide a comfortable site for bacterial growth. Using Vaseline (petroleum jelly) in the same manner should more safely provide lubrication and also serve as a pollen barrier.

Headache

THE AILMENT

Headaches in children always present a special challenge. To determine the cause, I recommend that parents keep a headache diary to record the times of discomfort, as wells as the meals, events, and activities that preceeded the headache. This information may help the doctor determine possible causes.

Questions for routine consideration include:

✦ Can your child tell you if the headache is throbbing like a drum beating or hurts like a tight band around his head?

✦ Has there been a recent fall, head bump, or any trauma involving the head?

✦ Does the child have a fever or any cold symptoms?

✦ Is this a high-pollen-count period?

✦ Has the youngster been in the sun for a prolonged period of time?

✦ Does your child get a headache when reading or while working on the computer?

✦ Has there been any recent disruption of the child's usual routine? A new family configuration? Change of home? New school? New caretaker?

✦ Has there been associated jaw discomfort, or are new teeth erupting?

✦ Does the headache fade with sleep or after a meal?

Children *can* have migraine headaches. If the child has throbbing head pain, usually on one side, nausea and/or vomiting, abdominal pain, an aura (some signal such as a special aroma, a flash of light, or a tingling feeling), and relief occurs with rest in a darkened, quiet space, coupled with a family history of migraines, you're almost certainly dealing with migraine.

When headache is associated with fever, stiff neck, vomiting, light sensitivity, or lethargy, a diagnosis of encephalitis or meningitis must be considered. Call your doctor immediately. If the headaches become increasingly frequent or more intense, or if they are associated with changes in vision, speech, clumsiness of gait, your child's pediatrician will need to evaluate further.

CONVENTIONAL TREATMENT

If a cause can be determined and eliminated, the headache usually fades. In most instances, acetaminophen or ibuprofen provides immediate temporary pain relief while the diagnostic workup takes place. Never give a child aspirin unless your doctor specifically prescribes it because of the risk of Reye's syndrome, a potentially life-threatening condition.

PARENTS' REPORT: WHAT WORKS

I have found that families frequently have favorite headache remedies. One mother rubs moonstone, a white gemstone, on the temple of the child with a headache. Some families routinely add ginger to recipes (it's believed that ginger can reduce pain caused by inflammation).

✦ Sliced raw potatoes placed across the forehead have been reported to help the headache to fade. I surmise that the cool, moist potato slices probably act like a cool compress.

✦ Some families use chilled mashed pumpkin as a cold poultice wrapped in cheesecloth and applied directly to the child's forehead.

✦ An editor, Norine, touts the benefits of lavender: She really doesn't like to leave home without it. "If I were trapped on a desert island and only allowed to have one remedy with me, it would be lavender. It's great for most of what ails you. When it comes to headaches, it is a pain reliever because it's a relaxer. Place two drops of lavender essential oil on the tips of your fingers and massage into the temples, behind the ears, and across the back of the neck. You can mix it with a vegetable oil and rub all over the forehead, temples, hairline, back of the head, top of the head, neck, and shoulders. You can also use lavender straight out of the bottle. It's one of only two oils that can be used safely without being diluted—the other is tea tree oil." Adding peppermint to the mix is a traditional headache remedy. Put lavender on one side of the head, peppermint on the other (the peppermint should be diluted in a vegetable oil first). Chamomile and rosemary essential oils can also be used, but they too need to be mixed with vegetable oil.

✦ A warm bath with an ice pack on the head is said to really work wonders. (If nothing else, it distracts the child.) Run a very warm, but not hot, bath for the child. Have the child soak in the tub with an ice pack on her head. The warm water dilates the blood vessels in the body to help move the blood from the head into the extremities. The ice pack constricts the blood vessels in the head so they return to normal size—pain comes when so much blood is being pumped through the blood vessels that they get overstretched. Shrinking them helps ease the pain. Add some essential oils such as lavender or peppermint to the bath to make it even more healing. If your child doesn't want a bath, just soaking her feet and hands in hot water will approximate the same result.

✦ Here's a remedy I *don't* approve of: I've been told that kids can eat 3 to 5 leaves of feverfew, found in perennial gardens, or the equivalent in capsule form. I'd stay away. First of all, they taste nasty, and second, they do absolutely nothing to stop a headache once it has started.

SUPPLEMENTS

✦ Calcium and magnesium can be given at levels not higher than 250 mg of calcium and 125 mg of magnesium once or twice a day. These help relax the muscles, allowing the headache to subside. Research indicates that a magnesium deficiency may be one cause of migraines. Check with your pediatrician first.

✦ Acidophilus supplements help with headaches that come from a buildup of toxins in the digestive system because they help to promote good digestion. This is a standard naturopathic remedy for migraines. You'll find these supplements in health food stores.

✦ Omega-3 essential fatty acids reduce inflammation in the body. You can find these as supplements—look for a high concentration of EPA. (See **Hay Fever** for an explanation of omega-3s.) Look for child formulas and follow directions on the package for dosage.

TEAS

✦ Chamomile tea is so gentle, most kids can drink it. It contains some relaxing chemicals, which makes it great for relieving tension headaches. Plus, just the act of taking a time-out to drink a cup of steaming tea is relaxing in itself.

✦ Pick up some peppermint tea bags at the health food store, or make peppermint tea for your child to drink: Chop 1 cup of peppermint leaves and add 2 cups of boiling water. Steep for five minutes. Sweeten and serve ½ cup at a time. (But no honey for children under one year old because of the risk of botulism spores.)

✦ Skullcap, an herb that is slightly stronger than chamomile, contains some mild sedative components that reportedly will help ease a tension headache in older kids (over the age of six). It can be given in either tea or tincture form. You'll find skullcap in the health food store. (See the dosage information on pages 10–11.)

✦ Wintergreen, willow bark (or white willow), and meadowsweet tea are pain relievers. Willow and meadowsweet both contain salicylic acids, which are the pain-relieving compounds found in aspirin. But because they are not metabolized the way aspirin is, they are safe for children. (See the dosage information on pages 10–11.)

✦ For a headache resulting from dehydration, mix 1 tablespoon sugar, 1/4 teaspoon salt, and the juice of half a lime into a pint of water. Have the child sip slowly. This helps restore the body's balance of electrolytes, relieving the headache.

MASSAGE

✦ An Ayurvedic remedy is to rub the shoulders, neck, upper back, and soles of the feet with sesame oil, followed by a very warm shower.

✦ Rub the top joint of each of the child's thumbs for three minutes. The stimulation of the thumb is believed to block the brain's pain sensors. This can't hurt, and your child may find it amusing.

ACUPRESSURE

✦ Accupressure releases the body's own pain relievers, the endorphins. There are many acupressure points that can work:

1. Between the index finger and thumb
2. Top of the foot between the big toe and the second toe
3. Top of the foot, between the bones of the forth and fifth toes
4. Between the eyebrows and the bridge of the nose

Press and hold for about fifteen to thirty seconds, then release. This should help with a minor headache. Press and release on and off for thirty minutes and it should take care of a bigger headache.

Ancient Chinese Exercise

✦ Called Li Shou, this works on the same principle as the hot bath: It gets the blood out of the head and into the extremities. It can be done when a headache strikes, or every day as a preventive measure. According to the mother of one of my patients, this is good for migraines. Have your child rub her palms together until they are warm. Then have her lightly stroke her face downward (from forehead to chin) with her fingertips thirty times. Then, with eyes half closed, she should stand with feet shoulder width apart, knees slightly bent, and bend from the waist slightly, focusing on her toes. Then she should vigorously wave her arms front to back one hundred times (front to back = one time). Good luck getting your youngster to do this!

Hemorrhoids

The Ailment

Hemorrhoids, sometimes called piles, are veins located in the rectum that have become overexpanded and collapsed because of increased pressure. Straining with bowel movements and passing hard, dry stools increase the pressure within the lower intestinal tract and cause the veins to enlarge and bulge. When visible in the anal area, these fleshy, soft protrusions are referred to as external hemorrhoids. They rarely occur during infancy. Occasionally infants will have harmless external skin tags at the anal opening, which parents sometimes confuse with hemorrhoids. Very young children who establish a pattern of not letting go of their stools become chronic holders, and those with frequent bouts of constipation and straining are the usual candidates to develop hemorrhoids. At times hemorrhoids may be itchy and uncomfortable. They are usually harmless and may go undetected for years unless itching, bleeding, or pain occurs. Any rectal pain or bleeding should be called to your doctor's attention.

Conventional Treatment

Treatment is targeted at relieving symptoms.

✦ Review your youngster's diet. It should include a variety of fruits, vegetables, and whole grains.

✦ Increase your child's water consumption and cut out sugary juices and soda.

✦ Use stool softeners occassionally to help reduce straining.

✦ Your doctor may prescribe anti-infective and anti-inflammatory medications to be applied directly to relieve itching and irritation.

✦ In very severe cases, liquid nitrogen (cryosurgical), laser, or conventional surgical removal of the hemorrhoid may be recommended.

Parents' Report: What Works

✦ To relieve itching hemorrhoids, make a solution of 1 teaspoon of powdered alum in a glass of water. Soak a clean cloth in this solution and apply frequently to the hemorrhoid area.

✦ Put 1 teaspoonful of echinacea extract in 1 pint of water, saturate a piece of clean cotton with the solution, and place on the rectum.

✦ Make a wash by mixing 1 ounce of lobelia extract, 1 ounce of baptisia extract, and 1 ounce of zinc sulfate with 13 ounces of water; shake well and apply frequently with a cotton ball to the hemorrhoids.

✦ Put extract of witch hazel on a wad of cotton and secure to the hemorrhoids at night with surgical tape. Use until cured. Ms. Grayson, a grandmother of five, told me that it works like magic.

✦ Here's a Gypsy remedy: Mix 1 tablespoon each of dried marjoram and thyme in 2 cups of boiling water. (Don't use the herbs from your kitchen rack, but the health food store variety.) Simmer for five minutes, remove, steep for fifteen minutes, strain out the herb parts, and refrigerate. When using, reheat to a tepid temperature. Soak a cotton ball in the solution and place at the rectum's opening.

Hiccups

THE AILMENT

Involuntary, uncontrollable contractions of the diaphragm, which separates the upper section of the torso from the lower section housing the stomach and intestines, are known as hiccups. The *hic* sound of the condition is caused by the protective reflex closure of the glottis in the back of the throat during the body's attempt to take in air. Although babies seem to have hiccups more frequently and for longer periods of time than older children or adults, they do not experience real distress during the episodes. The causes are not clearly understood, but hiccups are not usually serious. Swallowing an irritating substance may trigger a hiccup response. With time, most cases of hiccups gradually subside.

CONVENTIONAL TREATMENT

For infants, check to be certain that the airway is not obstructed. If the baby has recently completed a feeding, he may need additional time for another burp. If he is not distressed by the hiccups, relax; with time, they will go away naturally. If older children are bothered by hiccups, there are several exercises that make the lungs work harder and possibly speed resolution of the condition. I have recommended the usual—taking in a deep breath and holding it for at least ten to twenty seconds, then slowly exhaling. Or try breathing into a paper bag and rebreathing the exhaled air, or drinking a glass of cold water quickly. If hiccups persist for more than eight hours or if you feel that any respiratory difficulties exist, call your doctor.

Parents' Report: What Works

It seems that every family has a hiccup remedy.

✦ A colleague, Lee, insists her remedy is foolproof. As she describes it: To get rid of hiccups, just put a metal utensil in your mouth sideways and drink water over it. Although it doesn't matter if you use a fork or spoon (I'd skip the knife), she says her husband once stopped at a fast food restaurant to get her the required water and utensil, but he brought back a plastic fork, which didn't work at all. She insists her teenage son used the same remedy with a regular metal spoon and it worked like a charm.

✦ Have your child plug his ears and drink a glass of ice cold water. Or slowly sip a cup of warm water; you can even put a little honey in it (but not for children under one year of age). With babies, hiccups usually disappear in five to ten minutes. If they don't, give the baby a bottle of sugar water: Mix ¼ teaspoon of sugar with 4 ounces of water.

✦ Cover a glass of water with a clean cloth and drink through it.

✦ Slowly sip a glass of warm water mixed with 1 teaspoon of vinegar.

✦ Pull on the child's earlobes; this changes the pressure in the middle ear and can halt hiccups.

✦ This comes from a social worker born in Haiti: To stop baby's hiccups, pull a string off the baby's clothes. Put the string in your mouth, then place it on the so-called third eye of the hiccuping baby. (That's the space between and just above the two eyes, which takes on mystical qualities in several cultures.)

✦ Pour a cupful of boiling water over 1 teaspoonful of anise seed. Steep till cool. Give the baby 1 teaspoonful. It is said to cure the hiccups immediately.

✦ Have your child spread his arms out in a T and take a very deep breath. Repeat several times.

✦ Put 1 drop of chamomile essential oil in a brown paper bag. Hold the bag over the child's nose and mouth and have the child breathe in and out slowly and deeply through the nose fifteen times.

✦ Mix the juice of one lemon in half a glass of water and drink. Repeat in fifteen minutes if the first drink didn't stop the hiccups.

✦ If your youngster is old enough and brave enough, have him try this sour remedy: Put a teaspoonful of salt on half a lemon and then have child suck the juice out of the lemon.

✦ Have your child drink the juice from half an orange or take a few rapid swallows of pineapple juice.

Hives

THE AILMENT

Hives are red or white swollen, itchy areas that appear on the skin. They may begin as smaller raised bumps, which expand into wider raised lesions known as wheals. When the lesions are pressed, these pink-red raised areas generally blanch. They can be triggered by almost anything, such as certain foods, medications, inhalation of particular substances, or direct or indirect skin contact with certain metals or other substances. Even prolonged sun exposure, environmental temperature changes, strong emotional reactions, and stress can be triggers for a reaction. The body's immune system responds to all of those by producing histamines. High levels of circulating histamines can cause many changes in the body, including hives.

Some individuals react immediately with hives when an offending stimulus triggers their system. Others may have a delayed response and not show any reaction for several hours or days after exposure. Hives can quickly change size and shape and may be limited to a single area or appear over the entire body; generally they cause intense itching. Their sudden appearance may be alarming. If possible, try to identify the triggers so that your child can avoid them.

☛ WARNING: Pain at the site of the hives may be a sign of a more serious condition and cause for greater concern. Also, sudden or gradual swelling of the face—particularly around or inside of the mouth or tongue—could result in breathing difficulties and warrants immediate medical attention. The most severe allergic reaction—life-threatening anaphylactic shock—can result in respiratory arrest and death.

Conventional Treatment

✦ Cool compresses applied to the areas reduce the swelling while providing temporary relief for the intense itching. Over-the-counter antihistamine medications such as Benadryl may slow the process of new hives appearing and offer relief from itching.

✦ If swelling has caused wheezing or compromised your child's ability to breathe comfortably, your doctor may administer medications (epinephrine, Benadryl, or corticosteroids) by injection.

✦ Calamine, Caladryl, and other topical anti-itch preparations relieve swelling and itching.

PARENTS' REPORT: WHAT WORKS

Most of the following remedies, as either baths or pastes, give some relief for the intense itching.

✦ Add ½ cup of baking soda to lukewarm bathwater. Bathe the child twice a day if itching persists. You can also add two drops of chamomile essential oil to a baking soda bath to make it more healing.

✦ Oatmeal baths soothe; try colloidal oatmeal, found in health food stores. Pour a generous amount into the bath and have your child soak twice a day. Aveeno makes a full line of oatmeal products for sensitive, itchy skin.

✦ Powdered chickweed leaves, an herb found in health food stores, can be mixed with water and applied to the skin as a paste.

✦ Evening primrose leaves can be crushed and mixed with water to make a poultice or paste and applied to the skin. Evening primrose is full of gamma-linolenic acid, which is beneficial for skin conditions. You can get it in the health food store, where it comes in capsules. Just break open a capsule and apply topically. (Don't let your child ingest the capsules.) You can also prepare it as a tea and apply the tea as a wash to the affected areas once it has cooled down.

✦ Don't forget chamomile—our favorite gentle herb tea can also be applied topically to hives. Boost its effectiveness by adding one tea bag each of calendula, echinacea, and yarrow (a terrific skin healer), and toss in ½ teaspoon of baking soda to the brew. Use it to wash skin. If you want to make a poultice, add some bentonite to make it stick and some soothing slippery elm bark.

✦ There's always aloe vera, the ultimate skin healer. You can take the sap right out of an aloe leaf (keep a plant handy) or find the prepared gel in the health food store. Look for those that are at least 98 percent aloe. You can also use aloe vera juice (which is different from the gel) and add a few drops of lavender essential oil; put the solution in a spray bottle and spritz over the affected area.

✦ Mix one part lemon juice with two parts witch hazel and apply. It may sting, but it relieves the itching.

✦ My good friend Carol's great-aunt says relief can be found by washing the areas with dairy cream, half and half, or milk—preferably goat's milk or buttermilk—followed by a plain water rinse.

Indigestion (Gastroesophageal Reflux)

The Ailment

Indigestion is a nonspecific state of gastrointestinal discomfort characterized by any or all of the following: bloating, gas, pain, nausea, and vomiting. Sometimes called dyspepsia, this condition may result from an overproduction of stomach acids and can be triggered by what and how we eat (i.e., eating too much, consuming odd mixtures of food groupings, or eating too quickly). When infants have brief episodes of crying or spitting up after feedings, it's usually not very serious. Parents and physicians are likely to consider these periodic episodes harmless and may attribute them to gas or colic. And in most cases the discomfort is temporary.

However, when episodes are frequent and long-lasting, the condition, gastroesophageal reflux disorder (GERD), might be the culprit. Gastroesophageal reflux is the backflow under pressure of stomach contents into the esophagus after each feeding. This may be in the form of frequent but annoying small spit-ups or voluminous vomiting.

All infants experience occasional reflux. In older children and adults, this same phenomenon may produce a series of wet, sour-tasting belches. When this occurs with some frequency over time, the esophagus becomes irritated, and the result may be a burning sensation within the chest, commonly known as heartburn. In this condition, the muscular ring (sphincter) between the esophagus and stomach is not fully functional and the stomach contents can too easily reverse direction prior to entering the lower digestive system. Certain spicy or gassy foods are often the culprits. Pressure, due to an overfull stomach or lying down immediately after eating, may also cause some backflow.

Fortunately, older children are able to give us clues with their medical history and description of their symptoms. This information, coupled with parental instinct, will help you decide whether it's a simple upset tummy or a more serious diagnostic challenge for your physician to consider.

Conventional Treatment

Regardless of the patient's age, when digestive disorders are suspected, most physicians recommend some dietary modification. During infancy, milk is the first and primary food. If a breast-feeding baby has periodic gastric distress, some food the mom recently ate may be the offenders to a baby's less mature gastrointestinal system. It's important to remember that *everything* a breast-feeding mother consumes passes into her breast milk. I try not to ask mothers to make major modifications to their diets when they choose to breast-feed—I do not want them to feel deprived or penalized when they have elected to give their infants nature's perfect food. However, certain foods (beans, cabbage, cauliflower, broccoli, highly seasoned foods, spicy dressings, carbonated beverages, and caffeine-containing beverages) may cause gas in the baby. I also caution that alcohol passes into the breast milk. I suggest that if a breast-feeding mother decides to throw caution to the wind and have that spicy bowl of chili or attend a special event where she may consume some alcohol, she should pump her breasts in advance and refrigerate or freeze the breast milk to give to the baby during the twenty-four-hour period following her feast.

If it has been determined that the spitting up is due to gastroesophageal reflux, feeding the child milk with thickened cereal and sitting him upright for forty-five minutes following feedings may help. Also, offering smaller amounts at a single feeding and providing more frequent opportunities to burp may reduce the number of spitting-up episodes.

There are a few over-the-counter preparations designed to relieve baby's gassiness. For older children and adults, a variety of antacids exist. Check with your physician about which products may be appropriate for your children.

Parents' Report: What Works

✦ For gassiness, baking soda has been the remedy recommended by many of the grandmothers I have encountered over the years. They have often told me that a pinch of baking soda in a tablespoon of water is the miracle cure. I have wondered—is everyone's pinch the same? A safer bet would be a measured 1/4 teaspoon of baking soda dissolved into 4 ounces of room-temperature water. Just offer 1 tablespoon of this solution, and after a few minutes the baby should burp and or pass gas. Do not give this more than two times in a twenty-four-hour period. ☛ **WARNING:** There could be a danger of upsetting the baby's acid/base balance, which can affect respiratory and other systems, if you give this mixture too frequently.

✦ Dominique's dad, Marco, shared his family's North Carolina remedy for gas: Offer a teaspoon of freshly grated gingerroot daily (or 1,000 mg of the powder, which is available at the health food store). When Marco checked with his mother, she said that for infants over six months of age, mix 1 teaspoonful into 8 ounces of room-temperature water and offer 1 to 2 teaspoons of the solution (depending upon the age and size of the baby) not more often than every six hours. This family has found this remedy more effective than any over-the-counter or prescription medications. Ginger, either in capsules or powdered form, is helpful for indigestion, especially if it is due to eating spicy foods. Ginger can be taken any number of ways: sliced and eaten raw, grated or sliced and steeped as tea, in powdered capsules, in powder mixed in water, and even in ginger candy. I suggest that you check with your pediatrician if you are considering this for your infant.

✦ See **Gas** for more remedies.

Itching

The Ailment

Itching is a sensation not easy to describe, but you recognize it by the need to scratch. The cause may be as simple as dry air or as a result of some underlying systemic condition such as a kidney ailment. When infants itch, they may be observed trying to scratch the affected area by rubbing that body part on their bedding. This pattern may continue for some time before parents realize what is happening. After a while, reddish, thickened areas of skin may appear on the baby's cheeks, chin, arms, or knees. Scratching only promotes further itching. Insect bites, fungal infections such as yeast and ringworm, parasites, eczema, food and drug allergies, and even anxiety and stress can cause itching.

Conventional Treatment

If you review recent changes within your environment, you may be able to identify and eliminate the offending agent. Consider any new foods, medications, household plants, laundry detergents, skin soaps, lotions, and so on. Check your child's skin in good light daily to spot any new rash.

For younger children, I advise keeping the nails as short as possible. Short nails are less likely to cause and spread infection through broken skin. You can protect infants who scratch themselves by covering their hands with socks. In older children, sometimes an itch/scratch cycle may be temporarily relieved with an antihistamine such as Benadryl. Cool compresses are soothing, as is an Aveeno oatmeal bath. An over-the-counter low-potency hydrocortisone cream applied to the itching areas offers temporarily relief.

Parents' Report: What Works

✦ Mix 3 to 4 heaping tablespoons of baking soda into cool or room-temperature bathwater and let your child soak.

✦ Sprinkle a few drops of peppermint oil or two tea bags of yellow dock into the bath.

✦ One part lemon juice mixed with three parts witch hazel applied or spritzed on the itchy area offers relief.

✦ Combine 12 drops of lavender essential oil with 4 ounces of aloe vera juice. Put in a spray bottle, shake well, and spritz onto the itchy sites of the body.

✦ See **Hives** for more remedies.

Jaundice

THE AILMENT

Jaundice, a yellow or sometimes greenish hue in the skin and a yellow appearance of the whites of the eyes, is due to the presence of excess bilirubin, which is formed during the process of red blood cell creation and destruction. Jaundice signals some underlying disorder in the liver. Possible causes include hepatitis (a liver infection), types of anemia, malformation of the anatomy of the bile ducts, or a bile system blockage. Anything that interferes with normal liver function may cause jaundice.

Jaundice in newborns is usually due to a baby's immature liver, which cannot rapidly process the quantity of bilirubin produced because so many new red blood cells are being formed. Although usually not visible immediately following delivery, most newborns have some degree of jaundice after three or four days. Breast-feeding babies tend to maintain the yellowish skin hue for a bit longer than those who are formula-fed. This is *not* an alarming condition and is known as physiological jaundice.

However, when the blood type of the mother is different from that of the newborn, the mixing of the mother's and fetus's blood prior to birth may result in a more serious condition, erythroblastosis fetalis, which causes the baby's red blood cell disintegration to be accelerated. In most hospitals, lab studies are done on the newborn's umbilical cord blood. If the possibility for this adverse reaction exists, your pediatrician and nursery personnel will closely monitor the baby. The longer the bilirubin level is allowed to remain in the danger zone, the greater the likelihood for brain injury.

☛ WARNING: Any child who exhibits jaundice must be immediately seen by a doctor.

CONVENTIONAL TREATMENT

In newborns, observation and laboratory monitoring of bilirubin levels are key. My first recommendation is to increase the child's fluid intake, either breast milk or formula. If the elevated bilirubin levels are prolonged, I suggest the mother pump and freeze her breast milk and temporarily switch to formula, primarily to better monitor the infant's intake. At times it is necessary to use phototherapy (high-intensity blue lights), which accelerates the breakdown of bile pigments and, with increased fluids, speeds the bilirubin excretion from the body. If you are in a sunny region, exposing the baby to intervals of sunlight, with her eyes protected, also helps the process of bilirubin excretion. In severe and persistent cases, more extreme measures such as exchange transfusion may be considered by your baby's physician.

PARENTS' REPORT: WHAT WORKS

✦ A Pakistani father shared with me his family's custom: When a baby has jaundice, it is given a few sips of diluted beet juice daily (2 to 3 teaspoons of beet juice into 2 ounces of water) for a few days. The dad assured me that it works! Offer a few sips at a time over a few days—newborns can only take in small amounts.

✦ A naturopathic doctor suggests that since jaundice may be related to vitamin K deficiency, a breast-feeding mom should eat lots of green leafy vegetables—such as turnip greens, cabbage, and broccoli—which are high in vitamin K. The doctor further suggests that the mom should chew these vegetables well, which helps break down the food and makes the vitamin more available. Because vitamin K is fat-soluble, it's a good idea to eat the greens dressed up with a little olive oil, which helps the body absorb the vitamin better.

✦ A hands-on remedy is 1 drop of chamomile essential oil in ten drops of grapeseed or olive oil, massaged into the skin over the baby's liver to stimulate the excretion of bile pigments. (Essential oils are not for ingestion.)

Keloids

The Ailment

Keloids are shiny, smooth, pinkish or dark brown raised scars that form after skin has been injured, usually from punctures or lacerations. As healing progresses, excess new tissue may form beyond the margins of the original injury, creating a keloid. This overgrowth of tissue is more likely to occur if the injured site is picked, pinched, scratched, rubbed, or otherwise irritated. Keloids are usually painless and benign, but they tend to itch. Why keloids occur is not entirely understood. Genetics play a significant role, and these scars occur more frequently in people of color. Younger skin heals faster than that of older folks; however, if injured sites are irritated, keloids may form at any age.

Conventional Treatment

Depending on location, keloids may be better left undisturbed. Surgical removal can result in a larger scar, which then has the potential to form another keloid. Cryosurgery (freezing using liquid nitrogen), laser therapy, and corticosteroid injections into the scar may flatten the raised areas of the excess tissue.

☛ WARNING: Any keloid self-treatment or manipulation can result in a skin infection or a more severe scar. Be safe, try the suggestions below, and consult with your physician before trying other extreme unconventional suggestions, which may involve using heat, applying home-prepared creams or ointments under bandages, or drinking strange brews.

PARENTS' REPORT: WHAT WORKS

✦ Apply pure cocoa butter (it comes in stick form) at least twice daily to a healed wound.

✦ According to Chris, a naturopathic doctor, the key to managing keloids is to stop the scarring mechanism in the body. He recommends iodine—either Lugol's solution or SSKI (saturated solution of potassium iodide). Combine 15 drops of either iodine solution with 15 drops of arnica oil and massage into the keloid. This helps the body to stop making scar tissue. Arnica should never be ingested, so do *not* rub into broken skin. He also recommends essential oil of *Helichrysum italicum*, which my European colleagues applaud as great for breaking down scar tissue. I have been told that a drop massaged into the keloid twice daily is effective. You can also mix this with a drop of medicinal-grade lavender oil. Lavender helps promote healthy skin regeneration. These are not instantaneous cures; it takes time for the body to break down the keloid, but Chris says it works. Other oils that can be used include myrrh, sandalwood, and frankincense—all traditionally used to combat scarring.

✦ My mother suggests breaking open a capsule of vitamin E and rubbing the contents on the keloid.

Lice (Head)

THE AILMENT

Head lice are grayish insects the size of a sesame seed. They truly are blood-sucking parasites, thriving on the human scalp and hair. Head lice themselves do not transmit disease, but the saliva they leave on the scalp causes irritation and produces an inflammatory reaction, which creates an itchy scalp. The eggs, called nits, look like tiny white dots attached to individual hairs, usually near the scalp. Nits can also be found nestled behind the ears and at the nape of the neck. Sometimes it is difficult to distinguish these nits from dandruff. When a parent calls, I always suggest that they try the "flake test" by blowing on or shaking the hair shaft. Dandruff flakes off the hair; nits do not.

Lice are easily transmitted by close contact in cozy conditions, such as in school, where kids may work and play with their heads close together. Sharing headgear, such as helmets, headphones, hats, headbands, combs, and brushes can spread the problem. Contrary to popular belief, lice are not found only on dirty heads. Telltale head scratching by your youngsters' friends during car pools, sleepovers, or other gatherings should put you on alert for lice. Although annoying and irritating, lice and their nits are not a serious malady.

CONVENTIONAL TREATMENT

✦ Wash bed linens, pillows, blankets, and clothing of the affected person separately from the family laundry in extremely hot water. This includes your child's favorite teddy bear if it's washable. Any item that cannot be easily washed and dried must be put in sealed plastic bags and set outside on a porch or in a garage for two or three weeks; eggs can hatch in the bag, but the lice cannot survive if they are not able to feed on a scalp.

✦ Vacuum any mattress, couch, car seat, or carpet that your child may have used. Throw the vacuum cleaner bag away when done.

✦ There are several over-the-counter or prescribed medications (the permethrins) that kill the lice and their eggs. You may also find some sprays for bedding and furniture. Medications containing lindane, though effective, continue to generate concern about safety and the development of lice resistance.

✦ Washing the hair with a solution of white vinegar helps to loosen nits from the hair shaft before using a lice-killing shampoo. After shampooing, use a fine-toothed comb to remove the nits from hair strands. Repeat this process in seven to ten days as a precautionary follow-up. If the problem persists or if you suspect hair loss or scalp infection, consult your child's doctor.

PARENTS' REPORT: WHAT WORKS

Many of these remedies come from parents and friends who are teachers—the warriors on the front line in the war against lice, who have special expertise.

✦ Rub the head thoroughly with petroleum jelly and wrap it in plastic wrap or shower cap; leave on overnight and wash out in the morning. The petroleum jelly smothers the lice. Obviously, only use this method with older children because of the danger of suffocation from plastic with small children. This method is very effective but messy; you may have to shampoo several times.

✦ Mayonnaise or olive oil is a popular method of killing lice; it smothers them. Comb through the hair with mayonnaise or olive oil. Then use the nit comb. Olive oil washes out easily, but I've been told that it must be in the hair for eight hours to be effective. Mayo works on the same principle, but it's harder to wash out.

✦ Put peanut butter all over the child's hair, leave on for an hour or so, and then wash out. This is a teachers' favorite.

✦ At bedtime, wet the head with vinegar and wrap the head in a vinegar-soaked towel. Cover the towel with a dry towel and leave overnight. The eggs detach and will come out during a morning shampooing. ☛ WARNING: Don't let a child with a wet head sleep in a draft of cool air.

✦ Mix equal parts geranium, lavender, lemon, and rosemary oils and rub over the child's scalp; also apply to the bottoms of the feet. The oil destroys the lice, and perhaps this aromatic concoction is enough of a distraction to help your child relax and resist the urge to scratch. As always, don't let your child ingest essential oils.

Lips (Chapped)

The Ailment

Chapping occurs when the outer covering of the lips becomes very dry, without sufficient moisture to prevent cracking and peeling. Mouth breathing (which kids do when they have a stuffy nose), dry warm air, and medications (such as antihistamines) that dry secretions may all contribute to chapped lips. Adding moisture by licking the lips provides very temporary relief; dried saliva is not a lubricant but an irritant, so it actually promotes further peeling. When chapped, lips feel like potato chip crumbs are on them. This sensation makes kids try to peel off that annoying outer layer of lip covering, often causing bleeding and eventual discoloration.

CONVENTIONAL TREATMENT

Any oil, frequently applied, will provide temporary relief. Petroleum is the base of many costly lip balms; I recommend plain, inexpensive Vaseline petroleum jelly or its generic equivalent. Moisture added to the environment by way of a vaporizer or humidifier solves one aspect of the problem, as does drinking more water.

PARENT'S REPORT: WHAT WORKS

✦ Try udder balm (also called bag balm)—cow udders also get chapped! As a friend admits, "My mom used it all over her body when she lived through the harsh winters in Erie, Pennsylvania. She swears by it." If it keeps the skin moist, it undoubtedly keeps lips moist too.

✦ There are many commercial lip balms; Burt's Bees makes several, and they even have a line for babies. Burt's contains beeswax, which lasts longer than most commercial preparations. Most natural lip balms have beeswax as a base along with a variety of other ingredients.

✦ Honey also makes a great balm. You can use plain honey or mix it with 1 or 2 drops of lavender essential oil, which is healing to skin, anti-inflammatory, and analgesic (this small amount of essential oil is fine for lips). Apply to lips morning and night. No honey for children under the age of one, because it may contain dangerous spores.

✦ If you want to make your own, here's a recipe from a friend who whips up lip balm concoctions in her kitchen all the time. She starts with beeswax as the base. Melt it over a low flame. Unless you want vats of balm, stick with a few tablespoons of beeswax. Grate it with a cheese grater first, so it melts faster. Then add in enough coconut oil, canola oil, apricot oil, or oil of camphor to make a creamy consistency. Pour into clean jars and let cool. Apply to lips morning and night.

✦ Another herbalist friend highly recommends white oak

bark. If you can find this tea in your health food store, brew it to triple strength. Swab chapped lips several times a day with the liquid as needed.

✦ Mix a few drops each of chamomile and geranium essential oil with 2 teaspoons of aloe vera gel. Rub this tingling mixture onto chapped lips.

Loose Tooth

The Ailment

If it occurs at the age-appropriate time, a loose tooth may not be an ailment. During childhood, the first (baby) teeth are *deciduous*—that is, they are temporary, to be replaced by the permanent teeth. This process in childhood generally begins between the fourth and sixth birthdays and continues into adolescence. The emergence of the secondary teeth causes the primary ones to loosen. However, an active toddler may have a minor collision with another youngster, a tabletop, or the pavement, which results in a prematurely loosened or lost tooth. In addition to chewing and aiding the digestive process, our teeth help give us clear speech; their presence, as a boundary for our tongue, enables good articulation and enunciation. If teeth are lost too early, the clarity of your child's speech may suffer. If your child's permanent tooth is knocked out, drop it in a jar of cold milk and go to the dentist immediately. It may be possible to reimplant it.

Conventional Treatment

When a secondary tooth is erupting, its larger size generally displaces a smaller primary tooth. Allow the process to occur naturally. When a tooth is really loose and wiggly, it can pose a safety hazard, as the loose tooth can be accidentally swallowed and cause choking. When the tooth is sufficiently loose, a clean washcloth or handkerchief can be used to cover it so it can be gently pulled up or down in the plane of growth, usually with minimal discomfort. A promise of the tooth fairy's visit will occasionally diminish the anxiety and anticipated discomfort.

PARENTS' REPORT: WHAT WORKS

The following hints will help further loosen a tooth on its way out.

✦ Tie doubled sewing thread or string around the tooth and quickly pull on the tooth.

✦ Tie a string around the tooth, tie the other end to a doorknob, and slam the door. (Ouch!) This is the one we've seen many times in cartoon form.

✦ If a front tooth is loose, encourage your youngster to bite into an apple or other firm food.

✦ One mom said that as the teeth of each of her three kids loosened, she would serve take-out Chinese ribs, and sure enough, as the child would gnaw vigorously on a bone, the tooth would become more dislodged and succumb to a gentle tug.

✦ Have your child hold warm apple cider vinegar in her mouth for a few seconds, then swish and spit out. Have her do this several times. This will help to further loosen the tooth from its socket.

✦ Boil a mixture of sage with honey; cool to a temperature that is comfortable, and have the child swish it around in his mouth, then spit. Repeat a few times each day until the tooth is delivered! No honey for children under age one—and those kids should not have loose teeth anyway.

Motion Sickness

The Ailment

Motion sickness occurs when the organs of the inner ear, which affect balance, are malfunctioning. You feel like you're moving or spinning when you're actually standing still, and your sense of being upright is distorted. This malfunction causes the brain and the visual cues of motion to be out of synch. This lack of synchronization may cause light-headedness, dizziness, queasiness, chills, weakness, nausea, and sometimes vomiting. Although motion sickness is not serious, it is annoying and may limit the family's leisure options involving long automobile trips, boating, or train excursions. The tendency to experience motion sickness may run in families.

Conventional Treatment

If your youngsters have experienced motion sickness, talk with them in advance of the planned travel to reassure them that they will be okay. Suggest that they close their eyes and lie down (in your lap, if it seems practical) before the vehicle gets moving. Also offer a *small* snack well in advance of departure. It is better not to travel with a very full or very empty stomach. Keep cool washcloths handy to be used as a compress, and have plastic bags ready just in case.

There are many antihistamine (Dramamine) products available over-the-counter. Read and follow dosage recommendations. There are also skin patches, which permit the medications to be absorbed through the skin's surface. Prescribed medications (some of which act at the central nervous system or brain level), can be administered in the form of capsules, pills, or suppositories, or the doctor can give them by injection when necessary.

PARENTS' REPORT: WHAT WORKS

✦ It has been reported that a high-dose B-complex vitamin with at least 100 mg of vitamin B_6, taken in the morning and at night, may offer some protection. Check with your doctor before giving your child any vitamin supplement.

✦ If your child cooperates, have her chew five whole cloves just before the ride. ☛ WARNING: Do not give cloves to young children who do not yet have their molars for grinding or to those who may be at risk for a choking incident.

✦ Offer an older child 2 to 4 gingerroot capsules (500 mg each), or a ¼-inch slice of fresh ginger. A younger child may be able to take ½ to 1 teaspoon of powdered ginger dissolved in 8 ounces of water up to three times daily, depending on the circumstances; 4 ounces of ginger juice is another option. The best results will probably occur when the ginger is taken twenty minutes before departure on your trip, with 2 to 4 more capsules whenever the child just begins to feel motion sickness. Many children enjoy candied ginger slices.

✦ Make a tea of ginger and honey by mixing 1 teaspoon fresh ginger juice and 1 teaspoon honey in a cup of boiling water; have your child (over the age of one) drink as needed.

✦ Create an aromatic mixture of 1 teaspoon each of ginger and nutmeg with a handful of peppermint and spearmint leaves in a light vegetable oil and massage into the feet, temples, and wrists. An Irish friend, Rich, a gourmet cook, believes that all healing begins with the ingredients in your kitchen, and he shared this remedy one evening with me after a rough sailing trip with his daughter. If nothing else, it smells yummy.

✦ Have your child suck on a lemon.

✦ Since nausea is such a big part of motion sickness, see **Nausea** for more remedies.

Nausea

THE AILMENT

Nausea is a symptom not easily described. However, once you've had it, you won't forget it. Whether this feeling originates from brain signals, neurochemicals, hormones, gastric juices, or an infection, it creates that uncomfortable sensation of waviness, spinning, or movement, even when you are stationary. It is associated with feelings of queasiness, an unsettled stomach, a bitter taste in the mouth, a feeling of fullness, and a desire to burp, but with the worry that if you do, vomiting might follow. Dizziness, visual disorientation, and sometimes fever may be associated with nausea. When vomiting is imminent, it is usually preceded by the warning of nausea.

CONVENTIONAL TREATMENT

Often the best advice is to wait it out, do nothing, and allow the sensation to pass. However, if this sensation lasts too long, it becomes impossible to ignore. If the nausea is accompanied by the feeling of an upset stomach, it's better not to eat any food. If the sensation is associated with hunger, instead of attempting to eat a meal, try a few saltine crackers. Then wait, allowing at least twenty minutes for the brain and gastrointestinal system to synchronize. The sensation of nausea might fade. If a dry mouth is a part of the sensation, ice chips, as opposed to water, offer relief. Drinking liquids at this time may precipitate vomiting.

There are prescription medications, depending upon the suspected cause, that work in the brain to inhibit the release of certain neurohormones, abating the sensation. Another group of pharmacologic agents (atropine, scopolamine) inhibit nausea by acting at another level of the brain and by blocking the production of gastric secretions (stomach juices) as well as by slowing the activity of the smooth muscles in the digestive system.

PARENTS' REPORT: WHAT WORKS

✦ Hands down, the best, most effective natural remedy for nausea is ginger. Both Ayurveda and traditional Chinese medicine practitioners continue to recommend ginger. Ginger can be used in many different ways. You can slice or grate fresh gingerroot, pour hot water over it, and let it steep to make a tea. You can also brew ginger tea from powdered ginger, either right off the spice rack or in tea bags. Or, if your youngster wants something cold, you can mix powdered ginger into a glass of water and stir it up. Kids will also like chewing on crystallized ginger or ginger candy, found in gourmet, specialty food, and health food stores. If you're into juicing, try juicing an apple, some carrots, and some fresh ginger and have your child drink that down. You can also mix ginger tea with apple juice to sweeten it.

✦ Offer your child flat Coca-Cola (pour the liquid back and forth between two glasses for a few minutes). This is today's version of the old Coke syrup that was often on hand to cure nausea. (If you happen to have Coke syrup on hand, give 1 or 2 tablespoons.) Pepsi doesn't seem to work as well for this cure. It must be in the secret Coke formula.

✦ Chewable over-the-counter antihistamine tablets used for motion sickness also work for nausea.

✦ For nausea associated with a parasite infection, try mixing activated charcoal in a glass of water. Stir it and have the child drink it. Or offer activated charcoal capsules—follow the dosage instructions on the package. The charcoal binds with the toxins, preventing their dissemination throughout the circulatory system. Once bound, they are excreted with the rest of the body wastes. Check with your doctor before offering charcoal.

✦ Working on the same concept, use green clay found in health food stores and sold specifically to be ingested (Play-Doh doesn't count). Put 1 teaspoon into 8 ounces of water and then have the youngster sip it. If it tastes too yucky, let it settle for a while, and then try it again.

✦ There are several teas that reportedly tame rumbling tummies: chamomile, mint, raspberry, basil, meadowsweet, and lemon balm. Buy the ready-made tea bags. You can also use the tinctures of any of these—make sure it is the appropriate strength for younger children and infants. (See the dosage information on pages 10–11.)

✦ Here are some Ayurvedic remedies: 2 pinches of cardamom plus ½ teaspoon of honey in 1 cup of plain yogurt. (Remember, no honey for infants under one year of age.) Or try a pinch each of nutmeg and cardamom in warm milk. Both nutmeg and cardamom are carminatives; that is, they help combat gas. One cup of yogurt with live cultures contains beneficial bacteria to help fight off any bad bacteria that may be causing the stomach to be upset. Honey is antibacterial and antimicrobial in general. The milk may have some neutralizing effect. Perhaps it also soothes any inflamed areas within the digestive system.

✦ If your child is vomiting, mix 1 teaspoon of salt and 2 teaspoons of sugar into 16 ounces of lemon or orange juice. Add 8 ounces of water and have your child sip just 2 or 3 ounces from a small glass after each episode of vomiting. This mixture is packed with electrolytes, which are lost when there is a lot of vomiting.

✦ Gentle massage may be helpful. Mix a few drops of peppermint oil with a base of almond oil and gently massage the abdomen clockwise. Go with the curve of the intestines. This is good for all kids. For youngsters over the age of five, you can also try sandalwood. The combination of sandalwood, peppermint, basil, and melissa is considered fine for children older than seven. These herbs may be used individually or in combination, but not for ingestion.

✦ Put a cold can of soda or ice pack against the back of the child's neck for a minute or two.

Nervousness

THE AILMENT

Nervousness is usually described as a state of restlessness, agitation, and uneasiness. A nervous child may have difficulty sitting still or may fidget, scratch, and cry frequently. In children, these characteristics often accompany the diagnosis of attention deficit hyperactivity disorder. Tremors, muscle twitches, involuntary movements, teeth grinding, nail biting, and bed-wetting are behaviors often attributed to nervousness. It is now more readily recognized that some involuntary sudden jerkiness may be a tic or movement disorder, or one of several seizure disorders. These may indicate abnormal electrical discharges in the brain or other neurological-system concerns that warrant evaluation by a medical specialist—a neurologist.

CONVENTIONAL TREATMENT

As noted, some of these symptoms may be indicative of some disorder of the central nervous system. However, to understand a symptom's significance, the whole child must be evaluated. Once a source of the disorder is identified, appropriate treatment (medication or behavior modification) can be initiated.

Parents' Report: What Works

✦ Many parents believe that dietary modifications that include eliminating caffeine, sugars, and foods with red or yellow dye significantly alleviates the problem. I've had parents declare that their little angel turns into a fidgety devil after eating sugar or a specific food. There are mountains of anecdotal evidence but minimal supporting clinical evidence to back this up. Still, many parents believe that certain foods are stimulants for their children, while other foods act as downers. It is certainly worthwhile to cut sugar and caffeine out of your child's diet.

✦ Some foods, including pineapple juice and prune juice, are believed to calm nerves. Combine the two in equal proportions and offer 6 ounces two to three times a day. Strawberry, cherry, and celery juice are said to have similar calming effects.

✦ There are many soothing herbal teas—particularly chamomile. Also, sage may work both as a sipping tea and as a bath additive.

✦ Color therapy can be calming. One family says to wear red and green towels in bed. Shades of blue and violet are reported to be good for calming nerves. As one parent explained, "Any form of the color blue is said to be peaceful. Wear it, paint with it, carry a color swatch."

✦ Blue gemstones (there's that color again) are said to instill calmness when worn. Placing a blue gemstone, such as blue sapphire, aquamarine, or blue opal, around the child's neck at night is believed to ensure a good night's sleep (with no nightmares) and calmness during the day. Just make sure that the jewelry is worn safely—that is, without the possibility of it becoming a choking or strangulation hazard. I would definitely not suggest this for younger children.

✦ Some of my California colleagues, who have sworn me to anonymity, have suggested crystals for some nervous patients, but definitely not for young kids (under eight) who still put objects into their mouths and might swallow them. (You can find healing crystals in New Age–type stores that carry incense, candles, and lotions.)

✦ Nothing beats finding out what's making the child nervous. An acquaintance, Chris, who practices naturopathic medicine, says nervousness is usually associated with family strife—parents fighting, that sort of thing. One thing that he recommends for alleviating it is lavender oil rubbed on ears, wrists, and the soles of the feet. He also suggests visualization. Kids have great imaginations. Encourage your children to imagine problems away. Have them conjure up the most fun place they can. Then imagine the problem way off in the distance and make it seem ridiculous—maybe dress it up with mouse ears—and laugh it away. Chris believes once you've identified the problem, using visualization and lavender works ninety-nine times out of a hundred.

Nosebleeds (Epistaxis)

The Ailment

The inside of the nose is lined with delicate, thin tissues. The small blood vessels (capillaries) are very close to the surface of the mucous membranes and are easily ruptured. This may be caused by sneezing, hard nose blowing, rubbing, or picking in the nose. The common cold, allergies that make the nose runny or stuffy, dry air, cold air, some blood disorders, or head trauma can trigger nosebleeds. When a nosebleed initially occurs, the blood usually flows freely from one nostril. If the neck is hyperextended, with the head tilted all the way back, some blood drains to the back of the throat and may also flow from the mouth. Parents really panic when they see blood coming from the nose and mouth. Swallowed blood may cause stomach upset and vomiting, or it may get into the lower digestive tract and be passed in bowel movements. Nosebleeds are usually more of an inconvenience than they are serious. The volume of the blood lost is actually not as great as it may appear.

Conventional Treatment

Keep the child seated in an upright position or tilted forward. Have your child resist the temptation to lean back or to recline, for that will only allow the blood to flow into the back of the throat. With a cold compress or your fingers, pinch the nostrils together firmly, holding them for at least ten minutes or until the bleeding stops.

If bleeding does not stop in a reasonable period of time, call your child's physician. Sometimes the fragile nasal lining responds to chemical cauterization, which is a way to seal the ruptured bleeding vessels. Very severe and persistent bleeding may require packing the nose with gauze and referral to an ear, nose, and throat specialist. Applying a lubricant such as Vaseline inside the nose at bedtime prevents nasal tissue from cracking, and the nighttime use of a vaporizer adds moisture to air breathed during sleep.

Parents' Report: What Works

✦ Put a small piece of clean brown paper bag against the roof of the mouth. I can't imagine how this works, other than to absorb the blood as it drains from the posterior nasal area.

✦ Put a swab soaked in witch hazel inside the nostril; this causes the tiny blood vessels to constrict, halting the bleeding.

✦ Put a cold, wet washcloth on the nape of the neck for five minutes. Perhaps the cold compress stimulates an autonomic neurologic response, causing narrowing of the blood vessels. An ice pack on the bridge of the nose can work wonders.

✦ Cayenne pepper is one of the best remedies for stopping any bleeding, including nosebleeds. It helps the blood to clot and stops the pain. Either take cayenne pills, readily found in health food stores, or go to the kitchen spice rack, sprinkle some pepper into your hand and allow your child to sniff a little into his nostril. Just a pinch should work like a charm. Don't use too much; it can be very irritating.

✦ Yarrow is an ancient remedy for wound healing that dates to before the Trojan War. If you can find a yarrow leaf, put a small part of the leaf into your child's nostril and pinch his nose gently. Fortunately for us city folks, yarrow is found in health food stores. It can be used like cayenne—just a little bit sprinkled into the nose. This works well to stop the gushing. Also, try a cold compress made with tincture of yarrow (found in health food stores).

✦ The use of stinging nettles for nosebleeds is an Aztec remedy. Nettles from your garden that haven't been treated with *any* chemicals, either fertilizer or pesticides, can be mashed for the juice. Saturate a small cloth with this nettle juice and put it into the nostril that's bleeding. Nettles are rich in vitamins A and C, which strengthen mucous membranes. ☛ WARNING: Wear gloves when handling nettles because they really do sting. It's probably easier to just buy some nettle tea at the health food store. Brew the tea, let it cool, soak a clean cloth or saturate a cotton ball with it, and insert a small part of it into the nose. If you use capsules, open two and empty the contents into boiling water. Allow to steep for fifteen minutes, strain, and then use the liquid to saturate a small piece of cloth for nasal application. But don't use this remedy for children under four years of age.

✦ Parsley, dried or fresh, is another good herb to use inside the nostril to staunch bleeding. Insert a small bit and the bleeding should stop.

✦ I have been told that if your child stares at red things, it could stimulate the blood flow. Surround your child with blue, which reportedly slows bleeding. It could be blue clothing, a color swatch, or even a room decorated in blue.

✦ Put a drop of either lemon, lavender, rosemary, or chamomile oil on a tissue and have child inhale. This is said to be calming. The less anxious the child, the more likely the blood flow is to slow down.

✦ Once the nosebleed has stopped, try vitamin E. Puncture a capsule and squeeze out the liquid. Rub a tiny bit inside the nose to keep it moist.

✦ Aloe vera gel helps with wound healing, as may calendula.

✦ For recurrent nosebleeds, consider asking your doctor about supplemental vitamin K. If given in small amounts daily for two weeks, it helps increase the blood's clotting factors.

Pigeon Toes

The Ailment

An exaggerated inward turning of the feet toward each other is commonly known as pigeon toes. When this is noted in the newborn, it is considered a result of before-birth positioning in the close quarters of the uterus.

When pigeon-toed toddlers first start to walk, they generally turn in just the feet, with the knees facing forward. However, older children who are pigeon-toed turn their feet inward at varying angles and generally the entire leg from the hip down is involved. This is not a serious condition and does not impede your child's ability to walk, run, or play. If she trips over her feet when walking or running, I suggest an orthopedic referral for a detailed evaluation, with X rays if necessary, to determine if any type of correction is warranted.

Conventional Treatment

When I examine an infant, I note her position of comfort. If the child has some positional abnormalities, I always recommend a series of passive stretching exercises for the feet and ankles. I show parents how to gently rotate the baby's feet while holding the leg with one hand and the sole of the foot with the other, providing a slightly greater stretch to the inside part of the ankle. With time, the baby's position of comfort will be one with her foot pointing straight ahead.

Occasionally, in extreme or severe situations, orthopedic specialists have prescribed a restrictive horizontal metal bar with shoes positioned at a corrective angle, to be worn overnight. Today, some specialists have abandoned that recommendation, claiming it is not effective.

PARENTS' REPORT: WHAT WORKS

✦ Put the child's shoes on the wrong feet—that is, the right shoe goes on the left foot and the left shoe goes on the right foot. Try this shoe reversal for a month for your eighteen-to-twenty-four-month-old child to see if you note any improvement in position. Over the years, many families have told me that it straightened the young child's feet. Or it may just be the passage of time that does the trick.

Pinkeye (Conjunctivitis)

THE AILMENT

A red, weepy, itchy, or possibly painful eye may be due to conjunctivitis (pinkeye). This uncomfortable and unsightly condition is an inflammation of the clear membranes covering the inside of the eyelid and the eyeball. Frequently, children with pinkeye report an intolerance to light. Causes of pinkeye include viral or bacterial infections, allergic reactions, presence of a foreign body (dust, cinders, or eyelash) in the eye, chemicals, or other irritants. Pinkeye can involve one or both eyes and may be contagious. If your child gets pinkeye in daycare, she may be excluded until she has been medically evaluated and treated.

There are several types of conjunctivitis:

✦ *Bacterial conjunctivitis* is associated with redness, swelling, and a thick whitish discharge. There may be a similar type of mucoid discharge from the nose or an associated ear infection.

✦ *Viral conjunctivitis* may have similar symptoms, but the eye drainage tends to be more watery. This condition is frequently associated with coldlike symptoms.

✦ *Allergic conjunctivitis* may have any of the previous components, but the red, watery eyes are quite itchy and associated with sneezing, runny nose, and other allergic manifestations.

Conventional Treatment

Depending on the type of conjunctivitis suspected, your physician may prescribe anti-inflammatory and/or antibiotic eye drops. With clean hands and a moist washcloth, clear the drainage from the eyes before applying eye drops. The washcloth used by the infected child should not be used by anyone else. To apply eye drops, pull down the lower eyelid and drop the medication on the inside of the lower lid rather than directly onto the eye. Discourage your youngsters from rubbing their eyes. If allergies are suspected, an over-the-counter oral antihistamine may provide relief of the symptoms.

If only one eye is involved, after cleaning away any discharge to prevent friction between the lid and the eyeball, cover that eye with a sterile eye patch. These are available individually packaged in the drugstore.

☛ **WARNING:** If there is significant swelling of either the upper or lower lid with fever and discomfort, or if there is an itchy, red eye with discharge that does not resolve within seventy-two hours, your child's doctor should evaluate the condition.

Parents' Report: What Works

✦ I still vividly recall the day I entered the examination room to find a forty-one-year-old third-time mother with her newborn for a routine postdelivery visit. She held the child in one arm as she was squeezing her own breast with the other hand, squirting breast milk into her baby daughter's eyes. I asked, with some embarrassment for my intrusion, what she was doing. She patiently explained that she was treating her baby's runny eyes. Although pediatricians always promote the benefits of breast-feeding because of the immune qualities of mother's milk, I had never heard or read anything about the possible anti-infective properties of breast milk. I later discovered this was a common practice within many extended families in certain areas (particularly in the Appalachian regions of Kentucky and Tennessee) and has been used to treat—successfully, I might add—some types of conjunctival irritation in infants. This particular mom left my office without a prescription, because Mother Nature herself wrote the cure.

Here are some other remedies that families have shared with me:

✦ Put two or three drops into each eye of a solution of 1/4 teaspoon of salt dissolved in 8 ounces of warm water. Using a clean cotton-tipped applicator or a clean cotton ball for each eye, begin at the inner corner of the eye and wipe downward onto the skin. Do this three times daily for a few days.

✦ During my childhood, my mother would mix 1/4 teaspoon boric acid with 1 cup of water that had been boiled and allowed to cool. She would put this solution into a little blue eye cup and watch as she instructed me to bathe my eye. We repeated this ritual several times a day until my pinkeye had cleared.

✦ From an Italian family living in Brooklyn, New York, comes the use of cold brewed Bustelo coffee rubbed around the eyelids with a sterile cotton ball. The mild acidity of the coffee is similar to boric acid. The mother assured me it worked fine on all three of her sons. (The vasoconstrictive properties of caffeine may help reduce puffiness.)

✦ Put slices of raw potato over the closed eye. This works as a cool, moist compress.

✦ My color theorist family told me that wearing green gems such as emerald, green tourmaline, or peridot helps ease eye infections. Green is considered a balancing color and a tissue rebuilder. Looking at, holding, or wearing something indigo—deep blue—is also said to be healing for the eyes.

✦ The herb barberry contains the potent antimicrobial agent berberine. You can find barberry tincture in health food stores. Put a few drops in water and then soak a clean cloth and place over the affected eye. ☛ WARNING: Don't use as an eye wash; just hold the cloth over the closed eye. (If a little of the tincture gets in the child's eye, rinse with water.)

✦ Eyebright, just like its name implies, is recommended for eye irritations. It helps fight infection by increasing blood flow to the eye. Make a tea (you'll find eyebright tea bags in the health food store) or put a few drops of tincture into warm water. Let the tea cool a bit—you want it just a little warm. Then soak a clean cloth in the solution and use it as a compress for the eye.

✦ A Chinese remedy includes the use of chrysanthemum—it's like eyebright. Make a tea or put a few drops of tincture into some water, chill, and then soak a clean cloth and make a compress. Apply to closed eye.

✦ Echinacea/goldenseal combination tincture formulas are frequently mentioned by families. Taken orally, it's an immune booster and infection fighter. Carefully review the manufacturer's label and follow dosage recommendations. (Don't give to children under the age of three or who may be allergic to ragweed.)

Pinworms

THE AILMENT

These harmless but highly infectious and pesky white threadlike parasites may be found in kids without regard for age, ethnicity, or economic status. Pinworms most frequently affect those who play or live in group settings, such as preschoolers, college dormitory dwellers, and nursing home residents. These tiny worms usually enter the body as tiny eggs (not visible to the human eye) traveling on unclean hands or under fingernails. They also may be transmitted on bed linens, on clothing, and in house dust. Their cycle for development is quite short, allowing for rapid infection. The female worms lay their eggs in the host's lower digestive tract, near the anus. It takes only two to four weeks for the eggs to hatch and develop into adult forms, causing intense rectal itching. The host, in scratching for relief, picks up more eggs on the hands and under nails, thereby starting the cycle all over again.

Does your child have itching around his anus that seems more intense at night? Does he pull his clothing away from that area, seem more fidgety, or squirm a lot in his seat? Since these parasites can migrate to other areas, sometimes early clues include intense nasal itching. Some youngsters report that it feels like something is moving in their nose. Girls occasionally report vaginal as well as anal itching. These are all good reasons to suspect pinworms.

The essentials for this diagnostic endeavor include disposable rubber gloves, a flashlight, clear adhesive (Scotch) tape, one glass microscope slide (which you can request from your child's pediatrician), and your courage. With the flashlight in hand and disposable gloves on, about an hour after your youngster has gone to bed, look at his anal area and check for tiny white moving "threads." One more challenging step is to place a piece of the clear tape across the anus area in the early morning, before your youngster gets up. Wearing disposable gloves, remove the tape and apply it to the glass slide. Several worms and eggs may be trapped on this sticky tape. Label this slide with your child's name and return it to your child's pediatrician, who will send it to the laboratory for an accurate diagnosis.

Another sure albeit quite messy way to make the diagnosis at home is the actual inspection of a bowel movement using disposable gloves, newspaper, and a disposable wooden ice-pop stick or tongue depressor from your doctor's office. Wearing the disposable gloves, use the stick to separate the fecal matter on the newspaper as you inspect for moving, white, threadlike worms.

Conventional Treatment

Since the worms and eggs are so readily transmitted in close settings, an antiparasitic medication is prescribed not just for the identified sufferer but for all individuals in the same living space. Medication dosages are determined by age and body weight. The oral medication is generally effective after a few doses. Sometimes repeat therapy is necessary for the total eradication of pinworms. Prevent reinfection by laundering the sufferer's bed linens and clothing separately in hot water, cutting his fingernails, and encouraging frequent and careful hand washing for everyone.

Parents' Report: What Works

✦ I heard this remedy from a father at a conference in Arizona. He assured me it worked like a charm. Scald ½ cup of pumpkin seeds in boiling water and remove their outer skins. Add ½ cup of milk and grind into a paste with the back of a wooden spoon. Have the child eat the paste after fasting for twelve hours. Don't let the child eat anything else for two more hours. After that, give 2 teaspoons of castor oil in 6 ounces of orange juice with a light snack. The pinworms should pass in three hours.

✦ Make wormwood tea (the name of this herb seems appropriate) by mixing ½ teaspoon each of goldenseal and wormwood powder (found in health food stores) into 1 quart of boiling water. Cover, reduce to a simmer, and steep twenty minutes. Strain, cool, and have the child drink up to 1 cup between meals several times daily. For young children, the amount offered depends on their age and size. Under age three, offer up to 2 ounces; age five, offer 4 ounces; and over age eight offer 6–8 ounces. Be aware that wormwood tastes bitter.

✦ Garlic is one of nature's most potent antibiotics, able to slay many childhood parasites, including pinworms. One way to use it is to peel a single clove and prick it all over so the juices can flow out. Wearing a disposable glove, gently insert a tiny piece of the peeled garlic clove just inside the anal opening. Do not push or attempt to force it. If the area is too irritated from scratching, this could burn. If so, remove immediately. You could also cut a clove in half and rub it on the soles of the child's feet, as recommended by herbalist Kathi Keville. The reason: Garlic is absorbed through the skin and into the bloodstream.

Rashes

THE AILMENT

Changes in *texture* (rough, bumpy, stretched, puffy, shiny), *color* (pale, red, purple), and *sensation* (warm, burning, itchy, painful) of the skin's surface could be signs of a rash. Rashes may appear suddenly, sometimes as a result of infection (bacterial, viral, fungal, parasitic) or the immune system's (allergic) reaction to some offending substance either taken in as food, medication, or as a result of an irritant's direct contact with the skin.

When the skin's surface is irritated or ruptured by scratching, bacteria present on the skin may gain entry and infect the site. A sore at that scratched site can become a tender, pus-filled blister. Scratching these highly contagious sores may instigate spread to another part of the body. The resulting skin infection is known as *impetigo*.

Another rash associated with a sore throat, a strawberry-red tongue, fever, and a sandpapery feeling may be caused by streptococcal bacteria and is commonly associated with strep throat. This may not be an itchy rash. Strep throat can be confirmed by a laboratory test to determine the presence of this specific bacteria. With appropriate treatment for the streptococcal bacteria in the system, the rash will dry, peel, and fade along with the other associated symptoms within a short period of time.

A purplish splotchiness of the skin that is tender to pressure but not itchy may represent a reaction to medication or a serious bacterial infection. ☛ **WARNING:** The appearance of a purplish rash without a history of trauma to the site warrants an immediate call to your child's doctor; this may signal the presence of a serious underlying condition.

If a rash appears only after a specific encounter with a substance and fades after this substance is removed, inform your child's doctor. This is probably an allergic reaction. Rashes vary by when and how they appear. Some occur shortly after contact with a specific irritant (contact dermatitis), such as a member of the poison ivy (Rhus) plant family.

Generalized rashes include *eczema,* which appears as tiny bumps in clusters on particularly sensitive areas such as the skin on the back of the knees, in the folds of the arms, and around the neck. With eczema, rash areas are extremely itchy. Scratching produces raw, irritated patches that, with continued rubbing, thicken, form plaques, and result in the rash area darkening as healing occurs. The intense itching may interfere with your child's ability to focus and may cause many behavioral changes.

Viral rashes may appear as fine, flattened tiny pink to red dots under the surface of the skin. The skin may feel smooth to the touch. The rash is often visible on the palms of the hands and on the soles of the feet. Many of these rashes occur after a fever or a slight cold, and usually do not itch. Some viral rashes, such as that caused by chicken pox, cause intense itching. Most viral rashes fade as the infection subsides.

Fungal rashes, characterized by raised circular or ringlike lesions that may have scaly centers surrounded by a cluster of small bumps, may be caused by tinea, the fungus that causes ringworm. These areas are quite itchy and contagious; they can be spread from one site to another by scratching. When a fungal infection involves hair loss, proper treatment results in rash clearing and regrowth of hair.

Another frequent fungal rash is that caused by candida (monilia), which thrives in creases that trap moisture, such as in the folds of a chubby baby's neck, behind the ears, and particularly in the diaper area.

Parasites such as mites or lice cause intense itching with a resulting raised, fine bumpy rash. Treatment is required for the underlying condition before the skin can return to normal.

In younger children, the most common rashes include tiny bumps caused by heat frequently seen on the neck and in skin folds. Sweat glands regulate body temperature by allowing us to perspire. Since infants' sweat glands are less developed, they are also less efficient. The oil and sweat glands of infants become easily clogged and more readily result in the appearance of a faint red, bumpy, prickly heat rash.

Urine left in close contact with skin over a prolonged period of time results in splotchy red, raised, sometimes raw and burning areas, ideal sites for discrete clusters of lesions known as diaper dermatitis. A diaper rash, though generally not serious, may be quite annoying to the infant and can make baby and parents irritable and restless. More frequent diaper changing and applying a soothing diaper balm or petrolatum may provide a protective coating that shields that area from the sting of urine.

When diaper irritation is severe, I usually suggest that parents allow the child to go diaperless as often as possible for a few days; it may be a bit messy if you have an active toddler, but the bottom will remain drier and heal faster.

Conventional Treatment

When the source of irritation can be determined and eliminated, in most instances the rash spontaneously fades. Once any significant skin irritation has occurred, any product that reduces the discomfort at the sites helps to promote healing.

(Calamine lotion, which has been around for years, is an old hand at pimply, itchy rashes; just dab some on and let it dry.)

If you suspect bacterial, fungal, or viral diseases as the basis for skin eruptions, check with your doctor, who may prescribe antibiotics, antiviral medications, or fungicidal preparations.

PARENTS' REPORT: WHAT WORKS

✦ Remember the great-grandmother I discussed in the Introduction? She told me that a baby's first morning "pee," if applied to her facial rash, would heal it. I did not give the suggestion any serious consideration until some years later when I heard *another* parent speak of wiping her baby's face with her first wet diaper of the day, to keep her face clear of rashes! I have been told that it cannot be just anyone's urine, but must be urine from the person on whom it will be used. Imagine my surprise when an ancient-history buff told me that the men in Hannibal's army would treat their own war wounds by using their helmets to collect their own urine and mix it with a type of clay to create a paste with healing properties.

✦ My favorite tried-and-true recommendation for a rash is to take regular cornstarch, mix it with water to make a paste, apply it, and leave it on until it begins to flake; repeat the process three or four times a day. This paste will dry most rashes.

✦ To quiet an irritating or very itchy rash, try either 1 cup of oatmeal flakes or several heaping tablespoons of baking soda dissolved in room-temperature bathwater. Let your child soak.

✦ For a heat-related rash, a friend adds a few drops of lavender or chamomile essential oil to her child's bath. She also adds chickweed tea to the bath or bathes the area with chickweed tea. Chickweed can be bought in heath food stores or organic supermarkets. Lavender essential oil reportedly encourages the skin to discharge toxins. Essential oils are not for ingestion.

The following two remedies for rashes caused by poison ivy or poison oak come from my gardening families:

✦ Jewelweed, also known as impatiens and touch-me-not, can be used to stop the itch and dry the blisters. Rub the affected area with the leaves from this plant. The juice from the stems can also be used; rub it on gently several times a day and allow to dry. ☛ **WARNING:** Excessive rubbing will further irritate the area. Another variation is to boil the leaves, stems, and flowers until the water turns a deep orange. With cotton balls, swab the affected area, or saturate a clean cloth with this solution and apply as a compress. This method may work better for large areas affected by the rash. *Note:* Since jewelweed is also known as impatiens, people may think they can use garden impatiens, but that will do nothing for the rash. Jewelweed, by the way, is not readily available in health food stores. You may need to browse the Internet to find it.

✦ The common weed plantain, found along roadsides, meadows, and frequently in people's lawns, may be used to stop the itch and control the spread of the inflammation. Crush the leaf and rub it on the affected area. The skin may take on a green tinge temporarily, but plantain works quickly. One difficulty may be identifying this herb. It has broad leaves (4–10 inches in length) and long flowered spikes. To be safer, make a strong tea with the dried form, (which can be purchased in bulk from herbal suppliers and health food stores), strain the herb out, and let the liquid cool. Then apply with a swab or as a compress as needed. ☛ **WARNING:** The random picking of plants from the wild, from the roadside, or out of a neighbor's garden is risky. It's too easy to pick the wrong plant. Also, plants may be sprayed with pesticides and other chemicals; roadside plants are contaminated with car exhaust. I cannot overemphasize that it is safer to buy these plants in bulk from reputable herb retailers, health food stores, or organic farmer's markets. So crush fresh leaves only if you are an experienced botanist or have had one examine the plant (and I do have a few in my practice). That's not the average parent.

✦ Annabel, a dental hygienist from Kenya, told me that her village's custom was to use ashes left by burnt charcoal. Applied to the rash, they are soothing and drying.

✦ Some Native American groups use the following: Put two dozen or more cracked acorns into 1½ gallons of hot water and boil to reduce the liquid by half. Turn off the heat and let stand for several hours. Strain and cool, and put on the affected area with a cotton swab. You can also boil a 2-inch-by-4-inch section of sprig oak bark in a quart of water for five minutes and then allow to simmer for an hour; apply this liquid to affected skin areas to relieve itching.

✦ Within four hours of exposure to poison ivy, oak, or sumac, wash all exposed areas with soap and warm water and then apply rubbing alcohol liberally to the skin by gentle patting. Also, washing any clothing rubbed by these plants reduces the likelihood of recurring rashes.

✦ Aloe vera juice can be used to stop the itching and blistering of poison ivy, and it promotes the healing of rashes and sores.

✦ To relieve itching, mix equal parts of water and apple cider vinegar. Dab on affected areas, let dry, and repeat as often as needed.

✦ Baking soda to the rescue again! Put a tablespoonful of soda in a cupful of water. Wash the affected area with the solution and/or make it into a poultice. Change often enough to keep the application cool. Cover open blisters with sterile gauze. You can also make baking soda into a paste and apply it to the areas.

✦ Soak the affected area in a solution of Epsom salt and water for thirty minutes daily. Or make a paste with Epsom salt and apply to the rash.

✦ If you or your youngsters will be in a region where exposure to one of the poison plants is possible, as a precaution wear long-sleeved shirts and long pants with the pant legs tucked inside socks. As an additional step, rub your child's body with Fels-Naptha soap before going out and definitely afterward, leaving some soap residue on the skin to dry. If you've been exposed to poison ivy, wash off the plant's resin as quickly as possible with soap—or just plain water if that's all that is available.

✦ This advice comes from a colleague in Seattle, Washington: Make a skin wash by combining 1 teaspoon of powdered goldenseal root with 1 pint of hot water. When the solution cools, dab onto the affected areas. Goldenseal comes in liquid form and may be rubbed onto the skin. The herb's powerful anti-inflammatory and anti-infective properties will help the area dry rapidly. Goldenseal, mixed with water, will also dry a rash. (Mix some goldenseal tincture with water in equal parts and apply. The tincture may sting a bit if the rash is oozy, because of the alcohol in the tincture. This remedy is also beneficial for poison oak.)

✦ Oatmeal is another time-honored remedy for rashes. Cook some oatmeal, allow it to cool, and spread it on the affected area. If a lot of the body is affected, put 3 cups of oatmeal in waist-high warm water in your bathtub and have your child soak in it for a while. You can also put the oatmeal in a sock and swirl it around in the bathwater. Don't towel the child off when he gets out; as your child air-dries, the oatmeal will leave a powdery covering, which helps stop the itch.

✦ Dissolve a vitamin C tablet in water, and wash the affected area with this solution. The juice of an orange or lemon is also said to be very effective. You can obtain vitamin C in a powdered form in health food stores. Packets of vitamin C powder are sold by the box under various brand names; they dissolve faster in a tub than tablets. The packets generally contain 1,000 milligrams of vitamin C, and they fizz. For a small area, mix one packet with water, then bathe the area. If a lot of the body is covered in rash, put two to four packets in the bath and have the child soak. Still another method is to mix 2 tablespoons of powdered vitamin C with a 1/2 cup of aloe vera juice, then put in a spray bottle and spritz the affected areas.

✦ Vitamin E rubbed on raw areas can also be helpful. It's an antioxidant and helps the skin repair itself. Break open a capsule of vitamin E and apply the oil to a rash after the poison ivy resins have been washed off.

✦ Cut open a fresh watermelon and rub the area with the melon flesh and rind. According to a naturopathic practitioner, this might work because watermelon contains two potent antioxidants: lycopene and glutathione. Lycopene helps repair irritated skin. Glutathione helps eliminate the toxins that cause rashes.

✦ Chris, the naturopath, also highly recommends using bentonite, a type of clay found in health food stores, for poison ivy, sumac, and oak. The more severe the rash, Chris says, the drier the clay should be, as it absorbs the oils from the plants that cause the rash. Bentonite clay literally draws the toxins out of the skin.

✦ Another remedy is to apply cold cucumber slices to the rash area. This might work because of the cooling effect, which distracts from the itch. You could also chop up, finely dice, or juice some celery and put it on the rash.

✦ Calendula ointment or tincture, which is helpful for other skin wounds, can be helpful for the poison ivy/oak/sumac rash too. This also helps with prickly heat.

✦ Here's one from Mindy, an herbalist, for poison oak and ivy: Chinese White Flower Oil. This is the brand name of a combo remedy found in health food stores and Asian markets. It contains menthol, eucalyptol, and wintergreen oils. It is very drying and may tingle, but it shouldn't sting. Spread a few drops, undiluted, over the affected area.

✦ Here's a remedy I do *not* recommend. Household bleach can be used to remove the poison ivy resin and treat the itch, but the possibilities of tragedy, due to an accidental ingestion of the caustic bleach, far outweigh any possible benefits. Keep bleach away from kids.

✦ See **Acne** and **Diaper Rash** for more remedies.

Ringworm (Tinea Capitis)

The Ailment

When single or multiple areas of baldness with itchy scaling and prominent papules (small raised bumps) on the scalp appear, tinea capitis might be the culprit. This condition, caused by a fungus, is sometimes called ringworm, because of the whitish, circular patterns or rings it causes on the skin or scalp. A definite diagnosis can be established by examining a few of the scalp scrapings with the use of a Wood's lamp, fungal cultures, or other laboratory studies. Tinea capitis is contagious and spreads easily in children's group settings such as day care, camps, and schools, where youngsters too easily exchange clothing and headgear. A child with ringworm may scratch the affected areas, trapping fungal material under his nails, and transfer it to another child during the course of play.

Conventional Treatment

There are many effective topical preparations in the form of shampoos, creams, and solutions available by prescription. For severe or persistent cases, a prescription oral antifungal medication may be needed to supplement topical preparations. Treatment may take six to eight weeks to ensure elimination of the fungus.

PARENTS' REPORT: WHAT WORKS

✦ After trying two different preparations to clear a resistant case of ringworm on a youngster's scalp, a dad who hailed from the Caribbean asked my thoughts on his aunt's suggestion. She recommended soaking some pennies in half a cup of vinegar overnight and then applying the resulting solution to the lesion areas. I said that I had never heard of that particular cure, but since it did not seem risky and the child had already lost hair on his scaly scalp, I suggested he try it. To my amazement, at the follow-up visit just a few weeks later, the rash had cleared and new hair growth was occurring.

✦ Since ringworm is a fungal infection and tea tree oil is considered a good antifungal, there are several remedies that use this oil. Here are a few recipes:

1. Put 7–8 drops of tea tree oil in a cup of warm water. Make a compress and apply to the area three times daily. Throw away the cloth after each use.
2. Use undiluted tea tree oil on the affected area. One drop should do it for a child. Apply three times a day until it clears, which should be in about ten days.
3. Mix equal amounts of tea tree oil and lavender oil, and dilute with a small amount of vegetable oil such as almond or sesame. Rub over affected areas daily. Lavender is an all-round healer and pain reliever.

✦ Garlic oil—several cloves of garlic mashed into olive oil and steeped for a few days—can be rubbed on ringworm sites.

✦ Add tincture of myrrh, an antiseptic, found in health food stores, to bathwater. Or, if the area is small, dilute the myrrh with water and bathe the affected area at least twice a day.

✦ A family from India suggested neem oil as a remedy for many skin conditions, including ringworm. The neem tree is called the "village pharmacy" in India because it is believed to be useful for everything from lice to birth control. Neem is a potent antifungal as well as an antibacterial, but it does not have a pleasant aroma. You can find shampoos, creams, and soaps containing neem in health food stores.

✦ One Native American folk remedy is black walnut, reportedly a strong antifungal. If you can get walnut hulls—the green part that surrounds the nut—or fresh or dried leaves, boil them and soak affected area. One caveat: If you soak too long, the affected area can turn black, because this pigment is sometimes used to make black dye. It's harmless but funny-looking. Black walnut can also be drying, so you may want to use some skin moisturizer afterward if the skin feels chapped.

✦ Echinacea, goldenseal, and burdock root are immune boosters. You can use lotions with these ingredients, which you'll find in health food stores.

Sinus Problems

THE AILMENT

Each of us has eight (four sets) of sinuses, air spaces in the bones of our skulls that surround our nasal passages. They act as the filters of our entire respiratory system. At birth, all of the sinuses are not fully developed. Generally by age eight, all eight air cavities are formed and functioning. The *frontal* sinuses, the last to fully develop, are located above the ridge of the nose, just inside the borders of our eyebrows, and are the most frequent cause of sinus headaches. The two sinuses located in our upper jaw, on either side of our nostrils, the *maxillary,* are the largest. The *ethmoid* pair form multiple air pockets on either side of our nose, and the *sphenoid* sinuses are in the same region but more toward the center of the head.

Each of our eight sinuses is lined with the same tissues that are in the insides of our noses. Sinuses, when functioning properly, drain into the nose. Infections, allergies, or any irritants can cause the sinus' linings to become inflamed. Inflammation of these sinus tissues causes them to swell, which can block drainage into the nose. In addition to blockage, this swelling also causes tenderness and pain in and around the involved sinuses. Inflammation initially prompts excessive nasal secretions. The early secretions may be watery and thin, causing annoying sniffles and coughs. If it continues, these secretions may gradually progress to a thick yellow or green mucus, which drains forward and exits through the nose or may drain backward into the throat, prompting irritation and a hacking cough.

CONVENTIONAL TREATMENT

Once the doctor has determined the underlying cause for sinus discomfort, she can recommend the appropriate treatment. If a bacterial sinus infection is suspected, the doctor will prescribe antibiotic therapy. For the immediate relief of blocked sinuses, warm compresses across the bridge of the nose, on the forehead, or on each nasolabial fold may offer immediate, albeit short-term comfort. A steamy shower or inhaling the vapors of a warm-mist vaporizer or humidifier are other ways to open stubbornly blocked sinuses. Your pediatrician can help determine whether your child's symptoms are more characteristic of a cold or of a sinus infection.

PARENTS' REPORT: WHAT WORKS

✦ To relieve congested sinuses, try making this nasal flush: Mix 1/4 teaspoon salt and 1/4 teaspoon baking soda in 1 cup of warm water. Fill an ear syringe and squirt the mixture into the nose. You can also use 1 teaspoon noniodized salt and 1/2 teaspoon baking soda dissolved in 1 pint of water. Place the mixture in a nasal inhaler.

✦ Elder flower tea is said to encourage drainage of the sinuses. You can find elder flower tea bags in health food stores and reputable herb suppliers. Offer your child a cup or two of the brewed tea.

✦ Steam inhalations with essential oils are a good solution for clearing out a nasal infection since breathing in the essential oils gets them right to the site. All essential oils are antibacterial; some are also antiviral as well. Particularly useful for sinusitis are eucalyptus, rosemary, and thyme. Put 2 drops of each into a vaporizer or a big bowl of steaming water, tent the child's head with a towel, and let him inhale the steam, making sure his face is a comfortable distance from the steaming water.

✦ Massaging the sinus area with essential oils can help. Try eucalyptus and thyme—put 4 drops of each into a vegetable oil base, such as sesame, almond, or jojoba, and massage over and around the nose, forehead, and chest to help unclog breathing passages. You can also add a few drops of oregano oil (in the mint family) to some vegetable oil and use as a massage. But err on the conservative side with oregano—it's a little strong.

✦ Try a warm compress of ginger tea, made with sliced fresh gingerroot or tea bags, placed over the nasal area to unclog stuffy nasal passages.

✦ The first time I heard of using horseradish to help open sinus passages, I wasn't sure if you were supposed to sniff it or eat it. But an editor friend sheds light with this story: "My grandmother always grated her own fresh horseradish for Passover seder. Maybe it was the change of seasons or the change of weather since we were coming to Cleveland from Florida, but I inevitably had a stuffy nose during Passover. My grandmother would always give me a bit of horseradish to eat, which immediately unclogged my nasal passages. (It also seemed to sizzle to the top of my head.)" Since Japanese wasabi is similar, there's no reason this wouldn't work as well. I'd hesitate giving it to small children; it may be too strong.

✦ Not surprisingly, when in Hawaii, I often heard of remedies based on eating pineapple. Herbalist James Duke, author of *The Green Pharmacy* (Rodale, 1997), recommends pineapple as well. He says the enzyme it contains—bromelain—is helpful for clearing up sinuses.

✦ The herbs fenugreek and thyme, given in equal amounts, can also help alleviate sinus congestion. Mix a cup of each and dose according to the information on pages 10–11. Refrigerate any leftovers.

✦ Another sinus-clearing drink is hot lemonade that's made with fresh lemon juice, 1 tablespoon of maple syrup, and about 1/8 teaspoon of cayenne.

✦ Grandma was right—chicken soup is good for almost anything that ails you. Many studies have proven the viability of this "Jewish penicillin," but I think it's probably the hot broth and vegetables that do the work, in particular the carrots (full of vitamin A) and onions (cousin to garlic and full of its own antibacterial and antiviral compounds).

✦ The tincture combo of echinacea/goldenseal can be found in health food stores. It's mentioned frequently because it's a good immune booster, and the goldenseal helps soothe irritated mucous membranes. Follow dosage instructions on the label. (Do not give to children under the age of three or who are allergic to ragweed.)

Sleep Problems

THE AILMENT

When your baby spends his first night at home with you, keep him safe—*be certain to follow the recommendation of the American Academy of Pediatrics and place your baby on his back to sleep.*

Parents become quite concerned when they feel that their infants are either getting too much sleep or not enough. Most parents don't realize that newborns spend approximately twenty hours of a twenty-four-hour day sleeping. They awaken to be fed, returning to sleep when their tummies are full. New parents become quite anxious for their new baby to be awake and responsive. However, as babies begin to spend longer hours awake, some start to get their nights and days confused, taking long naps during the day and wanting to socialize at night. Then parents want to know when their baby will sleep through the night. Although there is no set pattern, most infants will sleep six to eight hours at night by age three or four months. This may change abruptly during any breaks of the usual routine, or if the baby isn't feeling well (colds, infections, the night after receiving immunizations, teething), is in a new environment, or is separated from you.

With time, babies adopt sleep patterns that generally work out for the family. I advise parents not to be alarmed about the baby's sleep schedule. There are wide variations within the range of normal. However, call your pediatrician if you feel that your baby is sleeping too much, not awakening during the usual feeding intervals, or seems less responsive.

Conventional Treatment

Establishing a sleep routine is a lifestyle and family pattern; for some, it is a cultural pattern. Ending your child's day with some consistent winding-down activity will make the going to bed process a bit smoother.

Newborns are very adaptable. Whatever the family's usual evening patterns, they should be continued, but with the respect and consideration that there is a new baby on board. Sometimes parents know in advance if they have a baby who's likely to be active at night. Infants' awake and quiet times may be somewhat predictable from their in utero activities. If they were quite active and kicking at night but calm during the day in the later stages of pregnancy, that pattern is unlikely to change spontaneously after birth.

For some infants, a warm bath followed by a small feeding and then quiet, gentle handling may be just enough to lull them into blissful sleep. For others, sound and movement are among the essential elements. It may be just the sound of your voice. With the baby's face or ear to your chest, it may be the magic of the rhythmic sound of your heartbeat. It could be the comfort of being cradled in your arms or the gentle sway and rocking of your pace that does the trick. However, consider that whatever regular pattern you initiate, if it works and you repeat it with any regularity, that becomes a routine.

Children's sleep expert Dr. Richard Ferber proposes a schedule that works for some. He suggests that parents should not rush to comfort the crying baby. He advises parents to follow a graduated schedule of allowing longer time periods before peeking in or cuddling the crying baby. Some experts disagree and think Ferber's routine just teaches children to cry for longer periods of time.

A common scenario is to put a crying baby into the parents' bed. My theory about the parental bed is that whatever works for the family is okay. In general, I caution that if you start allowing the crying child into your bed, you must be prepared for that extra bed partner nightly for perhaps a few years. I am certain that there will be many nights when you will be so exhausted that picking a child up and putting him into your bed not only is easy but feels like the most humane act you can perform at 3 A.M. Just understand that you are establishing a routine that will become increasingly difficult to break.

As children progress through early childhood, bedtime rituals such as storytelling, the favorite stuffed soft item, a pacifier, a warm beverage, bedtime prayers, a special cuddle, or a nightlight continue to be important. Rituals help children nod off and get the sleep necessary to promote feelings of security along with good growth and development. As your child gets older, you should know that scary stories, action videos, television, and nighttime reprimands do *not* contribute to restful sleep.

Parents' Report: What Works

✦ Grace said she prepared a special sleep pillow based on the advice of her Irish grandmother. Grace mixed a small amount of dried chamomile with some dried lavender and dried rose petals and stuffed this mixture into sachet packets made from cotton cloth. She sewed two packets into a small flannel wrap that she placed under the sheet at the head of each baby's crib. She insisted that this aromatic mixture helped her little ones sleep through the night. At first I questioned the allergenic possibilities of introducing dried plants to the respiratory system (via inhalation) at this early stage of development. But over the years other parents have told me of similar preparations, usually involving lavender. I have since discovered that lavender, with its pleasant aroma, has a mildly sedative effect and low toxicity. As long as it is not taken internally, a few drops of the essential oil placed on a baby's blanket can, in fact, have a calming effect. Other natural sleep enhancers include the Native American dream catcher and the use of special acupressure points to trigger good dreams. (Try pressing the ball of the thumbs.)

✦ Massage your baby with essential oils. This is particularly helpful when it's anxiety that is keeping the child up. The best remedy of all is lavender oil. It should be medicinal-grade oil, not the stuff sold in candle stores. A few drops, undiluted, rubbed onto the temples and the back of neck should relax the child enough to go to sleep. It won't knock him out, just slow him down. It is said that lavender slows nerve impulses, which is what makes it so relaxing. And it seems to be good for all ages. You can also use chamomile oil—this one is particularly good for babies because it's so gentle. Mix it in a small amount of vegetable oil, such as almond or sesame. For kids over one year, use geranium; for those over six years, you can mix the geranium and chamomile. Also, using a vaporizer can put the oils into the air to create a relaxing environment for the child. Just be sure to carefully wash the vaporizer so it doesn't become a breeding ground for bacteria and fungi.

✦ Warm baths increase blood circulation throughout the body and often induce a state of relaxation. A warm bath before bedtime might be enough to summon the sandman. But you can also add any of the oils mentioned above to the bath to make it extra relaxing. You can also add hops—the herb used to make beer. You can find hops tea bags; just float them in the tub. Or fill a muslin bag with loose hops and tie it to the faucet as you let the hot water run through it to fill the bath. Hops has a mild sedative effect on the central nervous system.

✦ Warm milk and tuna fish (both have the amino acids, which promote drowsiness) seem to constitute the perfect menu for putting your child to sleep!

✦ Along with warm milk, many teas and tinctures, like passionflower, chamomile, and lemon balm, are all soothing. Even a little catnip, which drives kitties wild, can be used to lull kiddies to sleep. (Just buy your catnip in the health food store, *not* in the neighborhood pet store.)

✦ A friend of Greek heritage describes his "bless pillow": "When I was a small child my grandmother would make the sign of the cross on a special pillow to ensure a safe journey, and so that God would let me wake. Knowing my grandmother, I wonder now if that was folklore magic or her neurosis. But it worked."

✦ Rub a light oil on the child's forehead, above and between the two eyes, on the spot known as the third eye. This is said to be relaxing and sleep-inducing.

✦ Simmer dill seeds in olive oil and rub on your child's forehead.

✦ Fill a sock with poppy seeds and lay it across the forehead.

✦ When children become afraid of monsters, make the bedroom monster-proof. Sprinkle invisible pixie dust or put up signs that say NO MONSTERS ALLOWED, or even help the child search to see there are no monsters. In other words, take your child's fears seriously. (One mom would let her child poke the hose of the vacuum under the bed to ensure that any bad dreams were all cleaned up.)

✦ On a trip to Mexico, I was informed that Mexican onyx puts kids to sleep. Perhaps it's because Mexican onyx is black, and that color seems to be protective, announcing, "Keep your distance." The idea is to place the onyx by the bed to protect your child's space.

Snoring

The Ailment

Snoring is loud, deep, throaty gurgling sounds caused by vibrations of the soft palate occurring with breathing during sleep, usually with the mouth open. Snoring is a condition that seems to be more prevalent in children with enlarged tonsillar and adenoid tissue, and in adult men. Snoring is *not* a normal state for young children. Enlarged adenoids are the usual culprits, though uneven breathing may be indicative of sleep apnea and should not be ignored. If this lack of rhythmic breathing is disturbing, consult your child's physician.

Conventional Treatment

A change of position is a cure for some. For young children, I recommend elevating their head and chest by placing two telephone books under the head of the mattress. This alters the position of the head, neck, and the soft palate. Persistent snoring may warrant an ear, nose, and throat consultation to check the extent of adenoid tissue obstruction of the breathing passages.

Drugstores sell nasal strips and other devices (parrot noses) to quiet snoring. Surgical procedures include the removal of the tonsils and adenoids, but these procedures are much less common then they were years ago.

Parents' Report: What Works

✦ Sew half of a tennis ball into the back of the snorer's pajamas. Snoring tends to occur when the child is on his back, and when he rolls onto the half ball, it will be uncomfortable and he'll roll back onto his front or side. ☛ WARNING: This should not be done with infants. They should be placed to sleep on their backs. Check with your pediatrician for instances when a child should sleep on his tummy.

✦ My naturopathic colleague, Chris, says that methylsulfonylmethane, MSM for short, a bioavailable form of sulfur, has been shown to have good results in Israeli studies. It is reportedly effective for halting snoring by strengthening connective tissue in the throat that helps keep the airways open during sleep. It is also said to be an immune system booster. You can find it in health food stores, but check with your pediatrician before giving it.

Sore Throat

The Ailment

A sore throat is a symptom of irritation or inflammation of a wide area from the back of the tongue and the upper back region of the nose, extending to the soft part of the roof of the mouth (the soft palate) and the pink fleshy tissue hanging from the soft palate (uvula). This inflammation may involve the tonsils (tonsilitis), and may extend to the larynx, causing irritation and swelling of the vocal cords (laryngitis), resulting in hoarseness. Sore throats may occur with a common cold, postnasal drainage, sinus infections, allergies, and viral infections. Streptococci are bacteria that cause strep throat, which, if untreated, may cause overwhelming, systemwide infection.

Conventional Treatment

Check for swollen or tender areas (which may feel like grapes beneath the skin) under the jaw ridge and around the neck. Look at your child's throat. With a flashlight, popsicle stick, or the handle of a spoon, press your child's tongue down and ask him to say ahh. Does the area you see appear red? Are there any white or yellow spots visible? Determine if your child has a fever. **Report these findings to your child's pediatrician.** If strep throat is suspected, a diagnosis can be made with a rapid strep test or a more definitive throat culture.

Once you've determined the cause, the next step it to make your youngster as comfortable as possible. If he has a fever, administer a nonaspirin fever-lowering agent such as acetaminophen, which will also relieve some of the discomfort. If he is old enough to gargle (and not swallow), prepare a warm salt water solution and encourage him to gargle several times a day. The warmth of the solution will soothe an irritated throat, and bacteria cannot thrive in a high-salt medium.

Your child may not want to eat because of the discomfort of a sore throat. Offer his favorite beverages, popsicle, ice cream, and crushed ice. As long as his fluid intake is adequate to avoid dehydration, he will not be harmed by a poor appetite during this period.

Parents' Report: What Works

There's a whole lot of gargling going on in my families:

✦ Have your child gargle with aloe vera juice two times daily.

✦ Mix 1 teaspoon of apple cider vinegar in a glass of water. Have your child gargle one mouthful every hour. This treatment can help the pain of a streptococcal sore throat in twenty-four hours. The acid in the apple cider vinegar is very helpful in soothing and minimizing the sore throat, and if the child swallows any, the extra potassium is also beneficial.

✦ Add 1/4 teaspoon of cayenne pepper to 1 cup of boiling water; stir well and let the child gargle while the mixture is warm. This brings more circulation to the area and helps draw away the infection.

✦ Add 4 teaspoons echinacea, 1 clove garlic, 2 teaspoons peppermint leaves, and 1 teaspoon cayenne to 2 cups of boiling water. Allow to cool to a safe level of warmth. Let the child gargle with this solution every two to three hours. (To be safe, don't give this mixture to children under three or those who are allergic to ragweed.)

✦ Grapefruit seed extract is a powerful all-around antimicrobial product and is an excellent disinfectant and antiseptic. Add 5 drops to a glass of water for a soothing gargle.

✦ Turmeric is a standard Ayurvedic remedy for sore throats because of its astringent and antimicrobial properties. Try 1 teaspoonful of powdered turmeric—the same stuff that's in your spice rack—in a cup of warm water. Let the child gargle with it.

✦ Use ginger tea bags or put fresh sliced root in a cup of hot water. Ginger is an anti-inflammatory. Encourage your child to gargle with the water once it's comfortably warm.

✦ Bayberry is a natural antibiotic found in health food stores. You can also use a few drops of the tincture in a cup of hot water. Some natural mouthwashes also contain bayberry because it fights germs. If your child is old enough to gargle, these are safe to use and can be effective.

✦ Thyme is antibacterial and astringent. For a gargling solution, try 1 teaspoon dried herbs in a cup of hot water. Allow to cool.

✦ Use a cinnamon stick in cold water. Cinnamon contains a water-soluble fiber called mucilage that coats the throat. Cold water seems to bring out the mucilage better. Slippery elm and marshmallow can also be used in this way. Again, colder is better.

✦ Have your child gargle with 2 tablespoons of sesame oil mixed in 1 cup of hot water.

✦ Add 2 sprigs of coarsely chopped parsley, 3 whole cloves, 1 teaspoon of powdered myrrh, and 1/4 teaspoon powdered goldenseal to 1 pint of boiling water. Steep. Stir occasionally while cooling, then strain, cool, and use as a gargle or mouthwash.

✦ Mindy Green of the Herb Research Foundation says you can boost the effectiveness of any of these gargles with some essential oils. Add one drop of lemon, cypress, or bergamot oil. You can also put a drop of any of these oils into a cup of hot water with a teaspoon of salt and have the child gargle with that. (The child shouldn't drink the mixture, but if a little bit is swallowed it isn't harmful.)

Teas can soothe a sore throat too:

✦ Offer several tablespoons of a mixture of honey and lemon juice several times a day. Do not follow with water or other liquid, let it sit in your child's throat a little while. This remedy (only for children over one year of age because of the honey) should also help alleviate that irritating throat tickle.

✦ Add 30 drops of an echinacea/goldenseal combination remedy to 1 cup of warm water; have the child drink the whole cup every two hours. (This is not for children under the age of three or those who are allergic to ragweed.)

✦ The Chinese herb schizandra can be made into a tea that can help soothe a sore throat. Schizandra is astringent, antimicrobial, and anti-inflammatory.

✦ Bake a banana in its skin; when cool, mash the pulp with fresh cream. Make a compress. Apply this banana cream compress to the throat; don't eat it!

Sprains

THE AILMENT

A sprain is caused by overstretching of a joint. Bones at the body's weight-bearing centers involved with movement are held together by strong fibrous tissues known as ligaments. When there is a sudden twisting action or stretching of one of those points beyond its limits, a tear in the ligament tissue may result. The tissue tearing may cause bleeding, swelling, and a great deal of pain when the child puts weight on the area. The most commonly involved joints are the ankles, knees, and wrists. Once youngsters are old enough to do handsprings, ride a skateboard, and run on playgrounds and sports fields, sprain injuries are more likely to occur. On occasion, it may be difficult to determine if the injury is a sprain, dislocation, or a fracture without a medical consultation or an X ray. **Check with your child's pediatrician if the area looks misshapen, or if the child cannot bear any weight on the area; there may be a fracture, which requires immediate medical attention.**

CONVENTIONAL TREATMENT

Remember the acronym RICE.

✦ **R, rest** the affected area. Isolate the painful joint and do not allow it to be active.

✦ **I, ice** the affected area. Apply a cold compress immediately; this slows the bleeding into the site, reducing the bruising, and provides some pain relief.

✦ **C, compress** the site by wrapping with an elasticized bandage. This helps to further immobilize the site and reduce the swelling.

✦ **E, elevate** the injured site to encourage good circulation to the area without allowing the blood to pool and collect at the injury.

Parents' Report: What Works

✦ Apply a cool compress made with 5 drops of chamomile, eucalyptus, lavender, or rosemary oil added to a cup of water.

✦ Witch hazel added to some cool water to make a compress will help reduce swelling.

✦ Calendula will help with swelling. You'll find calendula in creams, salves, and ointments in any health food store. If you can find calendula tincture, you can also make a compress with that—add a few drops of tincture to some cool water, soak a cloth, and hold it on the sprain site.

✦ St. John's wort oil is made by steeping St. John's wort in vegetable oil for several weeks. You can also find it in commercial preparations, but look for the essential oil. Long before it was discovered that St. John's wort helped with depression, it was used as a sprain and strain healer. This is applied topically—*never ingest essential oils.* You can use this straight or mix it with a few drops of lavender, marjoram, and chamomile essential oils.

✦ Apply arnica cream (found in health food stores) topically, but never apply over broken skin since it can be harmful if absorbed directly through an open wound. However, you can take *homeopathic* arnica orally. There is a difference in the preparations. The homeopathic arnica is safe when taken as prescribed orally. It comes in pellets and is also found in health food stores. Specify whether you want a topical cream or homeopathic oral treatment.

✦ As a topical healer, comfrey has been used for years to reduce swelling and promote healing. ☛ WARNING: Comfrey ingestion may lead to liver damage.

✦ See **Arthritis** for more remedies.

Stings (*see also* Bites)

THE AILMENT

Bites or stings by insects or jellyfish cause a sharp, sometimes burning pain, reddening, and swelling at the affected areas. Most stings are not serious, but some, in particularly sensitive individuals, may cause a severe, life-threatening allergic (anaphylactic) reaction.

CONVENTIONAL TREATMENT

Most stings cause immediate but brief discomfort. Some cause prolonged redness, burning, or itching at the site. If there is a stinger involved, remove it when possible. If left in place too long, it can cause inflammation. To remove a stinger, scrape the skin's surface with a fingernail, butter knife blade, or the edge of a credit card; when you can see the hairlike stinger upright, pull it straight out with your fingernails or tweezers. *Do not squeeze* the area; you may actually release additional harmful venom. If your child has a jellyfish sting, use sand or anything available that is slightly abrasive to wipe all remnants of jellyfish tentacles off the skin.

Wash the affected areas with soap and water if available. Applying vinegar to a jellyfish sting is reported to be immediately soothing. Cold water or ice compresses applied to the sites relieve the burning and irritation of the stings. For the irritation of itchiness, calamine lotion may offer some relief. Over-the-counter antihistamines (Benadryl elixir or capsules) will slow or stop an allergic reaction and lessen the irritation, swelling, and itching caused by the stings.

☛ WARNING: Shortness of breath, rapid pulse, sweating, clamminess, pale skin color, and sudden weakness are all signs of shock. Call for emergency medical assistance.

PARENTS' REPORT: WHAT WORKS

✦ It's fairly common to use meat tenderizer mixed with water to make a paste to relieve swelling; it's a good idea to pack meat tenderizer and baking soda (see below) along with your picnic lunches or in your beach bag.

✦ Make a paste using a teaspoon of baking soda and a little water and apply to the sting site. Leave it on for fifteen to twenty minutes. The alkalinity of the baking soda has a cooling effect and neutralizes the acid of the sting.

A colleague with a summer house in the woods has become an "expert" on stings. Here's her advice:

✦ For *bee and hornet stings,* apply a chamomile compress made with chamomile tincture or tea and cool water. Hold the compress on the site for as long as the child can stand it, then apply a drop of medicinal grade chamomile essential oil to the sting site three times a day.

✦ You can also use chamomile or lavender oil to alleviate *wasp* stings, but first wash the site with cider or wine vinegar to neutralize the sting. Then apply 2 drops of chamomile or lavender oil to the sting site.

✦ For other insect stings, rub on sage tea. The sage may act as an astringent.

✦ Mix equal parts of echinacea (the tincture is stronger than the tea form) with bentonite (found in the health food store) and add a few drops of lavender and apply to sting site. For not-so-serious stings, you can apply lavender oil, undiluted from the bottle, right onto the sting site. Use a drop at a time so that the skin absorbs it. If there's swelling, also add chamomile essential oil, a drop at a time.

✦ Stings can also be treated with aloe vera gel, calendula tincture or cream, or the popular echinacea/goldenseal tincture combo; apply the liquid right to the sting site.

✦ If your child is stung by a bee, rubbing marigold flowers right on the sting site (after the stinger has been removed) is said to reduce the swelling. Since stings often happen in gardens, if you can recognize marigold and you know the garden hasn't been sprayed with pesticides, just pluck the flowers. If all else fails, pat some mud on as a first-aid measure.

✦ See **Bites** for more remedies.

Stomachache

THE AILMENT

There are several uh-oh moments during parenthood when your alarm button goes off and you are catapulted into near panic. One of these occasions is often when your little one cries out, "My tummy hurts!" Over the past twenty-eight years of practice, "My child has a stomachache" has been one of the most frequent reasons for late-night phone calls.

There are many reasons a child might develop abdominal pain. It could be something as simple as indigestion, which fades over time without any special treatment, or a complex problem such as appendicitis, which warrants immediate medical evaluation and surgical intervention. General tummy discomfort, sometimes accompanied by vomiting and diarrhea, is often caused by a viral stomach flu, while severe cramping frequently accompanies bacterial infections, such as those associated with food poisoning.

The abdomen is that area on the trunk between the diaphragm, near the bottom of the rib cage, and the pelvis, near the groin crease. It houses several major organs, including the stomach, spleen, gallbladder, pancreas, liver, small intestines, large intestines, appendix, and kidneys.

Possible causes for discomfort can be categorized by the four quadrants of the abdominal area. A brief glimpse into each of these quadrants is offered here, not so you can diagnose a potentially serious illness at home, but just so that you can report troubling symptoms more efficiently to your doctor.

The *left upper quadrant* houses the stomach and the spleen. The *stomach* is where recently swallowed food mixes with gastric juices in preparation for the next step in the digestive process. Sometimes an unusual combination of foods will produce gases, which bloat or distend the stomach, making your child very uncomfortable. This can cause a variety of sensations, including cramping, belching, increased flatulence (gas), nausea, and possibly vomiting, all usually without fever. Generally, resting the tummy by withholding food for a few hours is adequate to allow time for the stomach to empty and for the discomfort to subside.

If any blunt trauma to the abdominal area occurs during contact sports such as football or soccer, this could result in severe pain, swelling, discoloration, or tenderness to the touch in the left upper region. There could even be an injury caused by an automobile seat belt. If this happens, the possibility of injury to the *spleen* must be considered. This could signal a medical emergency requiring an immediate medical evaluation.

The *left lower quadrant* houses a portion of the large intestines—*the left colon.* If there is discomfort in the lower area on your child's left side, have him lie on a flat surface and gently press on that area with the pads of your fingers. If he allows the pressure, try to determine if you can feel anything. Do you feel any small, movable lumps under your fingers? If so, check when he last had a bowel movement. His discomfort may be the result of constipation. This gentle massage, and the stimulus provided to the colon by the pressure of your fingers, may just do the trick, sending him to the bathroom and allowing him to get rid of the source of his discomfort.

On the other hand, slight discomfort in the region of the left or right lower back that began as a stomachache could indicate a kidney problem and should prompt a call to your child's physician.

The *right upper quadrant* is where the three lobes of the *liver* are situated. The *gallbladder* is also in this region. Although rare in children, some conditions and certain foods can trigger gallbladder disorders, which cause discomfort in the upper middle or upper right regions.

A few questions to consider: Is there any association of your youngster's discomfort with the recent ingestion of food? Also, can you recall what foods were eaten? How were they prepared—baked, fried? Were they highly seasoned or spicy? Is this food type or preparation a new experience for your child? The answers provide clues and perhaps reasons for some stomachaches.

Any discomfort in the lower middle or lower right region, the *right lower quadrant,* should sound an alarm for the *possibility* of appendicitis. The *appendix* is a small sausage-shaped, pouchlike protrusion of the large intestine near where it joins the small intestines in the digestive system. If partially digested food matter finds its way into this pouch, causing it to become blocked and inflamed, a painful condition, appendicitis, results. The symptoms include fever, nausea, vomiting, and persistent pain near the navel and the lower right side. If you suspect the appendix as the culprit, do not give any food or drink to your child until a physician has examined her. This could be a surgical emergency. (Okay, exhale now! It's important to note that only rarely does a stomachache turn out to be appendicitis.)

Other considerations when there is a stomachache are urinary tract infection, pneumonia, or perhaps overworked muscles from physical exertion. Even small sudden changes in family life structure produce stress and may trigger abdominal pain. Whenever the discomfort seems prolonged, becomes more severe with time, or interferes with eating, sleeping, or movement, these are signals for you to contact your doctor.

Considerations before calling the doctor:

✦ The pattern of the pain: Is it constant or intermittent?

✦ Associated symptoms: Has there been vomiting, diarrhea, or fever associated with the pain?

✦ The severity: Has the pain caused the child to bend over when trying to walk?

✦ Changes in the child's behavior: Has the pain made the child cry?

✦ Changes in the child's activities: Is the pain severe enough to stop her in her tracks and curl up on the floor?

The answers to these questions provide clues about the ailment and may help your doctor make the proper diagnosis.

☛ WARNING: **Consult a doctor immediately if you notice:**

✦ Vomiting of blood or a yellow bilelike substance
✦ Dizziness
✦ Sweating
✦ Pain in the scrotum or testicular area in a male
✦ Pain or discomfort lasting for more than four hours

Conventional Treatment

If you have answered the above questions and reviewed the **warnings** without reaching for the phone, you can probably encourage your youngster to lie still for a while, perhaps holding a warm-water bag or heated towel over the abdominal area. Parents frequently find relief for their child with over-the-counter preparations formulated for children that promise to break up the gas bubbles and neutralize or absorb the stomach acids. Offer small sips of clear liquids, electrolyte drinks, or ice chips to maintain adequate hydration. If a flu (viral gastroenteritis) is the culprit, a slightly modified diet of clear liquids, broth, or electrolyte solutions will replace the essential body fluids that have been lost, maintaining an adequate state of hydration until the "bug" passes.

Parents' Report: What Works

Try these remedies *only* if the answers to the above questions were no—that is, your child hasn't been vomiting or bent over in pain, and you feel comfortable not calling your doctor.

Since the beginning of time, the unsettled stomach has been settled various ways by many cultures. In my practice and during my travels, parents have shared their families' recipes for calming a rumbling stomach. Most of these remedies attempt to alter the acid/base balance of the stomach contents or seem to have some effect on the stomach's emptying time. And then there are always remedies suggested for which I can find no rational explanation. Once, while I was in Paris working on a health segment for a local news show, a crew member informed me that raw potato slices are good for an upset stomach. I was surprised to learn that you don't give them to the child to *eat;* rather, you actually place them on the child's stomach for about thirty minutes! I have not figured out how this comforts the child, but it certainly doesn't appear to do any harm.

The first set of remedies for stomachache are in the form of teas, which may be settling and will help to maintain proper hydration. They are most often served hot and seem to be soothing. You may have to experiment to brew a tea your child will drink. Many herbal teas have properties that can affect the way the gastrointestinal tract works. For example, regular orange pekoe tea contains a theophyllinelike ingredient, which relaxes smooth muscle spasms and has been a major home remedy for asthma as well.

✦ Peppermint tea has been mentioned to me by families with such frequency that I sometimes recommend it in a weak form as a remedy to settle an upset stomach. Menthol, its major active ingredient, has an antispasmodic action on the smooth muscles of the digestive tract, and it has a pleasant candy-cane aroma. You can also steep fresh mint in hot water to make a slightly bitter but very soothing brew. Have your child sip some over a twenty-minute period.

✦ Chamomile tea is a popular offering for a variety of ailments because it is believed to have anti-inflammatory and antispasmodic properties. Commonly used around the globe, many families continue to tout the benefits of sips of chamomile tea to calm an upset stomach.

✦ Almost two decades ago, while traveling in the Middle East, I heard that dill tea would help an upset stomach. Many years later a Lebanese grocer confirmed that it was the "tummy tonic" in his household. Just pick up some dill tea bags.

✦ In the Far East, particularly in China, lemon balm, catnip, and fennel are popular remedies. However, you could try a brew of equal parts anise seed, fennel, peppermint, and thyme. (In case you are wondering, catnip is generally safe for humans. It may jazz up kitties, but it is relaxing for your kiddies! But buy yours in the health food store, not the pet shop.)

✦ An herbalist acquaintance of mine swears by slippery elm, an herb commonly used by Native Americans. Slippery elm contains mucilage, which coats and soothes the digestive tract. Make your own tea (or you can find slippery elm in tea bag form in most health food stores), then let it cool and sit at room temperature until the water appears slimy. This makes the mucilage more effective.

✦ During my pediatric residency training, flat Coca-Cola or ginger ale was frequently recommended to help calm stomachaches, vomiting, and diarrhea. It was believed that these sodas restored some of the lost sodium and potassium while providing hydration. And they are often readily available in patients' homes. They were considered safer than the earlier generations' recommendations of a pinch of sugar and a pinch of salt mixed into boiled water—too often a pinch became heaping spoons of each, causing dangerous imbalances in the baby's system. These homemade drinks were the forerunners of the now popular and safer oral rehydration electrolyte solutions, such as Pedialyte.

✦ Another frequently mentioned remedy is a baking soda mixture. Forget using pinches. Try a measured 1/4 teaspoon of baking soda in 2 ounces of room-temperature water. If your child is under twenty pounds or twelve months, offer her 1 teaspoon of the baking-soda-and-water mixture. It should help the baby be less fussy. Wait an hour before offering another dose. For your one-to-three-year-old, you can offer 2 to 3 teaspoons. And over age three, you can try the whole 2 ounces. (Too much of this mixture can cause a metabolic imbalance, so be sure to follow dosage instructions.) This should aid the passage of gas. If the child is not more comfortable, check with your doctor.

✦ One of my Polish families recommended mixing about a cup of fresh blueberries with 2 teaspoons of sugar. Cover the mixture tightly and allow to sit for a day. Feed small amounts to the child, 1 tablespoon for each year of age.

✦ Massage can also be helpful for digestive upset, particularly if it's done with some healing essential oils. Because the skin readily absorbs these oils, they may offer an option for kids who don't like to take medicine orally. Good ones for tummy trouble include lavender, peppermint, lemongrass, chamomile, fennel, and geranium. Most essential oils (except lavender and tea tree oil) are too strong to apply directly to the skin, so mix 8 to 10 drops per ounce of a vegetable oil, like sesame, almond, or jojoba. Then gently massage the mixture into your child's stomach region in a clockwise motion for two to three minutes.

Stye

THE AILMENT

A stye is a common infection at the base of an eyelash. It is a pus-filled swelling on the edge of the eyelid, originating from inflammation of the eyelash (hair) follicles. Rubbing the eyelids or pulling at the eyelashes causes irritation and creates opportunities for bacterial or viral contaminants from the hands to infect the site. Styes that occur on the upper or lower eyelids are highly infectious, affecting both children and adults. They are more unsightly than they are serious. A stye forms a small red pimple that is uncomfortable and may come to a head in three to four days, after which it drains its contents before drying, shrinking, and disappearing.

Younger children frequently rub their eyes during play and may easily transfer contaminants from objects or other children, increasing the likelihood of developing styes and other eye infections.

Conventional Treatment

Rubbing or squeezing the area should be discouraged, as it will only further irritate the site and possibly transfer the organisms and spread infection.

The regular application of clean, warm, wet cloths for five to ten minutes three to four times a day speeds drainage and hastens resolution. If the swelling and discomfort persist, I usually prescribe an antibiotic eye ointment or eyedrops.

Parents' Report: What Works

The warm compress is the key to family stye remedies. The warmth seems to help bring the stye to a head and helps the healing process.

✦ You can make compresses with the following herbs, which are all anti-infective: goldenseal, Oregon grape, and barberry. These all contain berberine, which works against the staphylococci bacteria, a major culprit that causes styes. Compresses of thyme and chamomile can also be used, as can eyebright, which is a longtime favorite for eye infections.

✦ Some families like to use Lipton tea bags, or other regular orange pekoe tea bags, for many ailments. In this case, a tea bag placed on the site would work on the same principle as the herbal compresses. Make your cup of tea and sip it while your child rests the warm, moist tea bag on her eyelid.

✦ Scrape the inside of a potato and hold the raw potato shavings, wrapped in a clean cloth, on the eye for several minutes a few times a day. It should help reduce the inflammation. Potatoes are rich in vitamin C, which helps heal infections. I have also been told that placing raw potato slices across the eye is beneficial.

Swimmer's Ear
(Otitis Externa, Swimmer's Ear)

THE AILMENT

This condition—inflammation anywhere on the outer ear, particularly along the path from the lobe through the outer canal to the eardrum—is characterized by pain, itching, swelling, a discharge draining from the canal, and a sensation of fullness in the ear. Otitis externa (its official title) more commonly occurs when ears are frequently in water, hence the term swimmer's ear. Water, chemical irritation, overly vigorous cleaning, or any break in the skin of the ear can permit the entry of bacteria or fungal organisms and result in infection. An object lodged in the ear canal can cause irritation and an inflammatory reaction. Usually any attempt to move the involved ear upward or outward results in extreme discomfort. Since this infection does not involve the eardrum or any of the delicate hearing or balance mechanisms, otitis externa is an inconvenience, not a major malady. However, this infection should not be dismissed. If left untreated, a more serious infection involving deeper tissues, bone, and the bloodstream could result.

Conventional Treatment

Clean away any residual discharge from the ear canal with a washcloth and warm, soapy water. If there is irritation, use a dropper to put a few drops of hydrogen peroxide around the site to reduce the bacterial presence. It's wise not to use a cotton swab or any such object inside the ear. If a foreign object is observed in the ear, only a physician should attempt to remove it. You can offer a nonaspirin pain reliever such as acetaminophen or ibuprofen (a nonsteroidal anti-inflammatory) to relieve any discomfort. Check the label to be certain that you give the appropriate dose for age and weight.

For further pain relief, try a moist heat pack held to the affected ear. A heat pack can be made by placing a wet washcloth in an unzipped plastic bag into a microwave oven and heating one to two minutes. After carefully removing it from the microwave, seal the plastic bag and wrap in a towel, then place onto the affected ear. This wrapped heat pack will stay warm and can remain in place for twenty-minute intervals. ☛ **WARNING:** Test to make sure the heated plastic isn't too hot. Direct contact with skin could result in burns.

Depending upon the extent of the infection, your physician may prescribe a full course of antibiotic medications and special drops for the affected ear. An antibacterial, antifungal, or hydrocortisone cream may also be prescribed for any skin lesions.

Parents' Report: What Works

✦ Vinegar is a key remedy for swimmer's ear. Families give me lots of recipes for vinegar-based treatments. Here's an easy one: Make a solution that can be administered several times over two to three days: Mix 1 ounce white vinegar with 1 ounce rubbing alcohol, then put a few drops into the affected ear every six hours. Or use apple cider vinegar. Put 3 to 4 drops, diluted with an equal amount of water or rubbing alcohol, in the child's ear after showering.

✦ Make a wick out of a small piece of cotton cloth, handkerchief, or undershirt. Soak the cloth in vinegar. Twist the end of the cloth to fit gently into the canal. Vinegar changes the acid/base balance on the skin, acts as an anti-inflammatory, and draws out the pain.

✦ Use the warm (never hot!) setting of your hair dryer and place it at arm's length from your child's ear, moving it slowly back and forth for one minute. Test on your wrist first. The warm air will evaporate the trapped water.

✦ Garlic is a potent natural antibiotic—it fights bacteria, fungi, and viruses. You can buy garlic oil in health food stores. Or make your own. Just peel a few cloves, crush them, and let them steep in some olive oil for a few days. When the mixture is ready, warm slightly, put a few drops in the affected ear, and plug with a cotton ball.

✦ Use mullein oil, found in health food stores. Like garlic, mullein is an herb said to be an anti-infective agent. You can also mix a little mullein oil into the garlic oil mixture.

Teeth Grinding (Bruxism)

The Ailment

Teeth grinding—audible or visible movement of the lower teeth against the upper teeth—is known as bruxism. Bruxism is fairly common in children. Although the exact cause may not be easy to determine, over time it definitely causes wear on the margins of the teeth. (Not to mention what this sounds like to parents.) If a child's bite does not align properly or does not permit a "fit" closure, grinding may occur as the jaw attempts to find a comfortable position.

According to dentists' reports, approximately one-third of five- and six-year-olds were either reported by their parents to grind their teeth or demonstrated evidence of worn tooth margins during routine dental checks. In addition to misaligned or poorly positioned teeth, other possible causes may include the eruption of new teeth. At times children attempt to maneuver their jaw in such a manner to allow existing teeth to rub the gum margins where new eruptions are occurring.

Teeth grinding may be connected to psychological stress caused by disruptions to your child's usual routine. The arrival of a new baby, starting a new school, divorce or death in the family, or moving are among the most frequently reported events that trigger teeth grinding. Other causes may include pain, nutritional deficiencies, endocrine disorders, and allergies. If the problem seems severe and persists, a dental evaluation is recommended.

CONVENTIONAL TREATMENT

First, try to determine the cause of the teeth grinding. If a medical cause is suspected, the doctor will need a careful medical history and lab studies may be necessary. If a nutritional history reveals patterns that suggest certain deficiencies, you'll need to adjust your child's diet. If misalignment is found, orthodontic care to adjust the poorly aligned teeth may be necessary. Your child may need braces or a soft, pliable mouth guard worn at night to help eliminate the grinding. Many youngsters spontaneously stop grinding their teeth as they get older.

PARENTS' REPORT: WHAT WORKS

✦ Over the years, many grandmothers have informed me that a child's teeth grinding is indicative of worms (intestinal parasites). For years I dismissed this as folk talk. But after discovering that a few of these grandmothers were correct, I now ask the appropriate worm screening questions. That is, I ask whether the child is pulling on clothing in the genital area or seems to be itching in the rectal region. Depending upon the answers, occasionally I will send a stool specimen to the laboratory to be screened for the presence of intestinal parasites. If the lab report is positive, I initiate treatment with the appropriate antiparasite medicine.

✦ When all else fails, I share this recommendation from a parent I encountered early in my residency: Give chamomile tea to your child right before bedtime. It's very relaxing and a gentle soother that could easily lull a child to sleep. Actually, I recommend *any* sleepytime tea for the entire family, so that both the child and the family sleep well and no one hears the sound of teeth grinding. (Other soothing teas include passionflower for kids over the age of four, skullcap for kids over six, and valerian for kids over twelve. Beware—cats like valerian as well.)

Teething

The Ailment

Most babies experience the eruption of their first tooth between the ages of five and seven months. Teething is not an illness, but a rite of passage. Signs such as drooling, red and swollen gums, and fussiness may begin many months before the teeth actually erupt. As the teeth move closer to the gums' surface, babies will have a greater urge to bite and chew. You will notice that they want to mouth everything. At times, their drooling becomes excessive, soaking right through their clothing. As a result, the skin on the chest and around the mouth and chin may become quite irritated. In addition to the drooling, some youngsters experience a low-grade fever, exhibit symptoms resembling a cold, hit at their ears, and may have occasional diarrhea and fussiness. The teething process continues in some manner until all of the primary teeth have erupted, usually before the third birthday.

Conventional Treatment

✦ Sore and swollen gums may be relieved by massaging with your clean finger or a cool, damp washcloth.

✦ Over-the-counter teething gels (Numzit, Orajel) contain small amounts of topical anesthetics, which soothe and numb the gums temporarily. Exercise caution; use only age-appropriate versions that are alcohol-free, and get your doctor's okay.

✦ If your child is irritable and fussy, nonaspirin pain relievers such as acetaminophen or ibuprofen are quite effective. Follow the age-appropriate dosage recommendations.

✦ Teething biscuits may be welcomed by infants who are able to sit comfortably without support.

✦ A firm rubber teething ring that has been refrigerated allows the baby to gleefully bite and chew her way to soothing relief.

✦ Try to distract your teething baby with toys, music, and cuddles.

☛ WARNING: Teething discomfort can be confused with an ear infection. If fever, fussiness, hitting at the ears, loss of appetite, or other troubling symptoms occur and persist, give your doctor a call; it could be more than just teething.

PARENTS' REPORT: WHAT WORKS

✦ This remedy comes from an intelligent, experienced mother in my practice. Her grandmother passed it on to her mom, and now it belongs to her. She confided in me that whenever a child of hers was teething, she would place an uncooked egg on the highest shelf in her kitchen. If left undisturbed, this ensured that her youngsters would not experience teething problems. When I asked her just how long the egg should be left in place, I was told it should remain there as long as the child was teething and the egg was not emitting any unpleasant odors. I cannot fathom any scientific reason for this practice. It definitely comes under the banner of practices that have survived with time and do no harm. (If you try this, please let me know if it works!)

✦ Chamomile in various forms has been reported to help. Chamomile essential oil is a gentle soother and relaxer. Try 1 drop in ½ cup water. Dip your finger or a clean, soft cloth into this solution and rub it over your child's gums. (Essential oils are not for drinking, but used at this dilution and in this way, it is safe.) You can also mix a few drops of chamomile essential oil with an equal number of drops of vegetable oil and with this gently massage the skin around your baby's cheeks and jawline.

✦ From Hawaii comes still another use for the popular pineapple. Rub juice from fresh or canned pineapple onto the baby's gums. The stinging effect is a counterirritant.

✦ Clove essential oil has anesthetic properties, so if it is gently rubbed onto gums, it helps to relieve pain. Use sparingly, because it is one of the hot oils and may be too strong for young children. You can "cool" it by mixing in a few drops of light vegetable oil.

✦ Marshmallow tincture is soothing and an anti-inflammatory. Remember that it is also recommended for sore throats. Use this tincture, found in health food stores, and rub over sore gums.

✦ A colleague, Dan Mowrey, Ph.D., shared this remedy: "My daughter, Erin, did this with her child, Hazel, with great success: We located a source of marshmallow sticks and whenever Hazel seemed to be teething, we gave her a stick to chew on. It worked like a charm!! It's the best remedy I have ever seen for teething problems."

✦ A cold sensation usually works for teething. Put the baby's teething rings in the refrigerator (or the freezer) so they are nice and cold. You can try a large slice of apple—large enough not to worry about the child choking on it. Keep it in the fridge and give it to baby to gnaw on while you supervise. Other parents have recommended a small frozen washcloth or even a clean sock filled with ice chips with the end knotted as teething items. However, a large, long bib may be needed as these melt—beware of the mess and the damp clothing that results.

✦ I give a thumbs-down to any concoction involving bourbon, whiskey, or other distilled spirits mixed with sugar and rubbed onto the gums to effect numbing and calmness. ☛ **WARNING:** The use of alcohol for medicinal purposes in children is dangerous and should be discouraged. The potential adverse effects far outweigh any perceived benefits.

Thrush

THE AILMENT

The appearance of white, irregularly shaped patches on the inner surface of the cheeks, tongue, and gums is caused by the yeast fungus candida and is known as thrush. (Unlike milk residue, with which it is often confused, these patches cannot be wiped away easily with a cloth; if these affected areas are vigorously rubbed, red, raw, and bleeding areas may result.) Candida is normally found in healthy balance with other friendly microorganisms in our bodies. Any shift in our immune system due to illness, metabolic disorders, nutritional deficiencies, or an extended course of antibiotic medications may alter this natural balance. During infancy, the immune system is in an ever-changing state of maturation, and babies are more susceptible to microorganism imbalance. Occasionally an overgrowth of candida appears in areas that are prone to trap moisture—the mouth, the diaper area, the neck, and skin folds. Oral thrush causes mouth discomfort when the baby tries to suck or feed. During infancy, thrush is not usually regarded as a serious disorder. However, if it appears in older children or adults, it could be a sign of a more serious systemic disorder.

CONVENTIONAL TREATMENT

Antifungal medications (nystatin, mycostatin) are available by prescription as a suspension. These are quite effective, generally clearing the infection in seven to ten days. An older, less costly, tried-and-true over-the-counter treatment is gentian violet 1%. This purple liquid must be swabbed directly onto the white patches inside the mouth several times a day. This may be difficult to do without staining your hands, clothing, and everything else in reach. If you try gentian violet 1%, wear disposable rubber gloves, and cover the baby during the application.

For treatment to be effective and long-lasting, everything that enters the baby's mouth must be candida-free. Mothers who are breast-feeding a child with thrush should treat their nipples prior to feeding with the same medication they administer to the baby. So if your child is using nystatin drops, coat your nipples with the medication. Similarly, if you're using gentian violet, swab your nipples with it too. Rubber nipples from baby's bottles may be a source for continuing reinfection; discard them and buy new ones. New nipples should be boiled after use and similarly treated. Most cases of thrush clear with treatment and will not interfere with the baby's growth and development. If thrush seems resistant to treatment or if it recurs with great frequency, this may suggest an immune system disorder, which can be investigated through diagnostic laboratory studies.

Parents' Report: What Works

✦ Nursing mothers need to treat both themselves and the baby so they don't continue to pass the infection back and forth between them. A colleague, Stephanie, eliminated all sugar from her diet at the first sign of thrush in her infant. She believes that this one action helped to eliminate her baby's thrush. Stephanie excludes all obvious sugary foods as well as fruits and fruit juices. She explained that this starves the yeast, since they thrive on sugar. At the first sign of thrush, she also eliminates fats from her diet, with the exception of olive oil, which is said to halt yeast growth.

✦ Nursing moms can take grapefruit seed extract in capsules or liquid form. Readily found in health food stores, grapefruit seed extract is a potent antifungal. Follow label instructions for correct dosage.

✦ Ginger, which reportedly has some antimicrobial properties, is also good for nursing moms, who can drink a cup of ginger tea with their meals.

✦ Garlic, either in capsules or mixed into food, can also help. Garlic is a terrific antifungal and is often used to treat adult yeast infections.

✦ Many mothers promote the benefits of *Lactobacillus acidophilus* and *Lactobacillus bifidus* to repopulate the intestinal tract with friendly bacteria. One mom, Sandy, stated, "They kick butt when it comes to yeast." You'll find these products in health food stores. Mix ⅛ teaspoon of either *L. acidophilus* or *L. bifidus* with some water; older kids or adults with thrush can use it as a mouth rinse. For babies, use this mixture to completely bathe their gums, tongue, and inner cheeks to get all the thrush.

✦ You can go straight to yogurt. Just make sure you get the type with live cultures. Both the breast-feeding mom and her breast- or bottle-fed infant can take this. The live cultures will repopulate the intestinal tract and crowd out the invading yeast. You might even try getting your child to just hold a spoonful of plain yogurt in her mouth for a short period.

✦ Aloe vera gel is used by many parents. You need food-quality aloe vera gel because you're going to rub it on the baby's gums, tongue, and inner cheeks. Aloe vera juice is also popular. However, aloe vera juice has laxative properties. For older children or adults, try just 1 teaspoonful alone or mixed in vegetable juice. Also, if mixed with water, it can be used as a mouth swish or gargle—then have the child spit it out.

✦ Kids over three can gargle with 2 drops of tea tree oil in 1 cup of water. For candida that's also present on other skin areas, including the genitals, put a few drops of tea tree oil into a tepid bath and have the child soak in it.

✦ Try 1 tablespoon each of rosemary and sage in 1 cup of boiling water. Steep, then strain, cool, and use as a mouthwash for oral thrush.

✦ Rinse your child's mouth with a mixture of ½ cup water and ½ cup apple cider vinegar every few hours.

Thumb Sucking

The Ailment

Thumb and finger sucking are two of the common oral habits of children that concern parents. Most children who suck a finger begin the habit during the first year of life. In fact, ultrasonography has revealed that many begin this practice while still in the womb. For all healthy infants, sucking is a natural reflexive action. As a response to any light touch or stroke near the mouth, the baby's head reflexively turns toward the direction of this touch and the mouth starts sucking movements. Sucking enables the baby to meet nutritional needs necessary to facilitate growth and development and psychological needs to ensure comfort and security. As children become more socially aware of behaviors expected of a big boy or big girl, most will abandon the practice by age four or five.

Conventional Treatment

The best thing to do is nothing.

There is no doubt that a finger-sucking habit can affect the alignment of a child's teeth. The frequency, duration, and intensity of the practice determine the extent of any detrimental change. However, most children have minimal or no visible change in their bite because of thumb sucking. When the child is old enough to understand some of the cosmetic consequences, your appeals to stop the practice may be more acceptable. If the habit persists beyond the eruption of the first few permanent teeth, it would be wise to seek the counsel of your dentist. An orthodontic thumb guard appliance can be custom-made to fit into your child's mouth, making the finger's entry difficult and uncomfortable.

The most successful methods for stopping finger sucking are those that do not involve reprimands and punishments but use praise and reward as positive reinforcement for not sucking.

PARENTS' REPORT: WHAT WORKS

Many families have come up with their own concoctions to put on the thumb to stop the sucking.

- Pepper, hot sauce, and other unpleasant-tasting concoctions applied to the thumb may work for a while—until the child eventually figures out how to rub enough off so that the thumb is palatable again.
- A Martinique hotel executive told me how she cured her children of thumb sucking. She stuck her child's favored thumb inside a lime cut in half until it was saturated with the juice. After repeating this process on several occasions, the ritual and the tartness of the lime seemed to work as a deterrent.
- Many parents simply substitute a pacifier for a thumb as a reasonable alternative. Most children reach a developmental stage when they know sucking a pacifier will be frowned upon by the others in their play group or school. They will leave their pacifiers in the car or at home when they will be in the presence of disapproving others. Parents find the pacifier habit is often easier to stop (gather them up and say bye-bye). However, when they return to the sanctity of their parents and their space, some children may still seek the solace of their pacifier.

✦ A teacher in Schull, Ireland, who enjoys knitting explained how she made personalized little socks to place over her infants' hands as they slept. That made their thumb and other fingers less accessible for sucking. When the socks were no longer necessary, she framed them and hung them over the fireplace as decorative items.

✦ Gloves, like socks, can be worn on the favored hand of an older child who is motivated to stop sucking. The glove serves as a reminder and deterrent when, without thinking, that hand might reflexively go to the mouth.

Tonsilitis

The Ailment

Tonsilitis is inflammation (an infection) of the tonsils, which are round mounds of soft pink tissue located on either side at the very back of the throat. These clumps of lymphoid tissue are a part of the body's protective immune system. Tonsils and adenoids (similar lymphoid tissue positioned at the back of the nose) trap and destroy viruses and bacteria, preventing them from entering the respiratory tract. During early childhood, the tonsil and adenoid tissues are normally huge, even when they are not infected. When they are inflamed, they become even more enlarged, very red, and sometimes speckled with pus, causing fever, painful swallowing, swollen glands, unpleasant breath odor, and sometimes breathing difficulties. Bacteria such as streptococci are frequently found in infected tonsil tissues.

During the time of my pediatric training, it was common for children's tonsils and adenoids to be removed after a few episodes of infection. However, over time this practice has changed. It is now more common to treat multiple infections in an attempt to keep this tissue for its overall disease-prevention properties. Adenoid enlargement occurs with infections and in children who suffer with respiratory allergies. Children with enlarged adenoids often have a high-pitched nasal quality to their voice, are mouth breathers, and frequently snore loudly. As a child grows—usually after age eight, when resistance to infection increases—tonsil and adenoid tissues spontaneously shrink in size.

☛ WARNING: Sudden onset of unusual breathing problems with a sore throat, drooling, or difficulty swallowing saliva may signal peritonsillar abscesses. This constitutes a medical emergency, requiring immediate medical attention.

Conventional Treatment

If your child has a sore throat, check for fever and try to view the back of the throat. Use the handle of a spoon to depress the tongue, asking the child to say ahh. Look for large round mounds at the very back of the tongue.

- Are they red?
- Are there white or yellow spots?
- Are there tender lumps on the sides of the neck or along the jawline?
- Does your child have a fever?
- Is your child having any difficulty swallowing or breathing?

Report the answers to your child's doctor. A laboratory screen or culture may determine the infecting organism, and when appropriate, antibiotic therapy should be administered. Most episodes of tonsilitis are not life-altering if promptly treated.

However, your child's doctor may, after multiple episodes of infection, suggest you seek an ear, nose, and throat consultation. If your child's tonsils are no longer able to provide their intended protective barrier and are now only a source of continued infections, they should be removed.

Parents' Report: What Works

See **Sore Throat** for remedies.

Toothache

The Ailment

A toothache results when there is any disruption of the outer protective coating of a tooth. This allows exposure to the tooth's softer center, which contains the nerves. Pain is then experienced when anything very hot, cold, sweet, or sour comes in contact with that tooth. A toothache usually signals tooth decay. Without adequate treatment, the painful tooth may be lost, causing decay in or disruption of the adjacent teeth; it may also cause gum disease. A toothache is *never* normal and should not be ignored. (However, as new teeth erupt, expect some discomfort; the gum sites will be tender and swollen as tissue is broken.) Sometimes parents disregard decay in the primary (baby) teeth. This is a mistake, because the primary teeth provide the framework and foundation for the secondary (permanent) teeth. A boil or abscess in the gum represents a pocket of infection, which, if not properly treated, may result in tooth and bone loss and eventually a systemwide infection. Pain in the jaw, throbbing discomfort, or an earache may actually signal a problem tooth that needs immediate attention. Consult with a pediatric dentist.

Conventional Treatment

✦ While waiting for the dentist to check your youngster, give him a nonaspirin pain reliever such as acetaminophen or ibuprofen to reduce the discomfort. Warm saltwater mouth rinses to reduce the bacterial count and soothe the pain.

✦ Warm, wet cloths or a warm-water bottle (wrapped in a towel) against the cheek at the tender site may ease the pain.

✦ Brush, floss, or rinse to remove any trapped food.

PARENTS' REPORT: WHAT WORKS

The following are temporary measures and should only be used to hold the child over until you consult with the dentist.

✦ Many grandmothers have told me that they have used oil of cloves for a painful tooth. Oil of cloves is very popular as an anesthetizing agent; it turns up in many over-the-counter pain remedies. Here are two other remedies using cloves. Use the first on older kids who won't choke on the spice.

1. Place a whole clove between the aching tooth and your child's cheek. It can be held in place by holding your finger on the outside of the cheek. Have your child chew the clove a little to release its juice, then leave it in place for no more than half an hour to determine if the pain subsides.
2. Place two drops of clove oil on a sterile cotton ball; place the cotton ball between the aching tooth and the inside of the cheek until the pain subsides. ☛ **WARNING:** I have been advised by a dental colleague that pure clove oil placed directly into an affected area may damage an exposed nerve or raw gum tissue around a decaying tooth.

✦ Here are special acupressure points said to help relieve toothache pain:

1. Press gently on the bottom of the cheekbone, directly under the pupil of the eye.
2. Press in the webbing between thumb and forefinger.
3. Press in the hollow behind the earlobe.
4. Press in front of the ear, at the top of the jawbone.

✦ This Chinese remedy comes from a traditional physician who practices near San Francisco's Chinatown. Fry rhubarb, then soak the stalk in vodka to make a tincture. It should be kept in a dark brown jar with a tight lid. Shake the mixture every few days and top off with more vodka as some evaporates. After two to three weeks, strain out the plant material. Apply a few drops of this tincture to the aching tooth for a few minutes. Obviously, this is one of those remedies made in advance for the just-in-case toothache. You don't want to have a child sitting around with an aching tooth for two weeks! Despite my anxieties about using alcohol in children's therapies, this physician said he does not worry about the vodka in this preparation because most of the alcohol evaporates over the weeks. (Many tinctures are made with alcohol.) Also, he assures me he uses this remedy in minute amounts to gain temporary pain relief.

✦ Dissolve 2 tablespoons of salt in 1 cup of boiling water; cool slightly. Give the child a mouthful as hot as possible without scalding; have her slosh it around in her mouth near the tooth, then spit. Repeat as often as necessary.

✦ Put a towel-covered ice pack on the cheek for fifteen-minute intervals until you reach the dentist.

✦ Hawaiian healers recommend roasting or cooking a small piece of ginger and then shaping it to fit over the tooth. Have the child bite down and let his saliva flow over it. You can also mix powdered ginger with some water to make a paste. Use a cotton-tipped swab to apply it to the tooth, *not* on the gum. This acts as a counterirritant, creating some discomfort at the already painful tooth site, which then competes with the original toothache pain.

Umbilical Hernia (Navel Protrusion)

THE AILMENT

A painless bulge near the navel that balloons in size with crying, coughing, or straining may be an umbilical hernia.

The umbilicus (navel) is the only universal exterior leftover remnant of fetal life. The umbilical cord connects the unborn baby's circulatory system to the mother's. After the baby's delivery, the umbilical cord is cut and clamped. An antiseptic solution is applied to the stump and the skin around it. During the first two weeks, the cord, still attached to the baby, shrivels, becomes very dry, and spontaneously detaches itself. In many infants, within days of the completion of this process, the base of the attachment completely contracts, pulling some abdominal skin inward, creating the familiar belly button.

When there is a defect in the abdominal muscle wall or when the two inside borders of those muscles do not completely come together, the slight area of separation, notably larger at the navel, is known as an umbilical hernia. With time, most navel hernias close; they usually disappear spontaneously before the child is five years old. Rarely serious, those umbilical hernias that do not spontaneously resolve may cause some cosmetic concerns initially for the parents, and in later years for the child.

A protruding navel is not rare. The presence of an umbilical hernia is not unusual in African American infants. In fact, the appearance of protruding navels is noted in many African sculptures and other works of art.

☛ WARNING: If a portion of the bowel (the intestines) seems trapped in the hernia, it is a medical emergency.

CONVENTIONAL TREATMENT

Careful observation is important. Bath time is a good opportunity to check for an increase or decrease in size and to determine if the area is tender. Does it seem to cause discomfort if touched? Is there warmth in the area? Is there a color change? If the hernia goes inward with gentle pressure, there is no imminent danger. If the hernia area is hard or will not easily retract inward, notify your physician immediately. The condition has become a medically urgent situation, and corrective surgery may be necessary.

Regular "outtie" belly buttons—the result of an umbilical stump that wasn't tied very close to the body—are harmless and not of major concern. The classic umbilical hernia occurs when part of the intestine pushes out through any small opening in the connective tissue of the abdominal wall. Parents should never play doctor with this condition. If there are questions or concerns, call your doctor or go for a medical evaluation.

PARENTS' REPORT: WHAT WORKS

When parents want to do something to eliminate the navel bulge or to strengthen the abdominal wall, it's okay with me. There is a great sense of empowerment when a parent feels that her direct actions contribute to her baby's well-being.

✦ I think every grandmother over time has told me about some way to bind a navel hernia. In fact, my mother has preserved in her cedar chest a popular baby undergarment manufacturer's belly band, which she used to treat my navel hernia. She said that she watched me closely, holding me much of the time, fearing that if I cried too long, my navel might pop out and cause irreparable harm. She also believed that my umbilical hernia occurred because the newborn nursery staff allowed me to cry for prolonged periods. She has long resisted my insistence that there is no likely connection.

✦ Coins and other disclike objects have often been taped directly over the protrusion as a treatment. First be certain that any navel protrusion can be pushed in by hand. Completely cover a coin with adhesive tape or a soft cloth and place it directly over the navel. With more adhesive tape (I prefer three-inch-wide Elastoplast) stretched from one side to the other, pull the stomach muscles toward one another to close the hernia opening. Leave the tape in place for as long as it continues to adhere; change the tape as needed. You can continue baby's baths and all other activities. Since sensitive skin can have an adverse or allergic reaction to adhesive tape, I recommend using nonallergenic paper tape to avoid skin irritation.

✦ If your child requires surgery, and the hernia bulge has been pushed back with the muscles and skin sutured into place, it will be taped or trussed to keep the area stable while the injury heals. Chris, my naturopathic doctor colleague, suggests offering flavored gelatin or Jell-O, which he believes facilitates connective tissue healing.

✦ One folk remedy I've heard is to offer a tea of slippery elm bark and marshmallow root (you'll find both teas in health food stores). Drinking this tea after surgical correction reportedly speeds the healing of connective tissue. Your child's age determines the amount of this tea: For ages twelve months to two years, try offering 1/4 cup; for youngsters two to five years, offer 1/2 cup; for those older than five years, 1 cup can be given.

Urinary Stinging

THE AILMENT

If your child hesitates or cries when attempting to urinate, or starts the process and then winces and tries to stop in midstream, these are signals that it's probably painful. Urinary discomfort can be caused by many factors. Irritation and infection are the most common culprits. Bacteria, more so than viruses, are the usual germs identified as causing the problem. When you communicate with your pediatrician, be prepared to provide the following information:

- How often does your child urinate? Is he wetting himself after having been previously dry?
- Is the urine clear or cloudy, very pale or very dark? Is there any blood?
- What is the odor? Is it stronger than usual?
- Does your child have a fever?
- Is there abdominal pain?
- Have you used bubble baths or scented soaps in baths recently?
- Is there redness or other color change, swelling, or discomfort near the area around the bladder opening?
- Has there been any change in the child's state of alertness?

Careful hygiene can help avoid irritation and infection. Since the female urethral canal is shorter than the male's, bacteria and debris from the rectum can too easily contaminate that site and are more likely to initiate an infection. Therefore, girls seem to be more susceptible to urinary tract infections than boys. As a preventive measure, it's very important to teach young girls to always wipe from *front to back* after bowel movements.

Conventional Treatment

Once a urinary tract infection is suspected, your physician will need to collect some urine for laboratory analysis. In my practice, once I have obtained a "clean catch," I do an in-office urinalysis with a small portion of it, and send the remainder of the clean specimen to the lab for culture and sensitivity. If there are preliminary positives with the routine screening, as an interim measure I initiate antibiotic therapy while I await the laboratory reports. Once I have reviewed the final laboratory reports, I may need to alter my course of treatment. However, I advise eliminating foods containing caffeine from the diet, such as chocolate, coffee, tea, and colas, because they may contribute to bladder irritation. Drinking additional water is healthy and beneficial as a bladder flush.

Once a urinary tract infection is suspected or identified by your doctor, it is important to follow any prescribed treatment through to its completion. Urinary infections, if not promptly and properly treated, can have long-lasting consequences.

Reports have appeared in the medical literature supporting the increased consumption of cranberry and blueberry juices, which make the urine more acidic. An acidic environment makes it hard for bacteria to thrive.

Parents' Report: What Works

✦ Cranberry juice seems to be the ultimate natural urinary tract infection remedy. Its benefits continue to appear in consumer publications and have been reported in medical journals. Cranberry juice contains ingredients that prevent the bacteria that cause urinary tract infections from sticking to the bladder and urethra walls. The trick with cranberry juice is not to drink the sugary juice that you find in most grocery stores—the sugar content negates all the benefits, because it feeds the bacteria causing the infection. Pure cranberry juice would be the first choice, but it's generally way too tart to drink, particularly for picky kids. But you can find minimally sweetened cranberry juice in some supermarkets, health food stores, or organic supermarkets. Check labels and look for juices that are sweetened with grape juice or pear juice. As long as there are no added sugars, it should be fine. Strong extracts work the best; CranActin from Solaray Corporation is a good one to try.

✦ Blueberries can also be used for urinary tract infections. Try juicing them if you can't find blueberry juice. They are loaded with antioxidants, which helps fight the infection.

✦ Vitamin C, a potent antioxidant, works wonders on the bacteria that cause urinary tract infections. Do a triple-punch remedy with vitamin C, cranberry juice, and as much water as can be consumed to combat the infection and flush out the urinary tract.

✦ A parent of Cherokee heritage told me about the use of the herb uva ursi for urinary tract infections. She cautions not to mix this with cranberry juice, since they may counteract each other. This herb is considered as an antiseptic and astringent. However, since it may also be irritating in the urinary tract, check with your youngster's physician about its use or with an herbalist for the age-appropriate diluted dose.

✦ One herbal concoction that is said to help uva ursi's effectiveness is corn silk (the stuff that's left when you shuck corn) and parsley tea. Both corn silk and parsley have diuretic actions, which means they increase the excretion of urine. You can make this tea either with fresh corn silk—the water that unshucked corn is boiled in—or corn silk tincture and fresh parsley from your local health food store.

✦ I've even been advised that a handful of parsley placed over the bladder is a remedy!

✦ Pipsissewa is another Native American remedy for urinary tract problems. It is said to be gentler than uva ursi, but it is harder to find in health food stores. It can be ordered from bulk herb suppliers. (Give a dose three to four times daily. See the dosage information on pages 10–11.)

✦ Garlic, nature's own antibiotic, works to kill the bacteria that cause urinary tract infections. Use either deodorized garlic pills (follow package instructions for dosing) or small amounts of sliced raw garlic added to your child's food.

✦ Yogurt, the kind with live cultures, provides the beneficial bacteria to help combat the infection-causing bacteria.

✦ Don't forget the echinacea/goldenseal combination. While we normally think of this combo as a cold/flu remedy, echinacea is also beneficial for infections of the urogenital area. Echinacea is an immune booster, and goldenseal helps soothe mucous membranes; the linings and coverings of the urinary system are mucous membranes. (Reminder: Don't give this to children who are allergic to ragweed or who are under the age of three.)

✦ Marshmallow tea is very soothing to inflamed tissues, which is why it's also recommended for a sore throat. This tea can also soothe inflamed tissues in the urinary tract.

✦ Warm-water baths are also very beneficial for urinary tract infections to relax the muscles, which enables the child to "pee" more freely. An editor shared a memory from her childhood: "I was prone to urinary infections growing up, and my parents (Dad's a doc) would always put me in a sitz bath. Though it seemed kind of yucky, I was encouraged to pee right in the tub. Of course, I would always have to shower afterward."

Vaginal Itching and Irritation

The Ailment

Because the vagina and the bladder opening (the urethra) are anatomically so close together and near the anus, this region can be easily contaminated by bacteria from fecal matter, especially in young girls.

It is normal for females, even young girls, to have some vaginal secretions. These secretions consist of cells that are regularly shed from the vaginal walls as new cells are generated. The secretions are usually colorless or whitish, without odor, are not irritating, and do not cause burning or itching. With maturation, increased hormone production stimulates pubertal body changes and more obvious vaginal secretions (discharge). Although vaginal secretions increase and become more mucus-like at this stage, they should not be malodorous or cause itching or burning. Common causes of vaginal discomfort include irritating chemicals found in some soaps, bubble baths, lotions, and sprays.

After years of examining very young females with varied complaints of discomfort in the vulva region, I have learned to expect the unexpected. I have found small bits of crayon, paper, hair clips, and other small foreign objects hidden in tiny private places.

When vaginal irritation is accompanied by rectal itching, I suspect pinworms. Intense itching and irritation may occur after a few days of antibiotics prescribed for some other ailment—these medications can upset the body's healthy bacterial balance and promote the overgrowth of yeast and unhealthy bacteria.

Conventional Treatment

As a first step to relieve discomfort, try to identify and eliminate any offending agents. Reflect on recent events, any new underclothing purchases, or any change in laundry products. I advise parents to discontinue the use of bubble baths, scented soaps in bathwater, tight-fitting undergarments, leotards, or underwear made of moisture-retentive synthetic fabrics. I reinforce the need to teach young girls to always wipe from front to back, which reduces the likelihood of bacterial contamination. Avoid using powders and sprays in the region; they may aggravate the condition and cause further irritation. Check for the presence of scratches or cuts on the skin or the membranes around the area. Also check the pink tissue (mucous membranes) just within the labial folds and the skin space between the vagina and anus for any scratches, nicks, or other breaks of the surface. When bathing, take care not to scrub or further irritate the delicate tissues.

In an attempt to restore a healthy acid/base balance of the vaginal area, I have often recommended distilled white vinegar sitz baths. After your daughter's regular bath, add 2 cups of white vinegar into a clean tub filled waist-high with room-temperature water. Allow your child to sit in this solution for at least five minutes, then rinse her body with plain water and pat dry.

Parents' Report: What Works

A physician should check out this condition if home treatment doesn't offer complete relief in the first few days, since there are other infections that cause itchiness besides yeast. And some stubborn yeast infections may take a while to heal.

✦ For garden variety nonspecific vaginitis, lavender and tea tree oils are among the best remedies. They can be used in warm sitz baths. Try a few drops of either or both mixed together. Both are antimicrobial, and tea tree oil has antifungal properties.

✦ Probiotics such as powdered *Lactobacillus acidophilus* can be put into a warm-water bath. Probiotics can also be taken orally to enhance their activity. Follow package instructions for dosing. They restore the beneficial bacteria to the intestinal tract to help fight off the yeast.

✦ Yogurt has been suggested for use in a different way. You can deposit 1 tablespoon of yogurt in the vaginal area with your fingers, or use a large medicine dropper or even a poultry baster. It's best to do this at bedtime. Have the child wear a mini absorbent (sanitary) pad so the sheets don't get messy. Spike the yogurt with a dropperful of one or two of the following tinctures such as goldenseal or echinacea, *or* a drop or two of lavender or tea tree essential oil. (Eating some yogurt during the day enhances the remedy.)

✦ A colleague admitted: "I had one yeast infection that lasted on and off for months till I cut out all breads, yeast products, and sugars from my diet and then attacked it with antifungal herbs, which worked better than the over-the-counter stuff, which didn't work at all." If one of her daughters has a vaginal infection, she routinely banishes breads and yeast products from her diet for a while.

Other sitz bath possibilities include:

✦ One or 2 drops each of echinacea, goldenseal, and calendula tinctures and aloe vera juice in warm water—the echinacea is immune-boosting and beneficial for urogenital infections; goldenseal is also antibiotic and soothing to mucous membranes; calendula and aloe are both soothing to inflamed tissues.

✦ Equal parts vinegar and water—vinegar helps restore the vagina's acidity, which makes it inhospitable to overgrowth of yeast and other bacteria that may be causing the irritation.

Note: Over the years parents have asked about the use of douches with their children, but they are no longer medically advised. Similarly, I don't recommend any vaginal insertions for children because the risks for misuse are too great.

Warts

The Ailment

Most warts are viral in origin. These are usually small, raised, light-colored, irregularly shaped, sometimes scaly lumps of skin. For unknown reasons, some people are more prone than others to develop warts. They can appear anywhere on the body. Common locations include the hands (especially near the nails and on the palms), the soles of the feet, the knees, the face near the lips, and the genital area. Warts are usually painless, but depending on location, repeated pressure or irritation by rubbing or picking can cause bleeding and discomfort. Warts may be spread by direct contact with an infected person. Most warts, if not extremely bothersome, should be left alone and allowed to dry and gradually fade without any intervention. Despite the fact that most wart sufferers have never seen a live frog, folk tales continue to perpetuate the belief that warts come from touching or kissing a frog!

Conventional Treatment

The lesion should not be picked, squeezed, or irritated, but rather left undisturbed. With time, warts become very dry and eventually slough off. Many over-the-counter wart preparations include salicylic acid as an active ingredient. ☛ **WARNING:** Do not use any product with salicylic acid if your child has any history of aspirin sensitivity.

Your physician may recommend removal by a process called cryotherapy (an application of liquid nitrogen), or by surgical excision.

PARENTS' REPORT: WHAT WORKS

Most of these remedies involve rubbing with oils or fruit products with acidic properties that help slough off the excess skin tissue.

✦ Megan's mom soaks a small piece of cotton in aloe gel and tapes it over the wart. She adds more gel every few hours with an eyedropper and changes the cotton daily. She says that within a few days she can see drying in process, and in a few weeks the wart may actually disappear.

✦ Soak your child's wart in warm water for twenty minutes. Dry thoroughly, then apply full-strength apple cider vinegar with a cotton ball and leave on for ten minutes. Wash off with tepid water and dry. Repeat this process several times a week.

✦ Soya from Kenya said that in her home village, wood ashes are applied directly to the wart daily.

✦ Dissolve a regular aspirin in a few drops of water and apply to the wart, then cover with a Band-Aid. Repeat twice daily. (Remember: Don't use if your child is aspirin-sensitive.) If this method irritates the skin around the wart, apply some Vaseline around the area with a Q-tip before applying the aspirin solution.

✦ Rub the wart three times daily with a solution of baking soda and water.

✦ Here are two remedies that involve castor oil. (1) Apply castor oil to the wart and rub twenty times or so with your finger. Do this at night and in the morning. The wart should disappear in three to four weeks. (2) Apply a half drop of castor oil to the wart twice daily and cover the wart with some form of first-aid tape or bandage. Keep the bandage on twenty-four hours a day for three weeks, removing only to bathe the area and replace the bandage with a new one.

✦ Cover the wart with any kind of first-aid tape or a Band-Aid and leave on around the clock for three weeks, removing only to bathe and to change the tape. This keeps it less visible and will save the wart from constant irritation while awaiting resolution.

✦ Ms. Washington, a third-grade teacher, advises: Rub the wart daily with a piece of white chalk until the wart falls off.

✦ Break open the stem of a dandelion and rub the milky sap on the wart in a circular motion. Do this two or three times a day until the wart disappears. This was the favorite remedy of Will Greer, Grandpa Walton on the TV show *The Waltons*. The usual caution applies: Only use if the dandelion has not been sprayed with pesticides.

✦ Grapefruit seed extract is a powerful all-around antimicrobial product and is an excellent disinfectant. Apply a drop directly to the wart and cover with a Band-Aid; repeat twice daily. The wart should turn white and fall off in about a week.

✦ Dab 35 percent hydrogen peroxide on the wart with a cotton ball several times a day.

✦ Apply iodine to the wart daily.

✦ An Italian-American neighbor gently rubs lemon juice into the wart two or three times daily.

✦ Apply a drop of thuja tincture (an herbal remedy) directly on the wart from a dropper. You can also mix a few drops each of tea tree oil, thuja tincture, and castor oil to create a powerful mixture to rub on the wart.

✦ Put the contents of one 100 IU capsule of natural vitamin E on a Band-Aid and cover the wart. The warts may soon disappear.

✦ In the morning, crush a vitamin A capsule and mix it with

just enough water to make a paste. Apply the paste directly to the wart. In the afternoon, apply a drop of castor oil; in the evening, apply a drop of lemon juice.

Some of my families have discovered the healing properties of foods. Pick the fruits and veggies that seem to work for you.

✦ Cut an onion in half, scoop out the middle, and put in about ½ teaspoon of salt. After several hours, the salt will draw out the onion's juices, which can then be applied to the wart several times a day.

✦ Take a small piece of peel from a ripe banana and apply the pulp side to the affected area; tape securely. Change the peel daily. This remedy may take a while but has seemed effective with stubborn plantar warts. Other sources suggest using the peel of an unripe banana, as certain healing compounds are more concentrated in the peels before the fruit ripens. A dermatologist colleague has told me that in some tropical localities, health care providers routinely include bananas as part of the treatment regimen for warts.

✦ Cut a clove of garlic in half and rub the cut side on the wart.

✦ Rub a slice of fresh pineapple on the wart. Keep applying as frequently as needed.

✦ Rub the wart with raw potato peelings.

✦ Rub the wart daily with a radish.

✦ Take some green (not fully ripe) black walnuts and make a few incisions in the outer shell; rub the juice on the warts. There may be a slight stinging sensation or the area may turn brown, but this is only temporary.

✦ Elmer from Barbados said his mother used to apply the milky juice from a green papaya to his recurring finger wart several times a day. He declares that his wart would be gone in two weeks.

Yawning

The Ailment

Yawning is not an ailment; it's a reflexive response that everyone experiences. It is a deep, involuntary inspiration (taking air into the lungs), usually causing the mouth to open. It is interesting to observe children in various stages of a yawn—they often exhibit the characteristic open mouth, hyperextended neck, full body stretch, and noisy exhalation. We often associate yawning with fatigue or boredom. Some people will have cycles of yawning many times in succession.

Conventional Treatment

Make sure your child gets enough sleep!

Parents' Report: What Works

✦ Have your child hold his breath for one full minute, then exhale slowly. This is supposed to build up some carbon dioxide, which cancels the reflexic inspiration.

✦ When I feel a yawn coming, I stifle it by swallowing it.

✦ I also use biofeedback. When you feel a yawn, keep your mouth closed and focus on it going away.

✦ Have the child suck a slice of a raw potato or a strip of green bell pepper.

✦ Take one or two peach tree leaves, crush them, then fold them and put them in your child's mouth and have her hold them against the inside of her cheek.

These remedies are family tested, not laboratory-tested. I hope you consider them with a pinch of caution, a heaping tincture of awe, and multiple cups of smiles.

INDEX

About the Authors

LILLIAN M. BEARD, M.D., currently practices pediatrics in Silver Spring, Maryland. She practiced in Washington, D.C., for more than twenty-five years. She is associate clinical professor of pediatrics at the George Washington University School of Medicine and Health Sciences, assistant professor at the Howard University College of Medicine, and a child health consultant to industries. A fellow of the American Academy of Pediatrics and a frequent guest expert on national television, including *Good Morning America* and CNN's *Accent Health,* she is also the medical contributor on ABC's *Good Morning Washington.* She is the recipient of numerous professional awards and was cited by President Clinton in his 1993 Address on Health Care Reform.

LINDA LEE SMALL is the coauthor of seven books and the author of *Maybe Mother Did Know Best: Old-Fashioned Parenting the Modern Way.* Her articles have appeared in such publications as *Parents, Woman's Day, Redbook, Glamour, Self, Cosmopolitan,* and *Ms.,* where she was a contributing editor to the magazine.